ABITUR 2016
Original-Prüfungsaufgaben mit Lösungen

Englisch

Schleswig-Holstein

2011–2015

STARK

© 2015 by Stark Verlagsgesellschaft mbH & Co. KG
9. ergänzte Auflage
www.stark-verlag.de

Das Werk und alle seine Bestandteile sind urheberrechtlich geschützt. Jede vollständige
oder teilweise Vervielfältigung, Verbreitung und Veröffentlichung bedarf der ausdrücklichen
Genehmigung des Verlages.

Inhalt

Vorwort
Stichwortverzeichnis

Hinweise und Tipps zum Zentralabitur Englisch in Schleswig-Holstein

Die zentrale Abiturprüfung in Schleswig-Holstein I
Themenkorridore 2016 II
Wie sieht eine Abiturprüfungsaufgabe aus? II
Typische Teilaufgaben V
Bewertung der Prüfungsarbeit IX
Praktische Tipps zur Vorbereitung IX
Das Anfertigen der Prüfungsarbeit XII
Zum Gebrauch dieses Buches XIII

Englische Kurzgrammatik

Besonderheiten einiger Wortarten .... G 1
1 Adjektive und Adverbien – *Adjectives and Adverbs* .... G 1
2 Artikel – *Article* .... G 5
3 Pronomen – *Pronouns* .... G 6
4 Präpositionen – *Prepositions* .... G 8
5 Modale Hilfsverben – *Modal Auxiliaries* .... G 9

Infinitiv, Gerundium oder Partizip? – Die infiniten Verbformen .... G 10
6 Infinitiv – *Infinitive* .... G 10
7 Gerundium (*-ing*-Form) – *Gerund* .... G 11
8 Infinitiv oder Gerundium? – *Infinitive or Gerund?* .... G 13
9 Partizipien – *Participles* .... G 14

Bildung und Gebrauch der finiten Verbformen .... G 17
10 Zeiten – *Tenses* .... G 17
11 Passiv – *Passive Voice* .... G 24

Der Satz im Englischen .... G 25
12 Wortstellung – *Word Order* .... G 25
13 Konditionalsätze – *Conditional Sentences* .... G 25

Fortsetzung siehe nächste Seite

14 Relativsätze – *Relative Clauses* .... G 27
15 Indirekte Rede – *Reported Speech* .... G 29

Anhang .... G 31
16 Liste wichtiger unregelmäßiger Verben – *List of Irregular Verbs* .... G 31

Basiswissen zu den Themenkorridoren

Canada – A Land of Many Nations .... B 1
Ireland – A Country between Tradition and Modernity .... B 15

Abiturähnliche Übungsaufgaben

Aufgabe 1:	Mediation: „Nacktfotos als Tauschobjekt"	1
	Textaufgabe: Excerpt from *Death by Landscape* by Margaret Atwood	3
Aufgabe 2:	Mediation: „Man spricht Deutsch"	10
	Textaufgabe: "Canada – a linguistic battleground between the US and Britain"	13
Aufgabe 3:	Mediation: „Alkoholtestkäufe: Jugendliche dürfen losziehen"/ „Kein Alkohol mehr an der Tanke?"	19
	Textaufgabe: Excerpt from *The Snapper* by Roddy Doyle	21
Aufgabe 4:	Mediation: „Wohnprojekt für Studenten"	28
	Textaufgabe: "Bloody Sunday report"	30

Abiturprüfungen

Abitur 2011
Aufgabe 1:	Excerpt from: *A Great Deliverance* by Elizabeth George	2011-1
Aufgabe 2:	"How I Lost My Faith in London"	2011-8
Aufgabe 3:	"Samar and his Father" by Pankaj Mishra	2011-13
Aufgabe 4:	"Delhi Wedding for Runaway Romeo and Juliet"	2011-19

Abitur 2012
Aufgabe 1:	Excerpt from: *A Week in December* by Sebastian Faulks	2012-1
Aufgabe 2:	"The Fourth Night" from: *The White Tiger* by Aravind Adiga	2012-7
Aufgabe 3:	Blog entry: "Silver Jubilee" by Jonathan Gili	2012-14
Aufgabe 4:	"India in uproar over decision to include caste in national census" by Andrew Buncombe	2012-21

Abitur 2013

Aufgabe 1:	Excerpt from *Revolution 2020 – Love. Corruption. Ambition.* by Chetan Bhagat	2013-1
Aufgabe 2:	"After British Riots, Conflicting Answers as to 'Why'" by Ravi Somaiya	2013-9
Aufgabe 3:	"Loose Change" by Andrea Levy	2013-16
Aufgabe 4:	"Digital ID Program benefits the poor" by Lydia Polgreen	2013-23

Abitur 2014

Aufgabe 1:	"Belfast Riots Are the Symptom of a Community Left Behind" by Brian John Spencer	2014-1
Aufgabe 2:	"Eco-Warrior – Empire Oil Trailer" by Jamie Bastedo	2014-6
Aufgabe 3:	"Poor Pat Must Emigrate"	2014-11
Aufgabe 4:	"Canada's First Nations" by James Mackay and Niigaanwiwedam James Sinclair	2014-18

Abitur 2015

Mediation:	„Wenn sich Personaler nicht mehr für Persönliches interessieren" von Roland Preuß	2015-1
Aufgabe 1:	"Native despair: face to face with ennui on a reserve" by Richard Wagamese	2015-4
Aufgabe 2:	"The Magdalene Laundries" by Joni Mitchell and "I'm Not a Fallen Woman" by Patrick Soraghan Dwyer	2015-10
Aufgabe 3:	"Belfast's immoral 'conflict tourism'" by C. Jenkins and "After the fighting ends, the tourists come" by D. de Sola	2015-16
Aufgabe 4:	"Strawberries" by Drew Hayden Taylor	2015-22

Jeweils zu Beginn des neuen Schuljahres erscheinen die neuen Ausgaben der Abitur-Prüfungsaufgaben mit Lösungen.

Autoren:
Basiswissen: Rainer Jacob; Kurzgrammatik: Redaktion
Übungsaufgaben und Lösungen der Abitur-Prüfungsaufgaben:
Birte Bökel, Henning Christiansen

Vorwort

Liebe Schülerinnen, liebe Schüler,

bald werden Sie Ihre zentrale Abiturprüfung im Fach Englisch ablegen. Wir begleiten Sie auf Ihrem Weg zu einem guten Abschluss und helfen Ihnen, sich mit den Anforderungen des zentralen Abiturs in Schleswig-Holstein vertraut zu machen.

Dieser Band bietet Ihnen verschiedene Möglichkeiten, sich gezielt auf die Abiturprüfung im Fach Englisch vorzubereiten:

- Die **Hinweise und Tipps zum Zentralabitur** lenken den Blick auf die Hauptschwierigkeiten der Abiturprüfung und helfen Ihnen, Inhalt und Form der Klausuren besser zu verstehen.
- Anschließend finden Sie eine **Kurzgrammatik**, mit deren Hilfe Sie die wichtigsten Aspekte der englischen Grammatik wiederholen können, um so häufige Fehlerquellen zu vermeiden.
- Das **Basiswissen zu den Themenkorridoren** bündelt die wichtigsten Informationen zu den Themen „Canada – A Land of Many Nations" und „Ireland – A Country between Tradition and Modernity". Vergegenwärtigen Sie sich bereits Gelerntes und sammeln Sie weiteres Hintergrundwissen zu den beiden Themenbereichen.
- Mithilfe der **abiturähnlichen Übungsaufgaben** können Sie sich intensiv auf die Bearbeitung von Aufgabenstellungen zu den aktuellen Themenkorridoren vorbereiten. Jede Übungsaufgabe enthält zudem eine **Sprachmittlungsaufgabe**.
- Anschließend finden Sie die **Original-Prüfungsaufgaben 2011 bis 2015**. Anhand von **Musterlösungen** können Sie herausfinden, in welchen Teilbereichen Sie Ihre Kompetenzen weiter verbessern müssen.

Sollten nach Erscheinen dieses Bandes noch **wichtige Änderungen** im Zentralabitur 2016 vom Bildungsministerium Schleswig-Holstein bekannt gegeben werden, finden Sie aktuelle Informationen dazu im Internet unter:
www.stark-verlag.de/pruefung-aktuell

Schon jetzt wünschen wir Ihnen viel Erfolg bei Ihren Abiturprüfungen.

Birte Bökel, Henning Christiansen

Stichwortverzeichnis

Points of Special Interest

Alcohol abuse 19
Applying for a job 2015-1
Canada
~ First Nations 2014-6, 18; 2015-4, 22
~ language 13/14
~ relationship to Britain 14/15
~ relationship to the US 14/15
~ youth camp 3
Education 10
Environment 2014-6
Ethnic minorities 2011-8, 23; 2012-1; 2014-6, 18; 2015-1, 4, 22
Family 21; 2011-13
Financial crisis 2012-5
Growing up 3, 8; 2014-6; 2015-22
Immigration 2011-8; 2012-1; 2013-16
India
~ history 2011-13
~ religion 2011-13
~ society 2011-13; 2012-7, 21; 2013-1, 23
Integration 10
Internet 1
Ireland
~ abortion 25
~ emigration 2014-11
~ family 21; 2014-6; 2015-10
~ famine 2014-11
~ history 30; 2014-11
~ Magdalene Laundries 2015-10
~ Northern Ireland conflict 30; 2014-1; 2015-16
London
~ Acton 2011-1
~ cultural aspects 2011-8; 2012-14
~ historical and political development 2012-1
~ infrastructure 2011-4; 2012-14
~ riots 2013-9
~ social conditions 2011-5, 8, 19; 2012-1; 2013-11, 13, 16
~ urban living 2011-1; 2012-1, 14
Marriage/arranged marriage 2011-19
Multigenerational households 28
Racism 2011-8
Relationship 2011-19
Religion 2011-19
Revolution 2013-1
School life 10

Fortsetzung siehe nächste Seite

Stylistic Devices and Composition

Analysis 4, 6, 15, 17, 23, 25; 2011-4, 21; 2012-3, 9, 17, 24; 2013-4, 6, 11/12; 2014-2, 13, 20; 2015-5, 12, 18, 24
Article 2015-12
Blog entry 2012-14, 19/20; 2014-2
Blurb 2011-21
Cartoon 14, 17; 2013-3, 6
Characterisation 2013-4/5, 18/19; 2014-7
Comment 15, 18; 2011-23; 2012-5, 23
Comparison 2013-25, 27; 2014-20
Diary entry 23, 25
Essay 2012-11
Evaluation 2011-10

Explanation 2011-5
Homepage 2015-12
Letter 4, 5, 6, 32, 36; 2011-18, 22; 2012-5; 2013-4, 7; 2014-13; 2015-5
Mediation 1, 10, 19, 28; 2015-1
Petition 2014-20
Portrait 2011-10; 2012-3
Report 2011-4; 2012-9
Speech 2011-6; 2013-11, 14, 25, 27; 2014-6; 2015-18, 24
Story continuation 4, 8, 23, 27; 2013-18, 21
Testimony 2011-12
Tone/use of language 2011-4; 2012-17; 2013-11/12; 2014-13

Literature and Songs

Anonymous, "Poor Pat Must Emigrate" 2014-11
Aravind Adiga, *The White Tiger* 2012-7
Margaret Atwood, *Death by Landscape* 3
Jamie Bastedo, *Sila's Revenge* 2014-6
Chetan Bhagat, *Revolution 2020 – Love. Corruption. Ambition* 2013-1
Roddy Doyle, *The Snapper* 21
Patrick Soraghan Dwyer, "I'm Not a Fallen Woman" 2015-11

Sebastian Faulks, *A Week in December* 2012-1
Elizabeth George, *A Great Deliverance* 2011-1
Andrea Levy, *Loose Change* 2013-16
Pankaj Mishra, *Samar and his Father* 2011-13
Joni Mitchell, "The Magdalene Laundries" 2015-10
Drew Hayden Taylor, "Strawberries" 2015-22

Hinweise und Tipps zum Zentralabitur Englisch in Schleswig-Holstein

Die zentrale Abiturprüfung in Schleswig-Holstein

In Schleswig-Holstein findet die Abiturprüfung in den Kernfächern der Profiloberstufe in Form des Zentralabiturs statt. Das bedeutet, dass die Aufgaben für alle Fächer einheitlich vom zuständigen Ministerium gestellt und jeweils am gleichen Tag und zur gleichen Zeit von den Prüflingen bearbeitet werden. Dabei dürfen Sie als Prüfling zwischen zwei unterschiedlichen Aufgaben wählen, wobei jeweils ein literarischer und ein nicht literarischer Text zur Auswahl stehen.

Seit 2015 nimmt Schleswig-Holstein außerdem am länderübergreifenden Abitur teil. Neben der Textaufgabe müssen die Prüflinge nun eine Sprachmittlungsaufgabe (Mediation) bearbeiten, die in den Bundesländern Schleswig-Holstein, Bayern, Sachsen, Hamburg, Niedersachsen und Mecklenburg-Vorpommern gleich gestellt ist.

Die Abiturvorbereitung im Englischunterricht stützt sich vor allem auf den Lehrplan Englisch, der wesentliche Unterrichtsinhalte und -methoden festlegt. Für die sechs Halbjahre der Oberstufe sind folgende, in ihrer Reihenfolge schulintern festgelegte **Themen** vorgeschrieben:

- Spracherwerb
- *English in action* (z. B. Reisen, Arbeit, Lernen)
- Regionale Identitäten (z. B. Demokratie, Einwanderung)
- Individuum und Gesellschaft (z. B. Geschlechterrollen, Lebenswege)
- Globalisierung und globale Herausforderungen (z. B. Umweltthemen, Technik)
- Kunst und Literatur

Im Zentralabitur gibt es **Themenkorridore**, die die Prüfungsthemen für Sie eingrenzen. Das Bildungsministerium hat für das **Abitur 2016** zwei Themenkorridore festgelegt, die innerhalb der oben genannten Kursthemen bearbeitet werden müssen: *Canada – A Land of Many Nations* und *Ireland – A Country between Tradition and Modernity*.

Themenkorridore 2016

Thema I: *Canada – A Land of Many Nations*

Die Besonderheiten Kanadas in Bezug auf seine unterschiedlichen Bevölkerungsgruppen und seine kulturelle, soziale und regionale Vielfalt werden vor dem Hintergrund moderner Entwicklungen betrachtet.
Hierzu gehören folgende Themenschwerpunkte:
- kulturelle Gegebenheiten (u. a. indigene Bevölkerung, europäischer Imperialismus, Einwanderung aus Asien)
- soziale Bedingungen und politische Hintergründe
- wirtschaftliche Entwicklung
- die verschiedenen Regionen Kanadas
- Umweltschutz und -verschmutzung

Thema II: *Ireland – A Country between Tradition and Modernity*

Die Entwicklung Irlands wird vor dem Hintergrund der politischen und sozial-religiösen Konflikte untersucht. Zukünftige Entwicklungsmöglichkeiten werden betrachtet.
Folgende Themen stehen im Zentrum:
- historisch-politische Entwicklungen (z. B. Wellen der Emigration, Teilung, Streben nach Unabhängigkeit)
- soziale Bedingungen (z. B. religiöser Konflikt)
- wirtschaftliche Entwicklung (z. B. Wirtschaftskrise, demografischer Wandel)
- kulturelle Entwicklungen

Sicherlich sehen Sie, dass diese Themen nicht einem Halbjahresthema allein zuzuordnen sind, sondern in unterschiedlichsten Aspekten immer wiederkehren. Es gibt keine vorgegebene, einheitliche Literaturliste, die Sie auf das Abitur vorbereitet. Deshalb sollten Sie sich, falls Sie es im Unterricht nicht schon getan haben, die gegebenen Inhalte umso genauer erarbeiten. Bei der Vertiefung und Wiederholung hilft Ihnen das Kapitel **Basiswissen** in diesem Band, das **Hintergrundwissen zu den Themenkorridoren** in englischer Sprache zusammenfasst.

Wie sieht eine Abiturprüfungsaufgabe aus?

Die Kultusministerkonferenz hat in den „Einheitlichen Prüfungsanforderungen in der Abiturprüfung Englisch" (EPA) die Form der Abiturprüfungsaufgaben für ganz Deutschland einheitlich festgelegt. Es werden aber nicht alle in den EPA beschriebenen Aufgaben auch in jedem Bundesland eingesetzt; aus der großen Vielfalt der möglichen Aufgaben werden einige ausgewählt und in Rahmenrichtlinien für das jeweilige Bundesland festgelegt.

Seit 2015 besteht die Abiturprüfungsaufgabe in Schleswig-Holstein aus zwei Teilen.

Mediation (Sprachmittlung)

Schleswig-Holstein nimmt am länderübergreifenden Abitur teil. Im Fach Englisch wird in den Bundesländern Bayern, Hamburg, Mecklenburg-Vorpommern, Niedersachsen, Sachsen und Schleswig-Holstein die gleiche Mediationsaufgabe gestellt. Ihnen werden ein oder zwei deutsche Ausgangstexte vorgelegt, deren Inhalt Sie unter Berücksichtigung spezifischer Vorgaben auf Englisch wiedergeben sollen. Sie erhalten dazu eine Aufgabenstellung, die sowohl den inhaltlichen Rahmen als auch den Adressaten des zu erstellenden fremdsprachigen Textes vorgibt. Als Richtwert gilt, dass ein Ausgangstext von etwa 650 Wörtern auf einen Aufsatz von circa 250 Wörtern komprimiert wird.

Textaufgabe

Als **Textaufgabe** sind in den schleswig-holsteinischen Rahmenrichtlinien **zwei verschiedene Aufgabentypen** vorgesehen:

Aufgabentyp I (ausschließlich schriftliche Vorlagen)
- Literarische Texte (z. B. Gedichte, Liedtexte, Auszüge aus Romanen, Kurzgeschichten, Dramen)
- Sachtexte (z. B. journalistische Texte, Berichte, Essays)

Die vorgelegten Texte weisen eine Länge von 700–900 Wörtern auf. Es können unter Umständen auch mehrere Texte vorgelegt werden, die zusammen ebenso zwischen 700 und 900 Wörter umfassen.

Aufgabentyp II (schriftliche und nicht schriftliche Vorlagen)
Hier können neben schriftlichen Quellen auch audio-visuelle Produktionen und bildliche Darstellungen vorliegen. Dabei ist eine Verbindung mehrerer Vorlagen möglich, wobei die Vorlagen dann in der Regel auch thematisch verknüpft sind. Der Umfang der Texte ist bei diesem Aufgabentyp weniger streng geregelt, audio-visuelle Produktionen und Hörtexte dürfen nicht länger als fünf Minuten sein.

Die Materialien dienen als Grundlage für die Aufgabenstellung, die aus drei Teilaufgaben besteht. Diese Teilaufgaben sind so gestaltet, dass sie die drei folgenden, in den EPA näher beschriebenen Anforderungsbereiche abdecken.

Bei den Aufgaben im **Anforderungsbereich I** (Reproduktion/Textverstehen) sollen Sie darlegen, **was** im Text gesagt wird. Hier ist Ihr Leseverständnis gefragt. Manchmal muss auch nur ein Teilaspekt des Textes wiedergegeben werden. Typische Arbeitsaufträge (Operatoren) für Anforderungsbereich I sind die folgenden:

Arbeitsauftrag	Definition	Beispiele
brief	jemanden kurz über ein Thema informieren	*Brief the journalist about the incident.*
delineate	einen Sachverhalt ausführlich und verständlich darstellen	*Delineate the effects of the narrator's religious beliefs on her career.*

describe	eine genaue Beschreibung einer Person oder eines Sachverhalts anfertigen	*Describe her relationship to her sister.*
outline	die Hauptmerkmale oder wesentlichen Elemente eines bestimmten Sachverhalts wiedergeben	*Outline the Prime Minister's plan for the economic crisis.*
portray	eine Person oder einen Sachverhalt abhängig von der eigenen Meinung präsentieren	*Portray the speaker.*
state	einen Sachverhalt oder eine Diskussion knapp und präzise darstellen	*State the pros and cons given in the text.*
stress	etwas verdeutlichen	*Stress why the protagonist steals the briefcase.*
verbalize	eine nicht schriftliche Vorlage verbalisieren	*Verbalize the immigration statistics.*

Die Aufgaben im **Anforderungsbereich II** (Reorganisation/Analyse) zielen dagegen darauf ab, darzustellen, **wie** die Textaussage vermittelt wird. Es kann z. B. nach der Struktur, nach der Textsorte (z. B. Zeitungsartikel) oder nach der Wirkung auf den Leser gefragt werden. Folgende Arbeitsaufträge sind denkbar:

Arbeitsauftrag	Definition	Beispiele
analyze, examine	eine detaillierte Analyse des Textes anfertigen	*Analyze the President's views on terrorism.* *Examine the author's use of language.*
characterize	eine Person oder einen Sachverhalt charakterisieren	*Characterize Peter's behaviour towards George.*
classify	etwas (begründet) klassifizieren, in Gruppen einteilen	*Classify the families according to their lifestyles.*
compare	vergleichen und dabei Parallelen bzw. Unterschiede herausstellen	*Compare X and Y's views on capital punishment.*
contrast	zwei Aspekte miteinander vergleichen, um herauszustellen, wie unterschiedlich sie sind	*Contrast the behaviour of the two main characters.*
explain	einen Sachverhalt unter Berücksichtigung seiner Ursachen erklären	*Explain Prospero's behaviour towards Miranda.*
interpret	die Aussage eines Textes, einer bildlichen Darstellung o. Ä. individuell deuten	*Interpret the message the author wishes to convey.*
rank	eine Reihenfolge nach bestimmten Vorgaben erstellen	*Rank the language used by the characters in the play according to their social backgrounds.*

relate	mehrere Sachverhalte miteinander in Verbindung bringen	*Relate the statistics to the interview.*
speculate	eine mögliche Erklärung vorschlagen	*Speculate on how the plot would have developed if the protagonists were girls.*

Bei den Aufgaben im **Anforderungsbereich III** (Werten/Gestalten) sind Sie **persönlich gefragt**. Hier wird entweder eine begründete Meinungsäußerung oder eine kreative Leistung gefordert. Diese kann beispielsweise darin bestehen, dass Sie einen Brief oder eine Rede verfassen oder dass Sie sich einen alternativen Schluss bzw. eine Fortsetzung zu einer Geschichte ausdenken.

Alle Aufgaben beziehen sich auf den Prüfungstext bzw. die zugehörigen Materialien. Dieser Bezug muss auch dann hergestellt werden, wenn die Aufgaben auf Sachverhalte zurückgreifen, die im Unterricht behandelt wurden. Folgende Operatoren sind für diesen Anforderungsbereich typisch:

Arbeitsauftrag	**Definition**	**Beispiele**
assess	einen Sachverhalt durchleuchten, sich ein Urteil bilden	*Assess the influence of video games on children.*
conceive	sich eine Situation vorstellen, etwas konzipieren	*Conceive of a positive ending.*
design	etwas entwerfen	*Design a leaflet for the tour.*
determine	etwas ermitteln, Ursachen für etwas herausfinden	*Determine what caused the conflict.*
discuss	Argumente gegenüberstellen und begründet Stellung beziehen	*Discuss the implications of global warming as presented in the text.*
elaborate	etwas ausführen, Informationen und Details zu einem Sachverhalt darstellen	*Elaborate on the reasons for his decision.*
evaluate	einen Sachverhalt beurteilen	*Evaluate the effectiveness of the measures against climate change.*
explain	einen Sachverhalt verständlich erklären	*Explain the President's motivation for his speech.*
transform	eine Vorlage in etwas anderes umformen	*Transform the text into a scene from a play.*

Typische Teilaufgaben

Mediation

Mit der Mediationsaufgabe sollen Sie nachweisen, dass Sie Informationen in einer vorgegebenen Situation adressatengerecht vom Deutschen ins Englische übermitteln können. Die Ausgangsinformation umfasst in der Regel maximal 650 Wörter und soll innerhalb von 60 Minuten auf ca. 250 Wörter komprimiert werden. Da die Über-

tragung in einen Kontext eingebunden ist, wird unter Umständen auch Ihr interkulturelles Wissen geprüft. Das Thema des Textes muss nicht mit dem Themenkorridor übereinstimmen und wird daher häufig aktuelle Probleme aus deutschen Medien aufgreifen.
Ihnen wird bei diesem Aufgabentyp nur eine Aufgabe gestellt. Sie haben hier also keine Wahlmöglichkeit. Als Hilfsmittel stehen Ihnen ein- und zweisprachige Wörterbücher zur Verfügung.
Im Idealfall lesen Sie den Text zweimal und markieren beim zweiten Lesen die für die Lösung der Aufgaben relevanten Textstellen. Vokabeln sollten Sie nur dann nachschlagen, wenn sie für das Textverständnis von Bedeutung sind. Wichtig ist, dass Sie den Text nicht wörtlich übersetzen. Vielmehr sollen Sie die gefragten Informationen heraussuchen und neu strukturiert in der Fremdsprache wiedergeben. Die Aufgabe wird so gestellt sein, dass nicht alle im Text enthaltenen Informationen in Ihrer Lösung wiedergegeben werden müssen.

Leseverständnis

In Anforderungsbereich I wird Ihr Leseverstehen geprüft. Dabei sollen Sie – unter Beachtung der jeweiligen Aufgabenstellung – die wichtigsten Informationen zu einem Aspekt des Textes oder die Hauptaussage der Textvorlage herausarbeiten. In der Abiturprüfung geht es darum, zu überprüfen, ob Sie den Text verstanden haben und in der Lage sind, ihn in eigenen Worten adäquat wiederzugeben. Erfahrungsgemäß wird der Arbeitsauftrag so formuliert sein, dass Sie sich in Ihrer Lösung auf einen bestimmten Aspekt des Ausgangstextes konzentrieren müssen. Es ist möglich, dass die Aufgabe in einen situativen Zusammenhang gestellt wird, der auch Ihre stilistischen und kreativen Fähigkeiten fordert. So kann es beispielsweise sein, dass Sie die Handlung aus der Sicht eines Protagonisten in einer E-Mail wiedergeben oder mithilfe der Informationen im Text einen Lebenslauf einer Person oder den Klappentext eines behandelten Buches verfassen sollen.
Beim Anfertigen eines solchen Textes gibt es einige Regeln zu beachten:
- Werden Sie sich zunächst über die geforderte Textsorte klar. Handelt es sich um eine E-Mail unter Freunden oder eine Meldung aus der Tageszeitung? Passen Sie Stil und Wortwahl entsprechend an.
- Arbeiten Sie die für die Aufgabenstellung relevanten Informationen heraus und strukturieren Sie diese.
- Fügen Sie eigene Ideen oder Hintergrundinformationen nur hinzu, wenn die Aufgabenstellung es von Ihnen fordert – beispielsweise weil sonst zu große inhaltliche Leerstellen in Ihrem Text entstünden. So müssen Sie selbstverständlich Hintergrundinformationen über den Absender eines persönlichen Briefs an die Hauptfigur erfinden, wenn dieser im Text selber nicht vorkommt.
- Benutzen Sie Ihre eigenen Worte und vermeiden Sie Zitate.

Analyse des Sachverhalts

Für diesen Teilbereich Ihrer Arbeit gibt es eine wesentlich größere Auswahl an Aufgabenstellungen als für den ersten Teil. Dennoch finden sich auch für diesen Teil der Arbeit einige Regeln, die es zu beachten gilt:
- Markieren Sie zur Beantwortung der Frage relevante Textstellen. Dies vereinfacht den Umgang mit dem Text und spart Ihnen Zeit.
- Beginnen Sie Ihre Antwort, indem Sie die Frage umformulieren, um so sicherzustellen, dass Sie sie richtig verstanden haben.
- Benutzen Sie soweit möglich Ihre eigenen Worte, ohne dabei auf die Schlüsselbegriffe aus dem Text zu verzichten. Fügen Sie gegebenenfalls kurze Zitate an, um Ihre Ausführungen zu illustrieren. Dabei kommen Ihnen im Hinblick auf den Textzugriff wiederum die Textmarkierungen zugute.
- Schreiben Sie immer im *present tense*.
- Fügen Sie keine Informationen hinzu, die nicht aus dem Text hervorgehen, außer Sie werden in der Aufgabenstellung ausdrücklich dazu aufgefordert.
- Wird eine bestimmte Textsorte von Ihnen gefordert, passen Sie Stil und Wortwahl entsprechend an.

Mögliche Aufgabenstellungen wären:
- *Explain the dramatic development in the text.*
- *Analyze the author's attitude towards this trend.*
- *Examine in what way Gopal's reactions to Revolution 2020 reveal his character.* (2013-4)

Persönliche Stellungnahme

Anforderungsbereich III verlangt von Ihnen, dass Sie einen Sachverhalt bewerten oder diskutieren. In der Regel geschieht dies eingebettet in einen thematischen Kontext, wie z. B. eine politische Rede, einen Blog-Eintrag oder einen Brief. Ihre Argumentation muss daher auf jeden Fall in sich schlüssig, aber auch inhaltlich nachvollziehbar sein und sich eindeutig auf den vorgegebenen Kontext beziehen. Es geht den Prüfern nicht darum, Ihre persönliche Meinung zu bewerten, sondern Ihre Argumentation und die Art, wie Sie zu Ihrem Urteil gelangen.
- Werden Sie sich zuerst über die geforderte Textsorte klar und passen Sie den Stil Ihres Textes daran an.
- Stellen Sie Ihre Argumente möglichen Gegenargumenten gegenüber und entkräften Sie diese.
- Finden Sie eine sinnvolle Struktur für Ihren Text, beachten Sie dabei unbedingt die geforderte Textsorte. Im Folgenden finden Sie Beispiele für eine mögliche Struktur, die Sie an die jeweilige Aufgabenstellung anpassen müssen:

1. a) Schreiben Sie eine kurze Einleitung, in der Sie Ihre eigene Meinung deutlich darstellen.
   b) Liefern Sie die Argumente, die Ihrer Meinung zuträglich sind *(pros)*.
   c) Nennen Sie Gegenargumente *(cons)* und entkräften Sie diese.
   d) Ziehen Sie Ihre Schlussfolgerung *(evaluation of pros and cons; opinion repeated)*.
2. a) Schreiben Sie eine Einleitung, in der Sie Ihre eigene Meinung darstellen.
   b) Nennen Sie Ihrer Meinung entgegenstehende Argumente *(cons)*.
   c) Stellen Sie Ihre Argumente *(pros)* dar und entkräften Sie damit die zuvor genannten Gegenargumente.
   d) Ziehen Sie Ihre Schlussfolgerung *(evaluation of pros and cons; opinion repeated)*.
3. a) Schreiben Sie eine kurze Einleitung, in der Sie Ihre eigene Meinung deutlich darstellen.
   b) Stellen Sie Ihre Argumente und die Gegenargumente einander gegenüber.
   c) Ziehen Sie Ihre Schlussfolgerung *(evaluation of pros and cons; opinion repeated)*.

Machen Sie Absätze zwischen Sinnzusammenhängen, um das Lesen zu vereinfachen. Außerdem zeigen Sie so, dass Sie in der Lage sind, Ihren Text sichtbar zu strukturieren. Mögliche Aufgabenstellungen:

- *You have come across this article on the Internet. Explain your point of view concerning this topic in the comment section of the page.* (vgl. S. 15)
- *"Indians in London – a city of parallel societies?" Starting out from the reported case, write a commentary for a London weekly newspaper.* (vgl. S. 2011-20)
- *Because of her involvement in the riots Chelsea Ives, the young athlete, was excluded from the Olympic Games. In an introductory statement for a press conference of the British Olympic Committee she reflects on what she has done. Write this statement.* (vgl. S. 2013-11)

Kreativ-produktive Aufgabe

Der kreativ-produktive Aufgabentyp kann Ihnen in allen drei Anforderungsbereichen beggnen. Am häufigsten jedoch wird dies im Anforderungsbereich III der Fall sein, da Sie in dieser Aufgabenart kreativ mit den Informationen aus dem Text umgehen müssen. Dies kann beispielsweise bedeuten, dass Sie ein alternatives Ende zu einer Geschichte, einen Tagebucheintrag oder Ähnliches entwerfen müssen. In diesem Zusammenhang ist es wichtig, glaubwürdig zu erscheinen. Das können Sie nur erreichen, wenn Sie sich in die Person beziehungsweise Situation hineinversetzen. Dabei sollten Sie sich auf einem der Situation angemessenen Sprachniveau bewegen. Sollen Sie eine Fortsetzung zu einem literarischen Text schreiben, versuchen Sie sich – was Stil und Erzählperspektive angeht – am Original zu orientieren. Kommt im Text z. B. häufig wörtliche Rede vor, so bauen Sie diese ebenfalls in Ihren Text ein. Nutzen Sie Ihre Möglichkeiten, seien Sie kreativ.

Bewertung der Prüfungsarbeit

Ihre fertige Prüfungsarbeit wird zum einen nach inhaltlichen, zum anderen nach sprachlichen Kriterien bewertet. Bei der **inhaltlichen** Bewertung wird untersucht, inwieweit Sie den Text verstanden und die Aufgabenstellung erfüllt haben. Außerdem wird beurteilt, ob Sie Ihr Vorwissen adäquat eingebracht haben und ob Ihre Argumentation schlüssig ist. Der Inhalt jeder Teilaufgabe wird zunächst einzeln benotet, anschließend wird die Gesamtnote errechnet. Bei der Bewertung Ihrer **sprachlichen Leistung** achten Ihre Prüfer auf folgende Kriterien:
- Ist der Text logisch und übersichtlich?
  Werden *connectives* (vgl. S. X) verwendet?
- Ist die Wortwahl stilistisch angemessen?
- Werden die Regeln für die jeweilige Textsorte erfüllt?
- Ist die Syntax grammatikalisch richtig und abwechslungsreich?
- Beherrscht der Prüfling die Grundregeln der englischen Grammatik?
- Wie umfangreich ist der Wortschatz?
- Werden die orthografischen Regeln befolgt?

Bei der Ermittlung der Note wird Ihren sprachlichen Fähigkeiten mit 60 % ein höheres Gewicht beigemessen als dem Inhalt Ihrer Arbeit (40 %) – durchaus nachvollziehbar, da Sie ja am Ende Ihrer Schulkarriere vor allem nachweisen sollen, dass Sie die englische Sprache beherrschen. Leichte inhaltliche Schwächen Ihrer Arbeit können Sie also durch einen guten Stil wieder ausgleichen. Auf der anderen Seite machen Ihre inhaltlichen Aussagen mit 40 % immer noch einen großen Teil der Gesamtnote aus, sodass Sie trotz stilistischer Schwächen eine gute Note erreichen können, wenn Sie inhaltlich sehr sorgfältig arbeiten.

Die Gesamtnote für Ihre Klausur wird aus den Noten für Mediation und Textproduktion gebildet. Die Note für die Textproduktion macht dabei 80 %, die Note für die Mediation 20 % Ihrer Endnote aus.

Praktische Tipps zur Vorbereitung

Wie Sie im vorhergehenden Abschnitt feststellen konnten, geht die sprachliche Qualität Ihrer Arbeit im Vergleich zur inhaltlichen stärker in die Gesamtnote ein. Daher ist es sehr wichtig, dass Sie nicht nur über das oben genannte Grundwissen in Bezug auf die Prüfungsthemen verfügen, sondern sich vor allem einen flüssigen Stil und ein möglichst umfangreiches Vokabular aneignen – denn mit einer guten Teilnote im sprachlichen Bereich haben Sie schon den größten Teil der Gesamtnote in der Tasche.

Nehmen Sie sich also Ihre bisherigen Klausuren und evtl. Hausaufgaben vor, die Ihr Lehrer/Ihre Lehrerin korrigiert hat, und analysieren Sie Ihre persönlichen Stärken und Schwächen: ==Gibt es Fehler, die immer wieder auftauchen?== Welche Strukturen bereiten Ihnen Probleme? Wenn Sie Ihre persönlichen Problemfelder ermittelt haben, konzentrieren Sie sich darauf, diese Strukturen gezielt zu üben, bis Sie sie sicher beherrschen. Wenn Sie rechtzeitig mit dieser Analyse anfangen, können Sie Ihren persönlichen Fortschritt anhand der Klausuren kontrollieren, die Sie vor dem Abitur schreiben.

Erfahrungsgemäß sind es oft die gleichen Strukturen, die vielen Schülerinnen und Schülern Probleme bereiten. Häufige, leicht zu vermeidende Fehlerquellen sind beispielsweise:

- **conditional clauses:** Besonders in Aufgaben, in denen Sie sich in eine Situation hineinversetzen müssen, werden Sie mit Bedingungssätzen konfrontiert werden *(Speculate on what Miranda would have done if her parents had told her the truth. – What would you do if you were the narrator's mother?)*. Rufen Sie sich noch einmal ins Gedächtnis, welche Zeitformen im Hauptsatz und welche im Nebensatz verwendet werden.
- **reported speech:** Diese Struktur taucht z. B. in Zusammenfassungen und Analysen auf, wenn Sie die Aussagen eines Redners wiedergeben sollen. Achten Sie darauf, ob Sie in Ihrem Text *present tense* oder *past tense* verwenden – während Sie im ersten Fall die Zeitformen der Verben aus der direkten Rede einfach übernehmen können, müssen Sie sie im zweiten Fall in der indirekten Rede anpassen.
- **past tense / present perfect:** Diese vermeintliche Hürde können Sie leicht überwinden, indem Sie sich diese Regel merken: Wenn Sie Ereignisse beschreiben, deren Zeitpunkt, an dem sie stattfanden, eindeutig aus dem Kontext hervorgeht, verwenden Sie das *past tense (Miranda **became** very angry when she found out about her parents' secret. The two protagonists **met** when they were 16 years old.)*.
Dagegen verwenden Sie das *present perfect*, wenn Sie Handlungen oder Zustände beschreiben, deren Zeitpunkt keine Rolle spielt und sich auch nicht aus dem Kontext erkennen lässt *(Arnold Schwarzenegger **has given** a lot of interviews during his career.)*. Erinnern Sie sich auch an die Signalwörter für das *present perfect* wie beispielsweise *always, never, ever, since* und *for*, die ausdrücken, dass ein Zustand bis an die Gegenwart heranreicht. *("They **have known** each other since they were children"* bedeutet, dass die benannten Personen sich heute auch noch kennen.)

Neben der grammatikalischen Korrektheit Ihres Textes sollten Sie auch daran arbeiten, einen möglichst flüssigen Stil zu entwickeln. Statt Ihre Gedanken einfach mit *and, but* oder *because* aneinanderzureihen, sollten Sie Ihre Argumente mithilfe einer größeren Anzahl von Konjunktionen *(connectives)* strukturieren. Das erleichtert es Ihren Lesern, der Ideenführung zu folgen und Ihre Argumentation nachzuvollziehen. In der folgenden Tabelle sind einige solche Ausdrücke aufgeführt, die Sie auf jeden Fall kennen sollten:

Funktion	Konjunktion	Beispiel
Aufzählung	*First(ly) ..., second(ly) ..., third(ly) ...*	There are three reasons for my behaviour towards him: firstly, I don't like his haircut. Secondly, I hate his clothes.
	Finally ... / Lastly ...	And finally, his constant whistling makes me crazy!
	Additionally ... / In addition ... / Furthermore ...	Additionally, his flat is a mess!

Gegensatz	On the one hand ... on the other hand ...	On the one hand I'd love to have a dog, but on the other I'm allergic to fur.
	Nevertheless .../However ...	We could buy a fish tank, however.
	Although ...	Although everyone played well, the German team lost the match.
	In spite of .../Despite ...	She opened the trapdoor in spite of/ despite her fears.
Kausal-zusammenhang	As a consequence .../ Consequently .../As a result ...	Annie is allergic to dairy products. As a consequence, she never eats ice cream.
	Therefore .../Thus ...	You're only 14. Therefore you're not allowed to drink alcohol.
Schluss-folgerung	As a conclusion ...	As a conclusion, smoking should be forbidden in the classroom.
	To sum up .../ To put it in a nutshell ...	To sum up, the dangers of water-skiing are too grave to be ignored.

Inhaltliche Vorbereitung

Bei der inhaltlichen Vorbereitung auf die Abiturprüfung sollten Sie sich weder mit zu viel historischem Detailwissen (wie beispielsweise Jahreszahlen) noch mit ausführlichen Inhaltsangaben und Interpretationsansätzen für die im Unterricht behandelte Literatur belasten. Schließlich geht es im Abitur nicht darum, zu prüfen, ob Sie Sachwissen reproduzieren können, und es gibt auch keine vorgeschriebene Literaturliste, deren Kenntnis Sie nachweisen müssten.
Die schriftliche Abiturprüfung wird im Gegenteil darin bestehen, dass Sie mit unbekanntem Material konfrontiert werden, das Sie sich mithilfe der im Unterricht geübten Methoden und des erarbeiteten Vorwissens erschließen sollen.
Daher sollten Sie sich folgendermaßen auf die Prüfung vorbereiten:
- Gehen Sie die inhaltlichen Hinweise zu den Schwerpunktthemen für Ihren Abiturjahrgang durch, die Sie am Anfang dieses Buches finden. Stellen Sie sicher, dass Sie wissen, was sich hinter jedem Stichwort verbirgt – so können Sie ausschließen, dass Sie sich durch Missverständnisse inhaltliche Fehler einhandeln.
- Beschäftigen Sie sich noch einmal mit den literarischen und nicht literarischen Texten, die im Unterricht behandelt wurden. Möglicherweise werden Sie in der Abiturprüfung dazu aufgefordert, ein in der Aufgabenstellung beschriebenes Problem mit einem Ihnen bekannten Text oder Film zu vergleichen. Dafür ist es vorteilhaft, wenn Ihnen der Inhalt und die Namen der Protagonisten geläufig sind, um Unklarheiten zu vermeiden. Auch die Namen der Autoren sollten Sie sich einprägen.
- Fertigen Sie in diesem Zusammenhang Listen mit nützlichen Vokabeln zu beiden Themenkorridoren an. Sie haben dabei den Vorteil, dass die Wörter Ihnen nicht isoliert, sondern im Kontext begegnen, sodass Sie sich ihre Bedeutung leichter merken können.

Das Anfertigen der Prüfungsarbeit

Für die schriftliche Abiturprüfung ist eine Arbeitszeit von insgesamt 320 Minuten vorgesehen, die sich aus 20 Minuten zum Lesen und Auswählen sowie 300 Minuten zum Schreiben zusammensetzt.

Zu Beginn der Abiturprüfung werden Ihnen eine Aufgabe zum Teilbereich „Sprachmittlung" sowie zwei Aufgabenvorschläge zum Teilbereich „Schreiben" vorgelegt. Sie haben bis zu 20 Minuten Zeit, um sich für einen der Aufgabenvorschläge zu entscheiden, wobei Sie zwischen den Themenkorridoren bzw. der Textsorte (literarisch oder Sachtext) wählen können. Bei der (nicht korridorgebundenen) Sprachmittlung besteht keine Auswahlmöglichkeit.

Anschließend haben Sie 300 Minuten Zeit, Ihre Lösungen zu erstellen, wobei für die Bearbeitung der Aufgabe zur Sprachmittlung 60 Minuten und für die Schreibaufgabe 240 Minuten vorgesehen sind. Es steht Ihnen aber frei, die Reihenfolge und Zeitplanung individuell festzulegen.

Als **Hilfsmittel** werden Ihnen sowohl ein einsprachiges englisches Wörterbuch als auch ein zweisprachiges deutsch-englisches Wörterbuch zur Verfügung gestellt. Betrachten Sie letzteres als eine Art Sicherungsnetz, das Sie auffängt, wenn Ihnen einfach kein passender Ausdruck einfallen will und Sie nicht weiterkommen. Ruhen Sie sich aber nicht auf der Gewissheit aus, dass Sie fehlende Wörter nachschlagen können – Sie verschwenden damit kostbare Arbeitszeit. Investieren Sie also lieber vorher etwas Zeit und lernen Sie die Vokabeln, die Ihnen im Unterricht begegnet sind.

Zeitplanung ist ohnehin ein wichtiger Faktor: Wenn Sie die Aufgabenvorschläge erhalten haben, lesen Sie im Bereich der Textaufgabe zunächst die erste Textvorlage zügig durch, ohne Vokabeln nachzuschlagen oder Notizen zu machen. Lesen Sie anschließend die Aufgabenstellung und stellen Sie sicher, dass Sie sie verstehen. Dann wenden Sie die gleiche Vorgehensweise auf die restlichen Textvorlagen an. Entscheiden Sie dann recht zügig, welche Textvorlage oder welche Aufgabenstellungen Ihnen aufgrund Ihres Vorwissens oder Ihrer methodischen Fähigkeiten mehr liegen. Wenn Ihnen die Entscheidung schwerfällt, ist das wahrscheinlich ein Hinweis darauf, dass Sie alle Aufgaben ungefähr gleich gut lösen können – werden Sie also nicht nervös, sondern versuchen Sie, spontan eine Aufgabe auszuwählen.

Nachdem Sie sichergestellt haben, dass Sie die Arbeitsaufträge in den Teilaufgaben richtig verstanden haben, sollten Sie sich einen groben Zeitplan für die Bearbeitung machen. Dabei können Ihnen diese Grundregeln helfen:

- Planen Sie am Ende der Arbeitszeit eine Korrekturphase ein. Erstens wird Ihnen dann die Situation erspart bleiben, dass Sie mitten in der letzten Aufgabe abbrechen müssen, weil Ihnen die Zeit davongelaufen ist, und zweitens können Sie die sprachliche Qualität Ihrer Arbeit deutlich verbessern, wenn Sie sie noch einmal durchlesen und korrigieren.
- Legen Sie fest, wie viel Zeit Sie für jede Aufgabe verwenden wollen. Dabei können Sie sich an der Gewichtung der Aufgaben zueinander orientieren: Für eine Aufgabe des Anforderungsbereichs I, die möglicherweise nur zu 15 oder 20 % zur in-

haltlichen Gesamtnote beiträgt, müssen Sie höchstwahrscheinlich weniger Zeit aufwenden als für ein Rollenspiel oder eine sprachliche Analyse, die 30 oder 40 % ausmachen.

Wenn Ihre Zeitplanung steht, können Sie sich an die **Konzeptarbeit** machen. Lesen Sie die Teilaufgaben und die Textvorlage diesmal sorgfältig durch und markieren Sie wichtige Textpassagen. Vielleicht verwenden Sie für die unterschiedlichen Teilaufgaben verschiedene Farben oder Symbole? Versuchen Sie, bis zur Abiturprüfung eine Methode zu entwickeln, die zu Ihnen passt.

Notieren Sie sich anschließend die Punkte, die Sie erwähnen wollen, in Stichworten und ordnen Sie sie in der Reihenfolge, in der sie später in Ihrem Text vorkommen sollen (beispielsweise als Punkte in einer Zusammenfassung oder als Argumente in einem Kommentar). Indem Sie jetzt schon den Verlauf Ihrer Argumentation festlegen, stellen Sie sicher, dass Ihr fertiger Text übersichtlich strukturiert und logisch nachvollziehbar ist. Außerdem ersparen Sie Ihren Prüfern die (manchmal recht langwierige) Suche nach Absätzen, die Sie nachträglich mit Sternchen eingefügt haben. Der gute erste Eindruck, den eine übersichtlich strukturierte Arbeit schon zu Beginn der Korrektur macht, kann für Sie nur von Vorteil sein.

Außerdem sollten Sie darauf achten, dass Sie sauber und gut leserlich schreiben. Eine undeutliche Handschrift kann sich leicht negativ auf die Rechtschreibung auswirken.

Und zum Schluss noch ein Tipp: Fertigen Sie keine komplette „Vorschrift" an, die Sie anschließend in Reinschrift übertragen, denn auch hiermit würden Sie wertvolle Zeit vergeuden, die Sie zum Nachdenken oder zur Korrektur besser nutzen können.

Zum Gebrauch dieses Buches

Für dieses Buch sind **Übungsaufgaben** entwickelt worden, wie sie Ihnen in der Prüfung begegnen könnten. Sie sollen Ihnen vor allem ermöglichen, sich auf die Art der Aufgabenstellung vorzubereiten und die im Unterricht vermittelten Methoden zu üben. Für den Fall, dass Sie nicht sicher sind, ob Sie die Aufgabenstellung richtig verstehen, gibt es zu jeder Teilaufgabe zusätzliche **Hinweise und Tipps**, die Ihnen bei der Bearbeitung helfen sollen. Außerdem finden Sie zu jeder Aufgabe auch eine **Musterlösung**, mit der Sie Ihre Texte vergleichen können. Neben den Übungsaufgaben enthält dieser Band die **Original-Prüfungsaufgaben** des Zentralabiturs 2011 bis 2015, natürlich ebenfalls mit Musterlösungen und Hinweisen. Den Aufgaben 2011 bis 2014 liegen zwar andere Themenkorridore zugrunde, hier können Sie sich jedoch einen Eindruck verschaffen, wie „echte" Prüfungsaufgaben aussehen können. Bei der inhaltlichen Vorbereitung auf die Themenkorridore 2016 unterstützt Sie das Kapitel **Basiswissen**.

Kurzgrammatik

Besonderheiten einiger Wortarten

1 Adjektive und Adverbien – *Adjectives and Adverbs*
Bildung und Verwendung von Adverbien – *Formation and Use of Adverbs*

Bildung
Adjektiv + *-ly*   glad → glad<u>ly</u>

Ausnahmen:
- *-y* am Wortende wird zu *-i*   eas<u>y</u> → eas<u>i</u>ly
                                       funn<u>y</u> → funn<u>i</u>ly
- auf einen Konsonanten folgendes   simp<u>le</u> → simp<u>ly</u>
  -le wird zu *-ly*   probab<u>le</u> → probab<u>ly</u>
- *-ic* am Wortende wird zu *-ically* fantast<u>ic</u> → fantast<u>ically</u>
  Ausnahme: pub<u>lic</u> → public<u>ly</u>

Beachte:
- Unregelmäßig gebildet wird: good → well

- Endet das Adjektiv auf *-ly*, so
  kann kein Adverb gebildet werden; man verwendet deshalb:
  in a + Adjektiv + *manner/way*   friendly → in a friendly manner

- In einigen Fällen haben Adjektiv   daily, early, fast, hard, long, low,
  und Adverb dieselbe Form, z. B.:   weekly, yearly

- Manche Adjektive bilden zwei
  Adverbformen, die sich in der
  Bedeutung unterscheiden, z. B.:

Adj./Adv.	**Adv. auf *-ly***
hard	*hardly*
schwierig, hart	kaum
late	*lately*
spät	neulich, kürzlich
near	*nearly*
nahe	beinahe

The task is <u>hard</u>. (adjective)
Die Aufgabe ist schwierig.
She works <u>hard</u>. (adverb)
Sie arbeitet hart.
She <u>hardly</u> works. (adverb)
Sie arbeitet kaum.

G 1

Verwendung
Adverbien bestimmen
- Verben,

- Adjektive,

- andere Adverbien oder

- einen ganzen Satz
näher.

She <u>easily</u> <u>found</u> her brother in the crowd.
Sie fand ihren Bruder leicht in der Menge.
This band is <u>extremely</u> <u>famous</u>.
Diese Band ist sehr berühmt.
He walks <u>extremely</u> <u>quickly</u>.
Er geht äußerst schnell.
<u>Fortunately</u>, <u>nobody was hurt</u>.
Glücklicherweise wurde niemand verletzt.

Beachte:
Nach bestimmten Verben steht nicht das Adverb, sondern das Adjektiv:
- Verben, die einen **Zustand** ausdrücken, z. B.:

to be	sein
to become	werden
to get	werden
to seem	scheinen
to stay	bleiben

Everything <u>seems</u> <u>quiet</u>.
Alles scheint ruhig zu sein.

- Verben der **Sinneswahrnehmung**, z. B.:

to feel	sich anfühlen
to look	aussehen
to smell	riechen
to sound	sich anhören
to taste	schmecken

This dress <u>looks</u> <u>fantastic</u>!
Dieses Kleid sieht toll aus!

Steigerung des Adjektivs – *Comparison of Adjectives*

Bildung
Man unterscheidet:
- Grundform/Positiv *(positive)*
- Komparativ *(comparative)*
- Superlativ *(superlative)*

Peter is <u>young</u>.
Jane is <u>younger</u>.
Paul is <u>the youngest</u>.

Steigerung auf -er, -est
- einsilbige Adjektive

- zweisilbige Adjektive, die auf -er, -le, -ow oder -y enden

old, old<u>er</u>, old<u>est</u>
alt, älter, am ältesten
clever, cleve<u>rer</u>, cleve<u>rest</u>
klug, klüger, am klügsten
simp<u>le</u>, simp<u>ler</u>, simp<u>lest</u>
einfach, einfacher, am einfachsten
narrow, narrow<u>er</u>, narrow<u>est</u>
eng, enger, am engsten
funny, funn<u>ier</u>, funn<u>iest</u>
lustig, lustiger, am lustigsten

Beachte:
- stummes -e am Wortende entfällt
- nach einem Konsonanten wird -y am Wortende zu -i-
- nach kurzem Vokal wird ein Konsonant am Wortende verdoppelt

simp<u>le</u>, simp<u>ler</u>, simp<u>lest</u>

funn<u>y</u>, funn<u>ier</u>, funn<u>iest</u>

fi<u>t</u>, fi<u>tt</u>er, fi<u>tt</u>est

Steigerung mit *more ..., most ...*
- zweisilbige Adjektive, die nicht auf -er, -le, -ow oder -y enden
- Adjektive mit drei und mehr Silben

useful, <u>more</u> useful, <u>most</u> useful
nützlich, nützlicher, am nützlichsten
difficult, <u>more</u> difficult, <u>most</u> difficult
schwierig, schwieriger, am schwierigsten

Unregelmäßige Steigerung
Die unregelmäßig gesteigerten Adjektive muss man auswendig lernen. Einige sind hier angegeben:

good, better, best
gut, besser, am besten

bad, worse, worst
schlecht, schlechter, am schlechtesten

many, more, most
viele, mehr, am meisten

much, more, most
viel, mehr, am meisten

little, less, least
wenig, weniger, am wenigsten

Steigerungsformen im Satz – *Sentences with Comparisons*

Es gibt folgende Möglichkeiten, Steigerungen im Satz zu verwenden:
- **Positiv:** Zwei oder mehr Personen oder Sachen sind **gleich oder ungleich:** *(not) as* + Grundform des Adjektivs + *as*

  Anne is <u>as</u> <u>tall</u> <u>as</u> John (and Steve).
  Anne ist genauso groß wie John (und Steve).
  John is <u>not as</u> <u>tall</u> <u>as</u> Steve.
  John ist nicht so groß wie Steve.

- **Komparativ:** Zwei oder mehr Personen/Sachen sind **verschieden** (größer/besser ...): Komparativform des Adjektivs + *than*

  Steve is <u>taller</u> <u>than</u> Anne.
  Steve ist größer als Anne.

- **Superlativ:** Eine Person oder Sache wird besonders hervorgehoben (der/die/das größte/ beste ...): *the* + Superlativform des Adjektivs

  Steve is <u>the</u> <u>tallest</u> boy in class.
  Steve ist der größte Junge in der Klasse.

Steigerung des Adverbs – *Comparison of Adverbs*

Adverbien können wie Adjektive auch gesteigert werden.
- Adverbien auf *-ly* werden mit *more, most* bzw. mit *less, least* gesteigert.

  She talks <u>more</u> <u>quickly</u> than John.
  Sie spricht schneller als John.

- Adverbien, die dieselbe Form wie das Adjektiv haben, werden mit *-er, -est* gesteigert.

  fast – fast<u>er</u> – fast<u>est</u>
  early – earl<u>ier</u> – earl<u>iest</u>

- Manche Adverbien haben unregelmäßige Steigerungsformen, z. B.:

  well – better – best
  badly – worse – worst
  little – less – least
  much – more – most

Die Stellung von Adverbien im Satz

Adverbien können verschiedene Positionen im Satz einnehmen:
- Am **Anfang des Satzes**, vor dem Subjekt *(front position)*

  <u>Tomorrow</u> he will be in London.
  Morgen [betont] wird er in London sein.
  <u>Unfortunately</u>, I can't come to the party.
  Leider kann ich nicht zur Party kommen.

- **Im Satz** *(mid position)*
  vor dem Vollverb,

  nach *to be*,

  nach dem ersten Hilfsverb.

- **Am Ende des Satzes** *(end position)*

  Gibt es mehrere Adverbien am Satzende, so gilt die **Reihenfolge**: Art und Weise – Ort – Zeit *(manner – place – time)*

She <u>often</u> goes to school by bike.
Sie fährt oft mit dem Rad in die Schule.

She is <u>already</u> at home.
Sie ist schon zu Hause.

You can <u>even</u> go swimming there.
Man kann dort sogar schwimmen gehen.

He will be in London <u>tomorrow</u>.
Er wird morgen in London sein.

The snow melts <u>slowly</u> <u>in the mountains</u> <u>at springtime</u>.
Im Frühling schmilzt der Schnee langsam in den Bergen.

2 Artikel – *Article*

Der **bestimmte Artikel** steht, wenn man von einer **ganz bestimmten Person oder Sache** spricht.

Beachte: Der bestimmte Artikel steht unter anderem **immer** in folgenden Fällen:
- **abstrakte Begriffe**, die näher erläutert sind

- **Gebäudebezeichnungen**, wenn man vom Gebäude und nicht von der Institution spricht
- **Eigennamen im Plural** (Familiennamen, Gebirge, Inselgruppen, einige Länder etc.)
- Namen von **Flüssen** und **Meeren**

<u>The</u> cat is sleeping on the sofa.
Die Katze schläft auf dem Sofa. [nicht irgendeine Katze, sondern eine bestimmte]

<u>The</u> agriculture practised in the USA is very successful.
Die Landwirtschaft, wie sie in den USA praktiziert wird, ist sehr erfolgreich.

<u>The</u> university should be renovated soon.
Die Universität sollte bald renoviert werden.

<u>the</u> Johnsons, <u>the</u> Rockies, <u>the</u> Hebrides, <u>the</u> Netherlands, <u>the</u> USA

<u>the</u> Mississippi, <u>the</u> North Sea, <u>the</u> Pacific Ocean

Der **unbestimmte Artikel** steht, wenn man von einer **nicht näher bestimmten Person oder Sache** spricht.

<u>A</u> man is walking down the road.
Ein Mann läuft gerade die Straße entlang. [irgendein Mann]

Beachte:
In einigen Fällen steht **stets** der unbestimmte Artikel:
- **Berufsbezeichnungen** und **Nationalitäten**
- Zugehörigkeit zu einer **Religion** oder **Partei**

She is a̲n engineer. *Sie ist Ingenieurin.*
He is a̲ Scot(sman). *Er ist Schotte.*
She is a̲ Catholic. *Sie ist katholisch.*
He is a̲ Tory. *Er ist Mitglied der Tories.*

In diesen Fällen steht **kein Artikel**:
- **nicht zählbare** Nomen wie z. B. **Stoffbezeichnungen**
- **abstrakte Nomen** ohne nähere Bestimmung
- **Kollektivbegriffe**, z. B. *man, youth, society*
- **Institutionen**, z. B. *school, church, university, prison*
- **Mahlzeiten**, z. B. *breakfast, lunch*
- *by* + **Verkehrsmittel**
- **Personennamen** (auch mit Titel), **Verwandtschaftsbezeichnungen**, die wie Namen verwendet werden
- Bezeichnungen für **Straßen, Plätze, Brücken, Parkanlagen**
- Namen von **Ländern, Kontinenten, Städten, Seen, Inseln, Bergen**

Gold is very valuable. *Gold ist sehr wertvoll.*

Buddhism is widespread in Asia. *Der Buddhismus ist in Asien weit verbreitet.*

Man is responsible for global warming. *Der Mensch ist für die Klimaerwärmung verantwortlich.*

We went to school together. *Wir gingen zusammen zur Schule.*

Dinner is at 8 p.m. *Das Abendessen ist um 20 Uhr.*

I went to school by bike. *Ich fuhr mit dem Fahrrad zur Schule.*

Tom, Mr Scott, Queen Elizabeth, Dr Hill, Dad, Uncle Harry

Fifth Avenue, Trafalgar Square, Westminster Bridge, Hyde Park

France, Asia, San Francisco, Loch Ness, Corsica, Ben Nevis

3 Pronomen – *Pronouns*

Possessivpronomen – *Possessive Pronouns*

Possessivpronomen *(possessive pronouns)* verwendet man, um zu sagen, **wem etwas gehört**. Steht ein Possessivpronomen allein, so wird eine andere Form verwendet als in Verbindung mit einem Substantiv:

mit Substantiv	ohne Substantiv			
my	mine	This is my bike.	–	This is mine.
your	yours	This is your bike.	–	This is yours.
his/her/its	his/hers/–	This is her bike.	–	This is hers.
our	ours	This is our bike.	–	This is ours.
your	yours	This is your bike.	–	This is yours.
their	theirs	This is their bike.	–	This is theirs.

Reflexivpronomen – *Reflexive Pronouns*

Reflexivpronomen *(reflexive pronouns)* **beziehen sich auf das Subjekt** des Satzes **zurück**. Es handelt sich also um dieselbe Person:

myself
yourself
himself / herself / itself
ourselves
yourselves
themselves

I will buy myself a new car.
You will buy yourself a new car.
He will buy himself a new car.
We will buy ourselves a new car.
You will buy yourselves a new car.
They will buy themselves a new car.

Beachte:
- Einige Verben stehen ohne Reflexivpronomen, obwohl im Deutschen mit „mich, dich, sich etc." übersetzt wird.
- Einige Verben können sowohl mit einem Objekt als auch mit einem Reflexivpronomen verwendet werden. Dabei ändert sich die Bedeutung, z. B. bei *to control, to enjoy, to help, to occupy*.

I apologize ...
Ich entschuldige mich ...
He is hiding.
Er versteckt sich.

He is enjoying the party.
Er genießt die Party.
She is enjoying herself.
Sie amüsiert sich.

He is helping the child.
Er hilft dem Kind.
Help yourself!
Bedienen Sie sich!

Reziprokes Pronomen – *Reciprocal Pronoun* ("each other / one another")

each other/one another ist unveränderlich. Es bezieht sich auf **zwei oder mehr Personen** und wird mit „sich (gegenseitig)/einander" übersetzt.

Beachte:
Einige Verben stehen ohne *each other*, obwohl im Deutschen mit „sich" übersetzt wird.

They looked at each other and laughed.
Sie schauten sich (gegenseitig) an und lachten.
oder:
Sie schauten einander an und lachten.

to meet	*sich treffen*
to kiss	*sich küssen*
to fall in love	*sich verlieben*

4 Präpositionen – *Prepositions*

Präpositionen *(prepositions)* drücken **räumliche, zeitliche oder andere Arten von Beziehungen** aus.

The ball is under the table.
He came home after six o'clock.

Die wichtigsten Präpositionen mit Beispielen für ihre Verwendung:

- *at*
  Ortsangabe: *at home*
  Zeitangabe: *at 3 p.m.*

  I'm at home now. *Ich bin jetzt zu Hause.*
  He arrived at 3 p.m. *Er kam um 15 Uhr an.*

- *by*
  Angabe des Mittels: *by bike*

  She went to work by bike.
  Sie fuhr mit dem Rad zur Arbeit.

  Angabe der Ursache: *by mistake*

  He did it by mistake.
  Er hat es aus Versehen getan.

  Zeitangabe: *by tomorrow*

  You will get the letter by tomorrow.
  Du bekommst den Brief bis morgen.

- *for*
  Zeitdauer: *for hours*

  We waited for the bus for hours.
  Wir warteten stundenlang auf den Bus.

- *from*
  Ortsangabe: *from Dublin*

  Ian is from Dublin.
  Ian kommt aus Dublin.

  Zeitangabe: *from nine to five*

  We work from nine to five.
  Wir arbeiten von neun bis fünf Uhr.

- *in*
  Ortsangabe: *in England*

  In England, they drive on the left.
  In England herrscht Linksverkehr.

Zeitangabe: *in the morning*	They woke up <u>in the morning</u>. *Sie wachten am Morgen auf.*
• *of* Ortsangabe: *north of the city*	The village lies <u>north of the city</u>. *Das Dorf liegt nördlich der Stadt.*
• *on* Ortsangabe: *on the left,* *on the floor* Zeitangabe: *on Monday*	<u>On the left</u> you see the London Eye. *Links sehen Sie das London Eye.* <u>On Monday</u> she will buy the tickets. *(Am) Montag kauft sie die Karten.*
• *to* Richtungsangabe: *to the left* Angabe des Ziels: *to London*	Please turn <u>to the left</u>. *Bitte wenden Sie sich nach links.* He goes <u>to London</u> every year. *Er fährt jedes Jahr nach London.*

5 Modale Hilfsverben – *Modal Auxiliaries*

Zu den **modalen Hilfsverben** *(modal auxiliaries)* zählen z. B. *can, may* und *must.*

Bildung
- Die modalen Hilfsverben haben für alle Personen **nur eine Form**: kein *-s* in der 3. Person Singular.
- Auf ein modales Hilfsverb folgt der **Infinitiv ohne *to*.**
- **Frage und Verneinung** werden nicht mit *do/did* umschrieben.

I, you, he/she/it,
we, you, they } must

You <u>must</u> listen to my new CD.
Du musst dir meine neue CD anhören.

<u>Can</u> you help me, please?
Kannst du mir bitte helfen?

Die modalen Hilfsverben können nicht alle Zeiten bilden. Deshalb benötigt man **Ersatzformen** (können auch im Präsens verwendet werden).

- *can* (können)
  Ersatzformen:
  *(to) **be able to*** (Fähigkeit),
  *(to) **be allowed to*** (Erlaubnis)

I <u>can</u> sing. / I <u>was able to</u> sing.
Ich kann singen. / Ich konnte singen.

You <u>can't</u> go to the party. /
I <u>wasn't allowed to</u> go to the party.
Du darfst nicht auf die Party gehen. /
Ich durfte nicht auf die Party gehen.

Beachte: Im *simple past* und *conditional I* ist auch *could* möglich.

When I was three, I <u>could</u> already ski.
Mit drei konnte ich schon Ski fahren.

- **may** (dürfen) – sehr höflich
  Ersatzform: *(to) be allowed to*

  You <u>may</u> go home early. /
  You <u>were allowed to</u> go home early.
  Du darfst früh nach Hause gehen. /
  Du durftest früh nach Hause gehen.

- **must** (müssen)
  Ersatzform: *(to) have to*

  He <u>must</u> be home by ten o'clock. /
  He <u>had to</u> be home by ten o'clock.
  Er muss um zehn Uhr zu Hause sein. /
  Er musste um zehn Uhr zu Hause sein.

  Beachte:
  must not/mustn't = „nicht dürfen"

  You <u>must not</u> eat all the cake.
  Du darfst nicht den ganzen Kuchen essen.

  „nicht müssen, nicht brauchen" =
  not have to, needn't

  You <u>don't have to</u> / <u>needn't</u> eat all the cake.
  Du musst nicht den ganzen Kuchen essen. /
  Du brauchst nicht ... zu essen.

Infinitiv, Gerundium oder Partizip? – Die infiniten Verbformen

6 Infinitiv – *Infinitive*

Der **Infinitiv** (Grundform des Verbs)
mit *to* steht z. B. **nach**
- bestimmten **Verben**, z. B.:

to decide	(sich) entscheiden, beschließen
to expect	erwarten
to hope	hoffen
to manage	schaffen
to plan	planen
to promise	versprechen
to want	wollen

  He <u>decided</u> <u>to wait</u>.
  Er beschloss zu warten.

- bestimmten **Substantiven und Pronomen** *(something, anything)*, z. B.:

attempt	Versuch
idea	Idee
plan	Plan
wish	Wunsch

  We haven't got <u>anything</u> <u>to eat</u> at home.
  Wir haben nichts zu essen zu Hause.
  It was her <u>plan</u> <u>to visit</u> him in May.
  Sie hatte vor, ihn im Mai zu besuchen.

- bestimmten **Adjektiven** (auch in Verbindung mit *too/enough*) und deren Steigerungsformen, z. B.:

certain	sicher
difficult/hard	schwer, schwierig
easy	leicht

  It was <u>difficult</u> <u>to follow</u> her.
  Es war schwer, ihr zu folgen.

- **Fragewörtern**, wie z. B. *what, where, which, who, when, how* und nach *whether*. Diese Konstruktion ersetzt eine indirekte Frage mit modalem Hilfsverb.

We knew where to find her. /
We knew where we would find her.
Wir wussten, wo wir sie finden würden.

Die Konstruktion **Objekt + Infinitiv** wird im Deutschen oft mit einem „dass"-Satz übersetzt.
Sie steht z. B. **nach**
- bestimmten **Verben**, z. B.:

to allow	erlauben
to get	veranlassen
to help	helfen
to persuade	überreden

She allowed him to go to the cinema.
Sie erlaubte ihm, dass er ins Kino geht. / ... ins Kino zu gehen.

- **Verb + Präposition**, z. B.:

to count on	rechnen mit
to rely on	sich verlassen auf
to wait for	warten auf

- **Adjektiv + Präposition**, z. B.:

easy for	leicht
necessary for	notwendig
nice of	nett
silly of	dumm

She relies on him to arrive in time.
Sie verlässt sich darauf, dass er rechtzeitig ankommt.

It is necessary for you to learn maths.
Es ist notwendig, dass du Mathe lernst.

- **Substantiv + Präposition**, z. B.:

opportunity for	Gelegenheit
idea for	Idee
time for	Zeit
mistake for	Fehler

- einem **Adjektiv**, das durch *too* oder *enough* näher bestimmt wird.

Work experience is a good opportunity for you to find out which job suits you.
Ein Praktikum ist eine gute Gelegenheit, herauszufinden, welcher Beruf zu dir passt.

The box is too heavy for me to carry.
Die Kiste ist mir zu schwer zum Tragen.

The weather is good enough for us to go for a walk. *Das Wetter ist gut genug, dass wir spazieren gehen können.*

7 Gerundium (*-ing*-Form) – *Gerund*

Bildung
Infinitiv + *-ing*

read → read*ing*

Beachte:
- stummes *-e* entfällt
- nach kurzem betontem Vokal: Schlusskonsonant verdoppelt
- *-ie* wird zu *-y*

write → writing
stop → stopping

lie → lying

Verwendung
Die *-ing*-Form steht nach bestimmten Ausdrücken und kann verschiedene Funktionen im Satz einnehmen, z. B.:

- als **Subjekt** des Satzes

  Skiing is fun. *Skifahren macht Spaß.*

- nach bestimmten **Verben** (als **Objekt** des Satzes), z. B.:

to avoid	vermeiden
to enjoy	genießen, gern tun
to keep (on)	weitermachen
to miss	vermissen
to risk	riskieren
to suggest	vorschlagen

  He enjoys reading comics.
  Er liest gerne Comics.

  You risk losing a friend.
  Du riskierst, einen Freund zu verlieren.

- nach **Verb + Präposition**, z. B.:

to agree with	zustimmen
to believe in	glauben an
to dream of	träumen von
to look forward to	sich freuen auf
to talk about	sprechen über

  She dreams of meeting a star.
  Sie träumt davon, einen Star zu treffen.

- nach **Adjektiv + Präposition**, z. B.:

afraid of	sich fürchten vor
famous for	berühmt für
good/bad at	gut/schlecht in
interested in	interessiert an

  He is afraid of losing his job.
  Er hat Angst, seine Arbeit zu verlieren.

- nach **Substantiv + Präposition**, z. B.:

chance of	Chance, Aussicht
danger of	Gefahr
reason for	Grund
way of	Art und Weise

  Do you have a chance of getting the job?
  Hast du Aussicht, die Stelle zu bekommen?

- nach **Präpositionen** und **Konjunktionen der Zeit**, z. B.:

after	nachdem
before	bevor
by	indem, dadurch, dass
in spite of	trotz
instead of	statt

Before leaving the room he said goodbye.
Bevor er den Raum verließ, verabschiedete er sich.

8 Infinitiv oder Gerundium? – *Infinitive or Gerund?*

Einige Verben können sowohl **mit dem Infinitiv** als auch **mit der -ing-Form** stehen, **ohne** dass sich die Bedeutung ändert, z. B.
to love, to hate, to prefer, to start, to begin, to continue.

I hate getting up early.
I hate to get up early.
Ich hasse es, früh aufzustehen.

Bei manchen Verben **ändert sich** jedoch die **Bedeutung**, je nachdem, ob sie mit Infinitiv oder mit der -ing-Form verwendet werden, z. B. *to remember, to forget, to stop.*

- *to remember* + Infinitiv:
  „daran denken, etwas zu tun"

  to remember + *ing*-Form:
  „sich erinnern, etwas getan zu haben"

- *to forget* + Infinitiv:
  „vergessen, etwas zu tun"

  to forget + *ing*-Form:
  „vergessen, etwas getan zu haben"

- *to stop* + Infinitiv:
  „stehen bleiben, um etwas zu tun"

  to stop + *ing*-Form:
  „aufhören, etwas zu tun"

I must remember to post the invitations.
Ich muss daran denken, die Einladungen einzuwerfen.

I remember posting the invitations.
Ich erinnere mich daran, die Einladungen eingeworfen zu haben.

Don't forget to water the plants.
Vergiss nicht, die Pflanzen zu gießen.

I'll never forget meeting the President.
Ich werde nie vergessen, wie ich den Präsidenten traf.

I stopped to read the road sign.
Ich hielt an, um das Verkehrsschild zu lesen.

He stopped laughing.
Er hörte auf zu lachen.

9 Partizipien – *Participles*

Partizip Präsens – *Present Participle*

Bildung
Infinitiv + *ing*
Sonderformen: siehe *gerund*
(S. G 11 f.)

talk → talking

Verwendung
Das *present participle* verwendet man:
- zur Bildung der Verlaufsform *present progressive*,
- zur Bildung der Verlaufsform *past progressive*,
- zur Bildung der Verlaufsform *present perfect progressive*,
- zur Bildung der Verlaufsform *future progressive*,
- wie ein Adjektiv, wenn es vor einem Substantiv steht.

Peter is reading.
Peter liest (gerade).

Peter was reading when I saw him.
Peter las (gerade), als ich ihn sah.

I have been living in Sydney for 5 years.
Ich lebe seit 5 Jahren in Sydney.

This time tomorrow I will be working.
Morgen um diese Zeit werde ich arbeiten.

The village hasn't got running water.
Das Dorf hat kein fließendes Wasser.

Partizip Perfekt – *Past Participle*

Bildung
Infinitiv + *-ed*

Beachte:
- stummes *-e* entfällt
- nach kurzem betontem Vokal wird der Schlusskonsonant verdoppelt
- *-y* wird zu *-ie*
- unregelmäßige Verben (S. G 31 f.)

talk → talked

live → lived

stop → stopped

cry → cried
be → been

Verwendung
Das *past participle* verwendet man
- zur Bildung des *present perfect*,

He hasn't talked to Tom yet.
Er hat noch nicht mit Tom gesprochen.

• zur Bildung des *past perfect*,	Before they went biking in France, they had <u>bought</u> new bikes. *Bevor sie nach Frankreich zum Radfahren gingen, hatten sie neue Fahrräder gekauft.*
• zur Bildung des *future perfect*,	The letter will have <u>arrived</u> by then. *Der Brief wird bis dann angekommen sein.*
• zur Bildung des Passivs,	The fish was <u>eaten</u> by the cat. *Der Fisch wurde von der Katze gefressen.*
• wie ein Adjektiv, wenn es vor einem Substantiv steht.	Peter has got a well-<u>paid</u> job. *Peter hat eine gut bezahlte Stelle.*

Verkürzung eines Nebensatzes durch ein Partizip

Adverbiale Nebensätze (meist kausale oder temporale Bedeutung) und **Relativsätze** können durch ein Partizip verkürzt werden.	She watches the news, because she wants to stay informed. <u>Wanting</u> to stay informed, she watches the news. *Sie sieht sich die Nachrichten an, weil sie informiert bleiben möchte.*
Aus der Zeitform des Verbs im Nebensatz ergibt sich, welches Partizip für die Satzverkürzung verwendet wird:	
• Steht das Verb im Nebensatz im *present* oder *past tense* (*simple* und *progressive form*), verwendet man das *present participle*.	he finishes he finished } → finishing
• Steht das Verb im Nebensatz im *present perfect* oder *past perfect*, verwendet man *having + past participle*.	he has finished he had finished } → having finished
• Das *past participle* verwendet man auch, um einen Satz im Passiv zu verkürzen.	Sally is a manager in a five-star hotel <u>which is called</u> Pacific View. Sally is a manager in a five-star hotel <u>called</u> Pacific View.
Beachte: • Man kann einen Temporal- oder Kausalsatz verkürzen, wenn **Haupt- und Nebensatz dasselbe Subjekt** haben.	When <u>he</u> was walking down the street, <u>he</u> saw Jo. (When) <u>walking</u> down the street, <u>he</u> saw Jo. *Als er die Straße entlangging, sah er Jo.*

- Bei **Kausalsätzen** entfallen die Konjunktionen *as, because* und *since* im verkürzten Nebensatz.
- In einem **Temporalsatz** bleibt die einleitende **Konjunktion** häufig erhalten, um dem Satz eine **eindeutige Bedeutung** zuzuweisen.

As he was hungry, he bought a sandwich.
Being hungry, he bought a sandwich.
Da er hungrig war, kaufte er ein Sandwich.
When he left, he forgot to lock the door.
When leaving, he forgot to lock the door.
Als er ging, vergaß er, die Tür abzuschließen.
Tara got sick eating too much chocolate.
Tara wurde schlecht, als/während/da sie zu viel Schokolade aß.

Die Vorzeitigkeit einer Handlung kann durch ***after + present participle*** oder durch ***having + past participle*** ausgedrückt werden.
- Bei **Relativsätzen** entfallen die Relativpronomen *who, which* und *that*.

After finishing / Having finished breakfast, he went to work.
Nachdem er sein Frühstück beendet hatte, ging er zur Arbeit.
I saw a six-year-old boy who played the piano.
I saw a six-year-old boy playing the piano.
Ich sah einen sechsjährigen Jungen, der gerade Klavier spielte. / ... Klavier spielen.

Verbindung von zwei Hauptsätzen durch ein Partizip

Zwei Hauptsätze können durch ein Partizip verbunden werden, wenn sie **dasselbe Subjekt** haben.

Beachte:
- Das Subjekt des zweiten Hauptsatzes und die Konjunktion *and* entfallen.
- Die Verbform des zweiten Hauptsatzes wird durch das Partizip ersetzt.

He did his homework and he listened to the radio.
He did his homework listening to the radio.
Er machte seine Hausaufgaben und hörte Radio.

Unverbundene Partizipialkonstruktionen – *Absolute Participle Constructions*

Unverbundene Partizipialkonstruktionen haben ein **eigenes Subjekt**, das nicht mit dem Subjekt des Hauptsatzes übereinstimmt. Sie werden in **gehobener Sprache** verwendet.
Mit einleitendem *with* werden sie auf allen Stilebenen verwendet.

The <u>sun</u> having come out, the ladies went for a walk in the park.
Da die Sonne herausgekommen war, gingen die Damen im Park spazieren.

With the <u>telephone</u> ringing, she jumped out of bed.
Als das Telefon klingelte, sprang sie aus dem Bett.

Bildung und Gebrauch der finiten Verbformen

10 Zeiten – *Tenses*

Simple Present

Bildung
Infinitiv, Ausnahme 3. Person Singular: Infinitiv + *-s*

stand – he/she/it stand<u>s</u>

Beachte:
- Bei Verben, die auf *-s, -sh, -ch, -x* und *-z* enden, wird in der 3. Person Singular *-es* angefügt.

kiss – he/she/it kiss<u>es</u>
rush – he/she/it rush<u>es</u>
teach – he/she/it teach<u>es</u>
fix – he/she/it fix<u>es</u>
carry – he/she/it carr<u>ies</u>

- Bei Verben, die auf Konsonant + *-y* enden, wird *-es* angefügt; *-y* wird zu *-i-*.

Bildung von Fragen im *simple present*
(Fragewort +) *do/does* + Subjekt + Infinitiv

Where <u>does</u> <u>he</u> <u>live</u>? / <u>Does</u> <u>he</u> <u>live</u> in London?
Wo lebt er? / Lebt er in London?

Beachte:
Die Umschreibung mit *do/does* wird nicht verwendet,
- wenn nach dem Subjekt gefragt wird (mit *who, what, which*),

Who <u>likes</u> pizza?
Wer mag Pizza?

Which tree <u>has</u> more leaves?
Welcher Baum hat mehr Blätter?

- wenn die Frage mit *is/are* gebildet wird.

<u>Are</u> you happy?
Bist du glücklich?

Bildung der Verneinung im *simple present*
don't/doesn't + Infinitiv

He doesn't like football.
Er mag Fußball nicht.

Verwendung
Das *simple present* wird verwendet:
- bei Tätigkeiten, die man **gewohnheitsmäßig** oder häufig ausführt
  Signalwörter: z. B. *always, often, never, every day, every morning, every afternoon*

Every morning John buys a newspaper.
Jeden Morgen kauft John eine Zeitung.

- bei **allgemeingültigen** Aussagen

London is a big city.
London ist eine große Stadt.

- bei **Zustandsverben**: Sie drücken Eigenschaften / Zustände von Personen und Dingen aus und stehen normalerweise nur in der *simple form*, z. B. *to hate, to know, to like*.

I like science-fiction films.
Ich mag Science-Fiction-Filme.

Present Progressive / Present Continuous

Bildung
am/is/are + *present participle*

read → am/is/are reading

Bildung von Fragen im *present progressive*
(Fragewort +) *am/is/are* + Subjekt + *present participle*

Is Peter reading? / What is he reading?
Liest Peter gerade? / Was liest er?

Bildung der Verneinung im *present progressive*
am not/isn't/aren't + *present participle*

Peter isn't reading.
Peter liest gerade nicht.

Verwendung
Mit dem *present progressive* drückt man aus, dass etwas **gerade passiert** und **noch nicht abgeschlossen** ist. Es wird daher auch als **Verlaufsform** der Gegenwart bezeichnet.

Signalwörter: *at the moment, now*

At the moment, Peter is drinking a cup of tea.
Im Augenblick trinkt Peter eine Tasse Tee.
[Er hat damit angefangen und noch nicht aufgehört.]

Simple Past

Bildung
Regelmäßige Verben: Infinitiv + *-ed*

Beachte:
- stummes *-e* entfällt
- Bei Verben, die auf Konsonant + *-y* enden, wird *-y* zu *-i-*.
- Nach kurzem betontem Vokal wird der Schlusskonsonant verdoppelt.

Unregelmäßige Verben: siehe Liste S. G 31 f.

walk → walk<u>ed</u>

hop<u>e</u> → hop<u>ed</u>
car<u>ry</u> → carr<u>ied</u>

st<u>o</u>p → sto<u>pp</u>ed

be → was
have → had

Bildung von Fragen im *simple past*
(Fragewort +) *did* + Subjekt + Infinitiv

Beachte:
Die Umschreibung mit *did* wird nicht verwendet,
- wenn nach dem Subjekt gefragt wird (mit *who, what, which*),

- wenn die Frage mit *was/were* gebildet wird.

Bildung der Verneinung im *simple past*
didn't + Infinitiv

(Why) <u>Did</u> he <u>look</u> out of the window?
(Warum) Sah er aus dem Fenster?

<u>Who</u> <u>paid</u> the bill?
Wer zahlte die Rechnung?

<u>What</u> <u>happened</u> to your friend?
Was ist mit deinem Freund passiert?

<u>Were</u> you happy?
Warst du glücklich?

He <u>didn't</u> <u>call</u> me.
Er rief mich nicht an.

Verwendung
Das *simple past* beschreibt Handlungen und Ereignisse, die **in der Vergangenheit passierten** und **bereits abgeschlossen** sind.

Signalwörter: z. B. *yesterday, last week/year, two years ago, in 2008*

Last week, he <u>helped</u> me with my homework.
Letzte Woche half er mir bei meinen Hausaufgaben. [Die Handlung fand in der letzten Woche statt, ist also abgeschlossen.]

Past Progressive / Past Continuous

Bildung
was/were + present participle

watch → was/were watching

Verwendung
Die **Verlaufsform** *past progressive* verwendet man, wenn **zu einem bestimmten Zeitpunkt** in der Vergangenheit eine **Handlung ablief**, bzw. wenn eine **Handlung** von einer anderen **unterbrochen** wurde.

Yesterday at 9 o'clock I was still sleeping.
Gestern um 9 Uhr schlief ich noch.

I was reading a book when Peter came into the room.
Ich las (gerade) ein Buch, als Peter ins Zimmer kam.

Present Perfect (Simple)

Bildung
have/has + past participle

write → has/have written

Verwendung
Das *present perfect* verwendet man,
- wenn ein Vorgang **in der Vergangenheit begonnen** hat und **noch andauert**,
- wenn das Ergebnis einer vergangenen Handlung **Auswirkungen auf die Gegenwart** hat.

Signalwörter: z. B. *already, ever, just, how long, not ... yet, since, for*

Beachte:
- *have/has* können zu *'ve/'s* verkürzt werden.
- Das *present perfect* wird oft mit *since* und *for* verwendet („seit").
  - *since* gibt einen **Zeitpunkt** an:
  - *for* gibt einen **Zeitraum** an:

He has lived in London since 2008.
Er lebt seit 2008 in London.
[*Er lebt jetzt immer noch in London.*]

I have just cleaned my car.
Ich habe gerade mein Auto geputzt.
[*Man sieht evtl. das saubere Auto.*]

Have you ever been to Dublin?
Warst du schon jemals in Dublin?

He's given me his umbrella.
Er hat mir seinen Regenschirm gegeben.

Ron has lived in Sydney since 2007.
Ron lebt seit 2007 in Sydney.

Sally has lived in Berlin for five years.
Sally lebt seit fünf Jahren in Berlin.

Present Perfect Progressive / Present Perfect Continuous

Bildung
have/has + been + present participle

write ➔ has/have been writing

Verwendung
Die **Verlaufsform** *present perfect progressive* verwendet man, um die **Dauer einer Handlung zu betonen**, die in der Vergangenheit begonnen hat und noch andauert.

She has been sleeping for ten hours.
Sie schläft seit zehn Stunden.

Past Perfect (Simple)

Bildung
had + past participle

write ➔ had written

Verwendung
Die Vorvergangenheit *past perfect* verwendet man, wenn ein Vorgang in der Vergangenheit **vor einem anderen Vorgang in der Vergangenheit abgeschlossen** wurde.

He had bought a ticket before he took the train to Manchester.
Er hatte eine Fahrkarte gekauft, bevor er den Zug nach Manchester nahm. [Beim Einsteigen war der Kauf abgeschlossen.]

Past Perfect Progressive / Past Perfect Continuous

Bildung
had + been + present participle

write ➔ had been writing

Verwendung
Die **Verlaufsform** *past perfect progressive* verwendet man für **Handlungen**, die in der Vergangenheit **bis zu dem Zeitpunkt andauerten**, zu dem eine neue Handlung einsetzte.

She had been sleeping for ten hours when the doorbell rang.
Sie hatte seit zehn Stunden geschlafen, als es an der Tür klingelte. [Das Schlafen dauerte bis zu dem Zeitpunkt an, als es an der Tür klingelte.]

Will-future

Bildung
will + Infinitiv

buy → <u>will</u> <u>buy</u>

Bildung von Fragen im *will-future*
(Fragewort +) *will* + Subjekt + Infinitiv

<u>What</u> <u>will</u> <u>you</u> <u>buy</u>?
Was wirst du kaufen?

Bildung der Verneinung im *will-future*
won't + Infinitiv

Why <u>won't</u> you <u>come</u> to our party?
Warum kommst du nicht zu unserer Party?

Verwendung
Das *will-future* verwendet man, wenn ein Vorgang **in der Zukunft stattfinden** wird:
- bei Vorhersagen oder Vermutungen,
- bei spontanen Entscheidungen.

The weather <u>will</u> <u>be</u> fine tomorrow.
Das Wetter wird morgen schön (sein).
[doorbell] "<u>I'll</u> <u>open</u> the door."
"Ich werde die Tür öffnen."

Signalwörter: z. B. *tomorrow, next week, next Monday, next year, in three years, soon*

Going-to-future

Bildung
am/is/are + *going to* + Infinitiv

find → <u>am/is/are</u> <u>going to</u> <u>find</u>

Verwendung
Das *going-to-future* verwendet man, wenn man ausdrücken will:
- was man für die Zukunft **plant** oder **zu tun beabsichtigt**.

- dass ein **Ereignis bald eintreten wird**, da bestimmte **Anzeichen** vorhanden sind.

I <u>am going to work</u> in England this summer.
Diesen Sommer werde ich in England arbeiten.

Look at those clouds. It's <u>going to rain</u> soon.
Schau dir diese Wolken an. Es wird bald regnen.

Simple Present und *Present Progressive* zur Wiedergabe der Zukunft

Verwendung
- Mit dem *present progressive* drückt man **Pläne** für die Zukunft aus, für die bereits **Vorkehrungen** getroffen wurden.
- Mit dem *simple present* wird ein zukünftiges Geschehen wiedergegeben, das **von außen festgelegt** wurde, z. B. Fahrpläne, Programme, Kalender.

We <u>are flying</u> to New York tomorrow.
Morgen fliegen wir nach New York.
[Wir haben schon Tickets.]

The train <u>leaves</u> at 8.15 a.m.
Der Zug fährt um 8.15 Uhr.
The play <u>ends</u> at 10 p.m.
Das Theaterstück endet um 22 Uhr.

Future Progressive / Future Continuous

Bildung
will + be + present participle

work → <u>will</u> <u>be</u> <u>working</u>

Verwendung
Die **Verlaufsform** *future progressive* drückt aus, dass ein **Vorgang** in der Zukunft zu einem bestimmten Zeitpunkt **gerade ablaufen wird**.

Signalwörter: *this time next week / tomorrow, tomorrow* + Zeitangabe

This time tomorrow I <u>will</u> <u>be</u> <u>sitting</u> in a plane to London.
Morgen um diese Zeit werde ich gerade im Flugzeug nach London sitzen.

Future Perfect (Future II)

Bildung
will + have + past participle

go → <u>will</u> <u>have</u> <u>gone</u>

Verwendung
Das *future perfect* drückt aus, dass ein **Vorgang** in der Zukunft **abgeschlossen sein wird** (Vorzeitigkeit in der Zukunft).

Signalwörter: *by then, by* + Zeitangabe

By 5 p.m. tomorrow I <u>will</u> <u>have</u> <u>arrived</u> in London.
Morgen Nachmittag um fünf Uhr werde ich bereits in London angekommen sein.

11 Passiv – *Passive Voice*

Bildung
Form von *(to) be* in der entsprechenden Zeitform + *past participle*

The bridge was finished in 1894.
Die Brücke wurde 1894 fertiggestellt.

Zeitformen:

- *simple present*
  Aktiv: Joe buys the milk.
  Passiv: The milk is bought by Joe.

- *simple past*
  Aktiv: Joe bought the milk.
  Passiv: The milk was bought by Joe.

- *present perfect*
  Aktiv: Joe has bought the milk.
  Passiv: The milk has been bought by Joe.

- *past perfect*
  Aktiv: Joe had bought the milk.
  Passiv: The milk had been bought by Joe.

- *will-future*
  Aktiv: Joe will buy the milk.
  Passiv: The milk will be bought by Joe.

- *future perfect (future II)*
  Aktiv: Joe will have bought the milk.
  Passiv: The milk will have been bought by Joe.

- *conditional I*
  Aktiv: Joe would buy the milk.
  Passiv: The milk would be bought by Joe.

- *conditional II*
  Aktiv: Joe would have bought the milk.
  Passiv: The milk would have been bought by Joe.

Aktiv → Passiv

- Das Subjekt des Aktivsatzes wird zum Objekt des Passivsatzes. Es wird mit *by* angeschlossen.
- Das Objekt des Aktivsatzes wird zum Subjekt des Passivsatzes.
- Stehen im Aktiv **zwei Objekte**, lassen sich zwei verschiedene Passivsätze bilden. Ein Objekt wird zum Subjekt des Passivsatzes, das zweite bleibt Objekt.

Beachte:
Das indirekte Objekt muss im Passivsatz mit *to* angeschlossen werden.

Aktiv: Joe / buys / the milk.
       Subjekt   Objekt
Passiv: The milk / is bought / by Joe.
        Subjekt   by-agent

Aktiv: They / gave / her / a ball.
       Subjekt   ind. Obj. dir. Obj.
Passiv: She / was given / a ball.
        Subjekt   dir. Obj.

oder:

Aktiv: They / gave / her / a ball.
       Subjekt   ind. Obj. dir. Obj.
Passiv: A ball / was given / to her.
        Subjekt   ind. Obj.

G 24

Passiv → Aktiv
- Der mit *by* angeschlossene Handelnde *(by-agent)* des Passivsatzes wird zum Subjekt des Aktivsatzes; *by* entfällt.
- Das Subjekt des Passivsatzes wird zum Objekt des Aktivsatzes.
- Fehlt im Passivsatz der *by-agent*, muss im Aktivsatz ein Handelnder als Subjekt ergänzt werden, z. B. *somebody, we, you, they*.

Passiv: The milk is bought by Joe.
       Subjekt   *by-agent*
Aktiv: Joe buys the milk.
       Subjekt   *Objekt*

Passiv: The match was won.
       Subjekt
Aktiv: They won the match.
       (ergänztes)   *Objekt*
       Subjekt

Der Satz im Englischen

12 Wortstellung – *Word Order*

Im Aussagesatz gilt die Wortstellung
<u>S</u>ubjekt – <u>P</u>rädikat – <u>O</u>bjekt
(subject – verb – object):

- <u>S</u>ubjekt: Wer oder was tut etwas?
- <u>P</u>rädikat: Was wird getan?
- <u>O</u>bjekt: Worauf / Auf wen bezieht sich die Tätigkeit?

Für die Position von Orts- und Zeitangaben vgl. S. G 4 f.

<u>Cats</u> <u>catch</u> <u>mice</u>.
Katzen fangen Mäuse.

13 Konditionalsätze – *Conditional Sentences*

Ein Konditionalsatz (Bedingungssatz) besteht aus zwei Teilen: einem Nebensatz *(if-clause)* und einem Hauptsatz *(main clause)*. Im *if*-**Satz** steht die **Bedingung** *(condition)*, unter der die im **Hauptsatz** genannte **Folge** eintritt. Man unterscheidet drei Arten von Konditionalsätzen:

Konditionalsatz Typ I

Bildung
- *if*-Satz (Bedingung):
  simple present
- Hauptsatz (Folge):
  will-future

If you <u>read</u> this book,
Wenn du dieses Buch liest,
you <u>will learn</u> a lot about music.
erfährst du eine Menge über Musik.

Der *if*-Satz kann auch nach dem Hauptsatz stehen. In diesem Fall entfällt das Komma:
- Hauptsatz: *will-future*

- *if*-Satz: *simple present*

You <u>will learn</u> a lot about music
Du erfährst eine Menge über Musik,
<u>if</u> you <u>read</u> this book.
wenn du dieses Buch liest.

Im Hauptsatz kann auch
- *can* + Infinitiv,

- *must* + Infinitiv,

- der Imperativ
stehen.

If you go to London, you <u>can</u> <u>see</u> Bob.
Wenn du nach London fährst, kannst du Bob treffen.

If you go to London, you <u>must</u> <u>visit</u> me.
Wenn du nach London fährst, musst du mich besuchen.

If it rains, <u>take</u> an umbrella.
Wenn es regnet, nimm einen Schirm mit.

Verwendung
Bedingungssätze vom Typ I verwendet man, wenn die **Bedingung erfüllbar** ist. Man gibt an, was unter bestimmten Bedingungen **geschieht** oder **geschehen kann**.

Konditionalsatz Typ II

Bildung
- *if*-Satz (Bedingung):
  simple past
- Hauptsatz (Folge):
  conditional I = *would* + Infinitiv

If I <u>went</u> to London,
Wenn ich nach London fahren würde,
I <u>would</u> <u>visit</u> the Tower.
würde ich mir den Tower ansehen.

Verwendung
Bedingungssätze vom Typ II verwendet man, wenn die **Bedingung nur theoretisch erfüllt** werden kann oder **nicht erfüllbar** ist.

Konditionalsatz Typ III

Bildung
- *if*-Satz (Bedingung):
  past perfect

- Hauptsatz (Folge):
  conditional II = would + have + past participle

If I had gone to London,
Wenn ich nach London gefahren wäre,
I would have visited the Tower of London.
hätte ich mir den Tower of London angesehen.

Verwendung
Bedingungssätze vom Typ III verwendet man, wenn sich die **Bedingung auf die Vergangenheit bezieht** und deshalb **nicht mehr erfüllbar** ist.

14 Relativsätze – *Relative Clauses*

Ein Relativsatz ist ein Nebensatz, der sich **auf eine Person oder Sache** des Hauptsatzes **bezieht** und diese **näher beschreibt**:
- Hauptsatz:
- Relativsatz:

The boy who looks like Jane is her brother.
Der Junge, der Jane ähnlich sieht, ist ihr Bruder.

The boy ... is her brother.
... who looks like Jane ...

Bildung
Haupt- und Nebensatz werden durch das Relativpronomen verbunden.
- *who* (Nominativ oder Akkusativ),

Peter, who lives in London, likes travelling.
Peter, der in London lebt, reist gerne.

whose (Genitiv) und	Sam, whose mother is an architect, is in my class. *Sam, dessen Mutter Architektin ist, geht in meine Klasse.*
whom (Akkusativ) beziehen sich auf **Personen**,	Anne, whom/who I like very much, is French. *Anne, die ich sehr mag, ist Französin.*
• *which* bezieht sich auf **Sachen**,	The film "Dark Moon", which we saw yesterday, was far too long. *Der Film „Dark Moon", den wir gestern sahen, war viel zu lang.*
• *that* kann sich auf **Sachen** und auf **Personen** beziehen und wird nur verwendet, wenn die **Information** im Relativsatz **notwendig** ist, um den ganzen Satz zu verstehen.	The film that we saw last week was much better. *Der Film, den wir letzte Woche sahen, war viel besser.*

Verwendung
Mithilfe von Relativpronomen kann man **zwei Sätze miteinander verbinden**.

London is England's biggest city. London has about 7.2 million inhabitants.
London ist Englands größte Stadt. London hat etwa 7,2 Millionen Einwohner.

London, which is England's biggest city, has about 7.2 million inhabitants.
London, die größte Stadt Englands, hat etwa 7,2 Millionen Einwohner.

Beachte:
Man unterscheidet zwei Arten von Relativsätzen:
- **Notwendige Relativsätze** *(defining relative clauses)* enthalten Informationen, die **für das Verständnis** des Satzes **erforderlich** sind.

  The man who is wearing a red shirt is Mike.
  Der Mann, der ein rotes Hemd trägt, ist Mike.

  Hier kann das Relativpronomen entfallen, wenn es Objekt ist; man spricht dann auch von *contact clauses*.

  The book (that) I bought yesterday is thrilling.
  Das Buch, das ich gestern gekauft habe, ist spannend.

- **Nicht notwendige Relativsätze** *(non-defining relative clauses)* enthalten **zusätzliche Informationen** zum Bezugswort, die für das Verständnis des Satzes nicht unbedingt notwendig sind. Dieser Typ von Relativsatz wird **mit Komma** abgetrennt.

Sally, who went to a party yesterday, is very tired.
Sally, die gestern auf einer Party war, ist sehr müde.

15 Indirekte Rede – *Reported Speech*

Die indirekte Rede verwendet man, um **wiederzugeben, was ein anderer gesagt** oder **gefragt hat.**

Bildung
Um die indirekte Rede zu bilden, benötigt man ein **Einleitungsverb**.
Häufig verwendete Einleitungsverben sind:

to say, to tell, to add, to mention, to think, to ask, to want to know, to answer

In der indirekten Rede verändern sich die **Pronomen**, in bestimmten Fällen auch die **Zeiten** und die **Orts-** und **Zeitangaben.**

- Wie die Pronomen sich verändern, hängt vom jeweiligen **Kontext** ab.

direkte Rede	**indirekte Rede**
Bob says to Jenny: "I like y<u>ou</u>."	Jenny tells Liz: "Bob says that he likes <u>me</u>."
Bob sagt zu Jenny: „Ich mag dich."	*Jenny erzählt Liz: „Bob sagt, dass er mich mag."*
Aber:	Jenny tells Liz that Bob likes <u>her</u>.
	Jenny erzählt Liz, dass Bob sie mag.

- **Zeiten:**
Keine Veränderung, wenn das Einleitungsverb
im *simple present* oder
im *present perfect* steht:

direkte Rede	**indirekte Rede**
Bob <u>says</u>, "I <u>love</u> dancing."	Bob <u>says</u> (that) he <u>loves</u> dancing.
Bob sagt: „Ich tanze sehr gerne."	*Bob sagt, er tanze sehr gerne.*

In folgenden Fällen wird die Zeit der direkten Rede in der indirekten Rede **um eine Zeitstufe zurückversetzt**, wenn das **Einleitungsverb** im *simple past* steht:

simple present → *simple past*
simple past → *past perfect*

present perfect → *past perfect*

will-future → *conditional I*

- **Zeitangaben** verändern sich, wenn der Bericht zu einem späteren Zeitpunkt erfolgt, z. B.:

- Welche **Ortsangabe** verwendet wird, hängt davon ab, wo sich der Sprecher im Moment befindet.

Bob said, "I love dancing."
Bob sagte: „Ich tanze sehr gerne."

Joe: "I like it."
Joe: "I liked it."

Joe: "I've liked it."

Joe: "I will like it."

now	→	then, at that time
today	→	that day, yesterday
yesterday	→	the day before
the day before yesterday	→	two days before
tomorrow	→	the following day
next week	→	the following week
here	→	there

Bob said (that) he loved dancing.
Bob sagte, er tanze sehr gerne.

Joe said he liked it.
Joe said he had liked it.

Joe said he had liked it.

Joe said he would like it.

Bildung der indirekten Frage
Häufige Einleitungsverben für die indirekte Frage sind:

- **Fragewörter** bleiben in der indirekten Rede **erhalten**. Die **Umschreibung** mit **do/does/did entfällt** in der indirekten Frage.

- Enthält die direkte Frage **kein Fragewort**, wird die indirekte Frage mit *whether* oder *if* eingeleitet:

to ask, to want to know, to wonder

Tom: "When did they arrive?"
Tom: „Wann sind sie angekommen?"

Tom: "Are they staying at the hotel?"
Tom: „Übernachten sie im Hotel?"

Tom asked when they had arrived.
Tom fragte, wann sie angekommen seien.

Tom asked if/ whether they were staying at the hotel.
Tom fragte, ob sie im Hotel übernachten.

Befehle/Aufforderungen in der indirekten Rede
Häufige Einleitungsverben sind:
In der indirekten Rede steht hier **Einleitungsverb + Objekt + (not) to + Infinitiv**.

to tell, to order, to ask

Tom: "Leave the room."
Tom: „Verlass den Raum."

Tom told me to leave the room.
Tom forderte mich auf, den Raum zu verlassen.

Anhang

16 Liste wichtiger unregelmäßiger Verben – *List of Irregular Verbs*

Infinitive	Simple Past	Past Participle	*Deutsch*
be	was/were	been	*sein*
begin	began	begun	*beginnen*
blow	blew	blown	*wehen, blasen*
break	broke	broken	*brechen*
bring	brought	brought	*bringen*
build	built	built	*bauen*
buy	bought	bought	*kaufen*
catch	caught	caught	*fangen*
choose	chose	chosen	*wählen*
come	came	come	*kommen*
cut	cut	cut	*schneiden*
do	did	done	*tun*
draw	drew	drawn	*zeichnen*
drink	drank	drunk	*trinken*
drive	drove	driven	*fahren*
eat	ate	eaten	*essen*
fall	fell	fallen	*fallen*
feed	fed	fed	*füttern*
feel	felt	felt	*fühlen*
find	found	found	*finden*
fly	flew	flown	*fliegen*
get	got	got	*bekommen*
give	gave	given	*geben*
go	went	gone	*gehen*
grow	grew	grown	*wachsen*
hang	hung	hung	*hängen*
have	had	had	*haben*
hear	heard	heard	*hören*
hit	hit	hit	*schlagen*
hold	held	held	*halten*
keep	kept	kept	*halten*
know	knew	known	*wissen*

Infinitive	Simple Past	Past Participle	*Deutsch*
lay	laid	laid	*legen*
leave	left	left	*verlassen*
let	let	let	*lassen*
lie	lay	lain	*liegen*
lose	lost	lost	*verlieren*
make	made	made	*machen*
meet	met	met	*treffen*
pay	paid	paid	*bezahlen*
put	put	put	*stellen/setzen*
read	read	read	*lesen*
ring	rang	rung	*läuten/anrufen*
run	ran	run	*rennen*
say	said	said	*sagen*
see	saw	seen	*sehen*
send	sent	sent	*schicken*
show	showed	shown	*zeigen*
sing	sang	sung	*singen*
sit	sat	sat	*sitzen*
sleep	slept	slept	*schlafen*
smell	smelt	smelt	*riechen*
speak	spoke	spoken	*sprechen*
spend	spent	spent	*ausgeben/ verbringen*
stand	stood	stood	*stehen*
steal	stole	stolen	*stehlen*
swim	swam	swum	*schwimmen*
take	took	taken	*nehmen*
teach	taught	taught	*lehren*
tell	told	told	*erzählen*
think	thought	thought	*denken*
throw	threw	thrown	*werfen*
wake	woke	woken	*aufwachen*
wear	wore	worn	*tragen*
win	won	won	*gewinnen*
write	wrote	written	*schreiben*

Basiswissen zu den Themenkorridoren

Basiswissen zu den Themenkorridoren

Canada – A Land of Many Nations

The country

Canada is the second largest country in the world in area (after Russia), extending across the continent of North America from Newfoundland in the east to British Columbia in the west. It covers nearly ten million square kilometres, spans six time zones and borders three oceans (the Atlantic Ocean in the east, the Arctic Ocean in the north and the Pacific Ocean in the west). The largest region, which covers almost half of the country's surface area, is the Canadian Shield in east central Canada. It encircles Hudson Bay and stretches from the Great Lakes to the Arctic Ocean. The capital of the country is Ottawa, Ontario.

The most important regions of Canada

Geographical regions and population

Canada comprises ten **provinces** (Alberta, British Columbia, Manitoba, New Brunswick, Newfoundland and Labrador, Nova Scotia, Ontario, Prince Edward Island, Québec, and Saskatchewan) and three **territories** (Northwest Territories, Nunavut, and Yukon), which reflect the country's great **geographic diversity**. The main difference between a province and a territory is that that the federal government has more direct control over a territory, whereas each province has its own government with many more powers and rights.

In the far north, where it is too cold for trees of any kind to survive, herds of caribou and musk oxen graze on the land known as tundra. Further south, an evergreen forest stretches from the border with Alaska to the Atlantic coast, making it one of the largest in the world. In the centre, thick layers of sedimentary rock form a low, rolling landscape that rises gradually to the west. To the south the evergreens are mixed with trees such as sugar maple, red maple, beech, red oak and white ash.

The farthest western region bordering the Pacific Ocean is **British Columbia**, which is known for its spectacular scenery. With 950,000 square kilometres the province is four times the size of the United Kingdom and features snow-covered mountains, clear lakes and waterfalls, glaciers and lush rainforests. BC attracts visitors and outdoor activists throughout the year. Ski and snowboarding enthusiasts flock to

Whistler, the world-renowned centre for winter sports, whereas surfers come to Vancouver Island, the region's surfer capital, with its kilometres of white sandy beaches. The biggest city in British Columbia is Vancouver with a population of about 600,000.

Further inland, east of the Rockies, are the fertile **Prairie Provinces** (Alberta, Saskatchewan and Manitoba), which provide a stark contrast to the Arctic wastelands to the north. About 17 per cent of Canada's people live in these three provinces, which make up about a fifth of the country's land area. The plains were once grassy prairies, but today they are a farming region with vast fields of wheat and other grains. **Alberta** is the home of Canada's largest parks: Jasper and Wood Buffalo National Park. Great parts of the province are used for ranching. The urban centres of the province are Edmonton (820,000 inhabitants) and Calgary (about 1 million inh.). Next to Alberta is **Saskatchewan** with a population of just over one million.

Source: E. Pluribus Anthony, public domain

For thousands of years various indigenous groups (among them the Cree) inhabited the area before the first Europeans arrived in the 1680s. Agriculture, mining, and energy production are the major economic activities in modern-day Saskatchewan. Nature lovers are in their glory in the province of **Manitoba**, the land of 100,000 lakes, the largest of which are Lake Manitoba, Lake Winnipegosis and Lake Winnipeg, the tenth-largest freshwater lake in the world. Moose, beaver and polar bear are evidence of Canada's varied wildlife.

The oldest aboriginal settlements in Manitoba date back about 10,000 years when First Nations people came to the area shortly after the last ice age. Like in Saskatchewan, European discovery began in the 17th century. Manitoba's capital and largest city is Winnipeg (680,000 inh.). To the east of Manitoba lies **Ontario**, Canada's second-largest province. It is bound by the Hudson Bay in the north and the banks of the Great Lakes (Superior, Huron, Erie and Ontario) in the south. The Great Lakes area and the Saint Lawrence lowlands are Canada's industrial centres. Most of Ontario's population resides in two large cities in the south: Ottawa (880,000 inh.), which is Canada's capital, and Toronto, the capital of the province of Ontario and the nation's most populous city with more than 2.6 million inhabitants. Bordering Ontario to the east is **Quebec**, the largest province in the country, which extends to the Gulf of Saint Lawrence and the provinces of Newfoundland and Labrador. About 25 per cent of Canada's people live in the province, most of whom speak French, the official language in Quebec. Its urban centres are Montreal (1.7 million inh.), which is characterised by a diversity of cultures, and Quebec City (520,000 inh.), the provincial capital where European influence can best be observed in Canada. Several rivers in Canada rank among the world's largest. The longest of them is the Mackenzie, which flows for 1,738 kilometres.

Despite Canada's huge land area, almost 80 per cent of its population of more than 35 million people live on a narrow strip of land along the southern border. The rest of the country is thinly populated, because the land is too cold or mountainous for human settlement. Consequently, the population density is only 3.77 people per square kilometre, which makes Canada only slightly more "crowded" than Australia. More than three quarters of Canada's people live in cities or towns, the largest being Toronto, Ontario and Montreal, Quebec.

Climatic regions
Generally speaking, Canada has a **cold climate** because of the Arctic influence, with long winters and temperatures below freezing throughout most of the country. Along the Arctic Circle temperatures are below freezing for seven months every year. On the other hand, winter and summer temperatures are moderate along the Pacific coast. Vancouver, for example, has a mild climate, and average temperatures remain above freezing in winter.

Politics

Canada is a federal parliamentary democracy. Canada's past influenced the shaping of its political system, parts of which are based on the American and the British system respectively. Canadians combined a federal form of government with a cabinet system. They adopted the **federal system** of the United States with a **central government** (in Ottawa) which is responsible for national affairs and represents all the people of Canada. The provinces have their own governments with extensive powers to administer regional matters. The territories are self-governing, but the federal government plays a large role in their administration. The **cabinet system** – with a prime minister as head of the executive and his cabinet of ministers – is patterned on the system of the United Kingdom. Like in England the legislative power is vested in parliament, consisting of the **House of Commons** (Lower House, 308 members) and the **Senate** (Upper House, 105 members). Although Canada is an independent, self-governing nation, it is a member of the Commonwealth of Nations and recognizes the British monarch, **Queen Elizabeth II**, as queen of Canada and the official **head of state**, thus symbolizing the country's strong ties to Britain. The Queen has visited Canada more than 20 times, the most recent official visits of the monarch were in 2002, 2005, and 2010. A **governor general** acts as her representative and performs certain ceremonial and symbolic tasks; the actual running of the country lies in the hands of the **prime minister**.

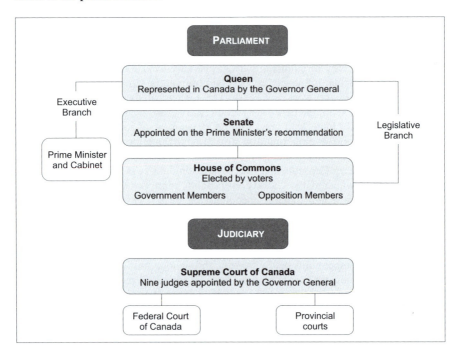

History

Like the USA Canada is a "nation of immigrants", which means all people living in Canada today are descendants of people who came to the land during numerous **waves of immigration**. About 40,000 years ago Canada's first settlers immigrated from Asia across the land bridge which then linked Siberia and Alaska. They were the ancestors of the different tribes of present-day Native Americans. The Eskimos of the Arctic followed later (about 4,500 years ago) along the same route. In the 1980s the words "Indian" and "Eskimo" came to be regarded as disrespectful and were consequently replaced by the terms **First Nations** and **Inuit**. These two groups together with the **Métis** (people of mixed European and Indian ancestry) make up Canada's aboriginal peoples which today account for less than 4 per cent of the country's total population. Together with the descendants of **Europeans** from various parts of the Old World they make up Canada's **ethnic diversity**.

The first Europeans to step on Canadian soil were the Vikings in about 1000 AD, who established a few settlements, but did not stay in the country. The search for the North-West Passage (a sea route from the Atlantic to the Pacific through the Canadian Arctic) and, above all, the discovery of Canada's natural wealth and resources really spurred **European immigration**. European explorers from France and England started a race to claim the riches in this new land – and a long rivalry which still influences Canadians today. The **French** explorer Jacques Cartier discovered the Staint Lawrence River in 1534 and claimed the land for France. To name the territory, Cartier was the first to use the word Canada, a Huron-Iroquois word for "village" or "settlement". French colonists founded Quebec in 1608. The **English** settlements were made possible by explorers such as Alexander Mackenzie, James Cook and George Vancouver and the formation of the Hudson's Bay Company by King Charles II (1670). Both nations competed in the trade of cod (= *Kabeljau*) and fur, which was in great demand in Europe and yielded enormous profits. The struggle for colonial domination between France and Great Britain also affected Canada's indigenous peoples and eventually resulted in a military conflict. France's Canadian colonies and American Indians joined forces to fight against Britain and its American colonies. The **French and Indian War** raged from 1754 to 1763. In one of Canada's bloodiest and most famous battles the British troops besieged Quebec. After the British victory, peace was concluded in the Treaty of Paris (1763), which gave Britain supremacy over almost all of eastern North America. The province of Quebec with its more than 60,000 French-speaking subjects came under British rule, increasing the tension between English- and French-speaking Canadians (cf. "Conflict between English Canadians and French Canadians", page B 7).

The **American Revolution** (1775–1783) brought another wave of immigrants. Thousands of settlers left the newly formed United States in search of cheap land in Nova Scotia and New Brunswick. About 8,000 moved to Quebec, thus increasing the anglophone community in the francophone city. Similarly to the development in the USA, the population of Canada increased quickly during the 19th century. To provide land for the newcomers – about 800,000 came between 1815 and 1850 alone – the Canadian government worked out a series of treaties with the indigenous tribes. However, these agreements were frequently not honoured by the whites.

In the 1850s the movement toward a union of Britain's North American colonies (Nova Scotia, New Brunswick and the provinces of Quebec and Ontario) began to gain momentum. In 1867 the British Parliament passed the British **North America Act**, which created the federation or Dominion of Canada. The act, with some amendments, served as the constitution of Canada for more than a century. It was proclaimed on July 1, now celebrated as Canada Day. In order to unify the country, Canada's first prime minister, John A. Macdonald, promoted the construction of the **Canadian Pacific Railway**. Its completion in 1885 facilitated Canada's westward expansion and led to another boom in business and immigration. The **discovery of gold** on the Klondike River in the far western Yukon Territory in 1896 started a gold rush – just as in California 50 years before – and caused another influx of people. Three million people (mainly Europeans) immigrated to Canada between 1894 and 1914. Not all hopeful adventurers found and washed gold from the rivers in the far North, but they discovered other precious minerals, which eventually made Canada a world-leading nation in mining.

In the 20th century, Canadians fought on Britain's side in both world wars (1914–1918 and 1939–1945). In 1931 Britain officially granted self-government to Canada. The country kept ties with Britain and entered World War II to support the allied forces. In 1982 the British Parliament replaced the British North America Act with a new **Canadian constitution**, making Canada a fully independent nation. After World War II another wave of immigration, especially from Europe, arrived in the country, contributing to Canada's industrial expansion and growth. The fact that Quebec was the only province that lagged behind made the traditionally strained relations between Anglos and Francophones worse.

Issues of ethnic diversity

Canada, the "land of many nations", has a total population of about 35 million. The two largest **ethnic groups** are residents with British (28%) and French (25%) origins, whereas people from other European and Amerindian origins account for 15% and 2% respectively. The number of immigrants with an Asian background is rising (4.3%) Most Canadians are Roman Catholics (43%) or Protestants (24%), with Muslims accounting for just about 2%. Three factors played an important part in the development of a **Canadian identity** from this mixture of races, religions and cultural traditions: the clash of Europeans with the country's aboriginal peoples, the rivalry between the British and French population groups and the desire of Canadians to distinguish themselves from their neighbour, the United States.

Conflict between aboriginal peoples and European settlers

As in the United States, Canada's native peoples (the **First Nations** and the **Inuit**) suffered when the Europeans began to settle in their territory. The Europeans drove them from their homes and re-located them in reservations. In addition, because of the diseases that the settlers brought, the aboriginal population declined. However, in contrast to the USA, Canada did not experience the massacres that accompanied the conquest of the West south of its border and nearly led to the extinction of the First Americans. Nevertheless, Canada's aboriginal population suffered **discrimination and violation of human rights**. In 1990, a band of Mohawk activists staged a violent protest in the town of Oka, Quebec, about unfair land distribution. As a result and to appease the aboriginal peoples, the government issued an **apology for past injustices**, which had included the removal of aboriginal children from their families. Like in Australia, they had to live in so called "Residential Schools", where they often suffered from physical and psychological abuse and where they were separated from their culture. The government pledged to give indigenous people greater control over their land and resources.

Conflict between English Canadians and French Canadians

The rivalry between the French and British has a long tradition. In the early 17th century French colonists settled in the territory now forming Nova Scotia and the Saint Lawrence River Valley and founded Quebec (1608). As a result of their victory in the **French and Indian War** (1754–1763) the British took over complete administrative control in Canada and strengthened ties with their mother country and the British Empire. In the course of time, the French-speaking majority in Quebec felt that their particular problems and interests did not receive proper attention and therefore demanded independence for the province. In the 20th century the issue of separation flared up during World War I when thousands of people from Quebec took to the streets protesting against sending Canadian troops to Europe to fight for Britain. In 1967 the French President Charles de Gaulle reinforced the separatist movement with the phrase "**Vive le Québec libre!**" ("Long live free Quebec!") which he proclaimed on his official visit to the Expo 67 in Montreal. To suppress violent demonstrations the federal government even had to impose martial law in 1970. The dispute seemed settled in 1980 after a majority of people of Quebec voted to remain part of the federation. However, separatist agitation continued and in another referendum in 1995 advocates of an independent Quebec were only narrowly defeated. Today, the Parti Québécois (PQ) campaigns for political, economic and social autonomy for the province of Quebec.

The mighty neighbour across the southern border

Outsiders might think that Canadians are just like Americans. However, although both countries show many parallels as far as colonisation and industrialisation are concerned, Canadians stress the fact that they are not Americans and try to maintain their own identity. One of the main differences in the development of the two neighbouring states was the fact that Canada's creation as a nation was **not achieved through revolution** like in the USA, **but through evolution**. Generally speaking, the founding of the nation occurred with less bloodshed and cruelty than in the newly founded USA. Although Canada's native peoples were often at a disadvantage, they were not threatened with near-extinction. The numerous waves of immigration contributed to mutual **understanding and tolerance**.

Multiculturalism

The large numbers of people from different backgrounds who came to set up homes helped make Canada a country where diverse nationalities and cultures could live side by side peacefully. In fact Canada became the first country in the world to pass a national **multiculturalism act** (1988) and to establish a federal Department of Multiculturalism, with the aim of respecting and preserving the languages, religions, customs and traditions of any ethnic group. The word multiculturalism was coined in

Canada in the 1960s. Today the country is proud of its acceptance of ethnic diversities, proof of which are the Greek, Italian or Chinese quarters in all major cities.

Timeline: Canada and its relationship to Great Britain and France

1534	Jacques Cartier explores the Gulf of St Lawrence, claims its shores for France
1583	Newfoundland becomes England's first overseas colony
1605–1608	Samuel de Champlain establishes the first successful New France Colony at Port Royal and founds the first permanent settlement at Québec City
17th century	Conflict between France and England increases (fur trade rivalry)
1670	Hudson Bay Company established; obtains exclusive trading rights in all the territory draining into Hudson Bay (GB)
1690	British assault on Québec fails
1713	Treaty of Utrecht: France loses its claim to Hudson Bay and Newfoundland
1756–1763	French and Indian (Seven Years') War
1763	Treaty of Paris: Britain acquires all French colonies east of the Mississippi including New France, which becomes the colony of Québec
1791	Constitutional Act passed by the British House of Commons: Québec divided into Lower Canada (present-day Québec) and Upper Canada (present-day Ontario)
1812	War between US and Britain following an American invasion of Upper Canada around the Great Lakes and the Canadian frontier
1818	Canada's border is defined as the 49th Parallel from Lake of the Woods to the Rocky Mountains
1837/38	Armed rebellions in Upper and Lower Canada, caused by disaffection with the ruling elites, poverty and social divisions. The "Canadian question" becomes a leading issue in British politics.
1840	Act of Union: Formation of the United Province of Canada = Canada East (Lower) and Canada West (Upper); Canada reunited
1867	British North America Act unites Ontario (formerly Upper Canada), Québec (formerly Lower Canada), New Brunswick, and Nova Scotia under the Dominion of Canada

1914–1918	World War I: Canada fights on the side of Britain and France
1931	Statute of Westminster grants British dominions complete autonomy
1939–1945	World War II: Canada fights on the side of Allies (USA, Britain and France)
1967	French President Charles de Gaulle visits and declares 'Vive le Québec libre' (Long live free Québec) = Rise of Québec Separation Sentiment
1970	Members of a radical Québec separatist group, the Front de Liberation du Québec, kidnap a British trade official and murder a Québec minister
1980	First Québec independence referendum is defeated
1982	Queen Elizabeth II signs the Canada Act, giving Canada complete sovereignty; Canadian constitution adopted ("Patriation")

Economy

Today Canada is an economic powerhouse and one of the strongest economies in the Western world. It is a member of the "**Group of Eight**" (G 8), the club of the world's wealthiest countries, and ranks 27th in the list of the richest countries with a GDP per head of $ 41,500 (in comparison: USA $ 49,800, Germany $ 39,100, UK $ 36,700)[1]. Like the USA, Canada relies on a free-market economic system and keeps close trade links with its neighbour. In recent years, two trade agreements – the **Free Trade Agreement** (FTA) of 1989 and the **North American Free Trade Agreement** (NAFTA) of 1994 (which includes Mexico) – intensified economic integration and led to an increase in trade activities. Canada exports 75 per cent of its goods to the USA and is also the largest foreign supplier of energy, including oil, gas, uranium, and electric power of the United States.

When the country was first colonised Canada's wealth was based on the exploitation of its **natural resources**. This **primary sector of the economy** (agriculture, forestry, and fishing) still plays an important role and contributes a large part to the country's export earnings. Canada is one of the world's leading exporters of natural gas and mineral products such as gold, copper, zinc, nickel, iron ore, potash and cement. The forest industry ranges from local sawmills with a handful of employees to multinational companies with thousands of employees and accounts for almost 2 % of the total gross domestic product (GDP). In recent years, the country's petroleum sector has emerged as a considerable economic force. The exploration of Alberta's oil sands promises significant earnings and increases Canada's oil reserves, ranking the country third in the world behind Saudi Arabia and Venezuela.

1 2012 figures supplied by CIA World Factbook

On the whole, however, today the trend has shifted from the primary to the **secondary** and **tertiary sector of the economy** and Canada now makes more money selling **services** and **manufactured goods**. In modern plants Canada's highly trained and qualified workers produce cars and other transportation equipment, electrical and electronic products, processed foods, chemicals and metal products. A large part of Canada's labour force is employed in the service industries, which include finance, property, insurance, healthcare, education and tourism. Although agriculture has lost its originally overwhelming importance, Canada is still one of the **leading food producers in the world**. Wheat, barley (= *Gerste*) and oilseeds are among Canada's main grain export crops.

The global economic crisis of 2008 also hit Canada's economy and led to a recession, from which the country was able, however, to recover because Canadian banks had been more reserved and less daring in their financial transactions.

Environmental issues

Tourist brochures advertise Canada as a country of unspoilt wilderness with thousands of clear rivers and lakes and bountiful wildlife. However, although this is still largely true, Canada's environment is under attack because environmental needs frequently run counter to economic interests. The warning signs that centuries of **exploitation** have left some scars have become visible everywhere. In an OECD study of 1995 which compared the environmental track record of 28 industrial nations Canada ranked among the three worst environmental offenders. Since then the country has made progress towards improving its environmental record and a number of laws have been implemented to protect Canada's nature. However, continued efforts are necessary to face the challenges of **air pollution**, **climate change** and **logging** (= *Abholzung*).

In 2009, Canada was ranked seventh in total greenhouse gas emissions behind Germany and Japan. **Air pollution** is responsible for acid rain, which severely affects the water quality and life in Canada's lakes and damages forests. Most of these toxic gases are associated with the **burning of fossil fuels** to generate energy and heat homes. Canada still has a number of coal-fired electricity plants, which use traditional technology to generate power to cover energy demand in manufacturing, construction and mining industries. Because of the cold climate and long winters the **heating of houses** contributes to air pollution. In view of the considerable distances which have to be covered to **transport** people and goods between far away regions of the country, domestic transportation accounts for a large proportion of toxic emissions. Heavy-duty vehicles, trains, aeroplanes and, above all, private cars produce more than a quarter of Canada's greenhouse gases. Car fumes affect in particular the metropolitan areas of southern Ontario and southern Québec. Canada is also worried about pollution from US factories near the border.

The increase in toxic emissions into the atmosphere is the main reason for the worldwide problem of **climate change**. Environmentalists in Canada point to the disturbing fact that between 1949 and 2000, the average annual temperature in the country increased by 0.9 °C. To many, this increase may seem rather modest, but the consequences to nature are enormous. For example, when the weather is getting warmer fish migration patterns begin to change. **Sockeye salmon**, which normally live in the Pacific Ocean, have been spotted in the Arctic. In a milder climate, insects multiply immensely, and forests in British Colombia become infested with myriads of flies, moths and beetles. In addition, climate change causes **extreme weather conditions** such as prolonged droughts in the Canadian prairies and ice storms in the Maritimes (the provinces of New Brunswick, Nova Scotia and Prince Edward Island). To avert the dangers resulting from a heating of the earth Canada played an active role in the negotiations that led to the **Kyoto Protocol** in 1997. In this agreement Canada committed itself to reducing its greenhouse gas emissions by 6 per cent (compared to 1990 levels) within 15 years. However, the ambitious target was missed, in part due to disagreements between the central government and the politicians in the provinces. Critics of the Climate Action Network Canada blame the government in Ottawa of disregarding the demand of the Kyoto Accord in favour of market-centred policies.

Another major environmental issue in Canada is the long-standing problem of **logging**. One of Canada's greatest natural possessions is its enormous green band of tree growth, which covers the southern portion of the Canadian Shield and stretches from the border with Alaska to the Atlantic coast. The boreal forest (the term used for the forest of the climatic zone south of the Arctic) accounts for four fifths of the nation's forested area. From early on, when European settlers arrived in Canada, the forests became valuable sources of timber used in shipbuilding and other construction. Today, logging is a key sector in the country's economy, and many people work in the logging and wood-processing industries. Conservationists have long been concerned that excessive – and illegal – logging, they call it clear-cutting, will destroy the complex forest ecosystem, lead to **deforestation and the extinction of wildlife**. In 1993 protests against logging resulted in the largest act of peaceful civil disobedience in Canada. Protestors climbed 1000-year-old redwood trees, which loggers had wanted to cut down, and some lived in them for over two years. Environmental activists such as the Ancient Forest Alliance group in British Columbia demand a complete stop of logging in endangered old growth forests and campaign for sustainable logging in second growth forests.

The Department of the Environment of the Government of Canada is responsible for coordinating the country's environmental policies and programmes. High on the agenda is the **conservation of energy resources** to slow the depletion of such non-renewables as petroleum and natural gas and further **development of renewable resources**. Cutting down fuel consumption through conservation, would help reduce the amount of toxic gases released into the atmosphere. The federal department is also concerned with the **clean-up of hazardous waste and oil spills**. Canada has oil reserves in Alberta, Saskatchewan and off Newfoundland and possible accidents in the exploitation of oil deposits in Alaska are constant threats to Canada's coasts. Although it happened more than 25 years ago, Canadian environmentalists vividly remember the greatest catastrophe which affected Alaska's untouched nature. In 1989 the supertanker **Exxon Valdez** caused an enormous oil spill which covered hundreds of kilometres of the Alaskan coast, killing wildlife in the Prince William Sound.

Culture

Canada is often described as **a land of many nations** and a nation of immigrants. All Canadians are descendants of people who brought their hopes, their way of life, religion, culture and tradition to the new shores. All these different peoples exercised their influence in forming what we now call the "Canadian" culture. It combines **First Nations**, **British**, **French**, **Asian** and **American influences**. Canadians have conflicting feelings about the United States – a country with which they have much in common, but against which they define themselves. On many occasions the country recognises the achievements of the different communities in making Canada the culturally diverse nation it is today. For example, Black History Month in February or Asian Heritage Month in May are organised to acknowledge the contributions of these cultures to the nation of Canada.

Literature

An integral part of Canada's cultural diversity is the country's heritage of its indigenous peoples. There are no written documents of **First Nations culture**, but European trappers, traders, explorers, and missionaries recorded much of the **oral tradition** which goes back thousands of years. To protect and preserve the culture of Canada's native peoples the federal government adopted an official policy of multiculturalism in 1971.

One of the **earliest books of Canadian literature** was Marc Lescarbot's *Histoire de la Nouvelle France* (History of New France), from 1609, published in France and intended for European readers. The first major contribution in English was Thomas Chandler Haliburton's *The Clockmaker* (1836), the humorous adventures of a character named Sam Slick. Ralph Connor, whose real name was Charles William Gordon (1860–1937), was the first novelist to write about the Canadian West. His book *The Sky Pilot* was a frontier adventure and sold more than 1,000,000 copies. Another popular writer was Mazo de la Roche (1879–1961), author of a most successful family saga, the Jalna novels.

The 20th century witnessed the rise of the so-called Québécois fiction, a term for the experimental writings of **Canadian-French** authors Gabrielle Roy (1909–1983) and Hubert Aquin (1929–1977).

Two modern Canadian novelists of world fame are Margaret Atwood (born 1939) and Michael Ondaatje (born 1943). Margaret Atwood was born in Ottawa, Ontario, and wrote her first book of poetry in 1961 while attending the University of Toronto. Her first novel, *The Edible Woman*, was published in 1969 to wide acclaim. In her works she frequently discusses feminist topics (*The Handmaid's Tale*, 1985, deals with the consequences of a reversal of women's rights) and takes an interest in double identities (*Double Persephone*, 1961, *Two-Headed Poems*, 1978 and *Alias Grace*, 1996). Margaret Atwood is also one of Canada's leading environmental activists. Philip Michael Ondaatje was born in **Sri Lanka** and came to Canada in 1962. He won the Booker Prize for his novel *The English Patient*, which was adapted into a successful film.

Irish-born Brian Moore (1921–1999) explores Canada's past in his historical novel *Black Robe* – the name given to priests by the First Nations. Set in New France in the 17th century, the novel tells the story of a French Jesuit and his missionary work with the Huron Indians.

The novelist Thomas King (born 1943) is of **Cherokee** and Greek descent and writes about **First Nations people** and North America's relationship with its Aboriginal population. His works include *Medicine River* (1990) and *Green Grass, Running Water* (1993).

Visual arts
The earliest examples of Canada's visual arts are the **sculptures and handicrafts of the native peoples**, including the stone carvings of the Inuit and the totem-pole carvings of the Northwest Coast Indians. With the arrival of Europeans Canadian artists focused their interests on **painting**. The most influential landscape painters were the artists of the **Group of Seven** (1920–1933), sometimes referred to as the Algonquin school after a Native American tribe. Among the English-Canadian writers who were influenced by the Group of Seven were the poets E. J. Pratt, F. R. Scott, A. J. M. Smith and Dorothy Livesay, the "senior woman writer in Canada" during the 1970s and 1980s.

Music
Canada's ethnic groups (Aboriginals, the British, and the French) and the neighbouring American culture contributed to the musical heritage of Canada. **Choral music** societies developed across the country, and **opera** was available not only in such metropolitan areas as Toronto, Montreal, and Vancouver but also in remote parts of the country through touring productions. The Toronto Symphony Orchestra (TSO, founded in 1922) and the Orchestre symphonique de Montréal (OSM, Montreal Symphony Orchestra) enjoy international reputations. Among the most important **composers** of the 20th and 21st century are Jean Coulthard, Jacques Hétu, Colin McPhee, Ann Southam, Claude Vivier and Healey Willan. During the 1960s and 70s Canadian **folk singers and songwriters** rose to international fame, for example Joni Mitchell, Leonard Cohen, Gordon Lightfoot and Neil Young.

Media
Every major Canadian city (e. g. Edmonton, Vancouver, Quebec and Winnipeg) has its daily **newspaper**, most of which also publish editions on the Internet. Canada's newspaper with the highest circulation (nearly 400,000 copies daily) is *The Toronto Star*. Its print edition is distributed almost entirely within the province of Ontario. *The Globe and Mail,* which is also based in Toronto, is the second-largest daily paper (circulation: about 305,000). It is distributed nationwide and regarded as Canada's national newspaper. A national news agency, the Canadian Press, which was established in 1917, supports the country's dailies in the exchange of news and information.

The centre of the Canadian **film** industry is the National Film Board of Canada (NFB), which was established in 1939. As an agency of the Government of Canada the NFB concerns itself with the production and distribution of films and digital media in English and in French. Several of its productions received Oscar nominations. Although the national Canadian film production plays an important part, over 95 % of Canada's annual box office returns are for Hollywood foreign films. A major event for filmmakers, producers and cinema enthusiasts around the world is the annual Toronto International Film Festival (TIFF) held in September in Toronto, Ontario. Other festivals are held in Vancouver, Montreal and Halifax.

In recent years Canada has also become an attractive place for film producers, because Canada offers not only spectacular locations, but also excellent studio facilities and experienced film crews. In addition, the Canadian government supports foreign productions with tax breaks. Consequently, many Hollywood studios shoot big budget films and TV series in Canada. The cities of Vancouver and Toronto have become known as "Hollywood North".

In a huge country like Canada **broadcasting** serves not only as a source of information and entertainment but also as a link between the urban centres and the various regions up to the remote Arctic settlements. Canadian broadcasting is regulated by the Canadian Radio-Television and Telecommunications Commission, which was established in 1968. It authorizes the establishment of networks and private stations and specifies how much of the broadcast content must be Canadian in origin. This is especially important in view of the increasing influence of US media since the spread of cable stations and satellite connections. The publicly owned Canadian Broadcasting Corporation (CBC) provides two national networks for both radio and television, one in English and one in French, and a special northern service in Indian and Inuit-Aleut languages.

One of the most influential analysts of the influences **of electronic media** on people's lives was the Canadian philosopher and educator Herbert Marshall McLuhan (1911–1980). As early as 1962 he predicted that the electronic age would turn all humanity into a "global tribe". The term "global village" is attributed to him. His most famous books include *Understanding Media: The extensions of Man* (1964) and *The Medium is the Message: An Inventory of Effects* (1967).

Ireland – A Country between Tradition and Modernity

Historical and political developments

Northern Ireland and the Irish Republic

Ireland, often referred to as the "Emerald Isle" because of its beautiful green countryside, is the second largest island of the British Isles, separated from Great Britain by the Irish Sea and St Georges Channel. The island of Ireland is divided into four large provinces (former kingdoms): Leinster, Munster, Connacht and Ulster. The first three provinces occupy about five sixths of the island and make up the **Irish Republic** (in Gaelic language: *Éire*) with its capital Dublin. The northern province Ulster, known as **Northern Ireland**, takes up the remaining one sixth and is part of the United Kingdom. Its capital is Belfast. The patron saint of all Ireland is St Patrick. Patrick ("Paddy") is also a popular Irish first name. **St Patrick's day** is March 17, when Irishmen wear the shamrock (= *Kleeblatt*). The Irish symbol of the shamrock was adopted because St Patrick used this plant as an illustration of the Trinity (= *Dreieinigkeit*) – three leaves forming one leaf. His flag is a diagonal red cross on a white background and forms part of the Union Jack. About 6.5 million people live on the island altogether, 4.6 reside in the Republic. Almost 90 per cent are Catholics.

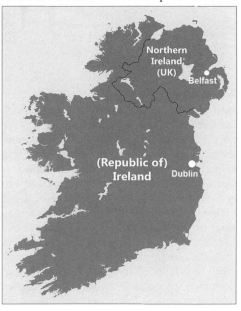

Jonto, lizenziert unter cc-by-sa-3.0.
URL: http://commons.wikimedia.org/wiki/ File: Ireland-capitals.PNG

Politics

The Irish Republic has a president as official head of state and a prime minister as head of the government. The legislative is vested in the **Irish Parliament** which consists of the President of Ireland and two Houses. The **Lower House** (also referred to as House of Representatives) has 166 members, the **Upper House** (the Senate), which serves mainly as an advisory body, has 60 members. The **prime minister**, usually the leader of the party with a majority in the House of Representatives, is called the *taoiseach* in Gaelic. The main **political parties** are Fine Gael (centre-right), Fianna Fáil (Republican Party), Labour Party, Sinn Féin (Irish republican party), Green Party and the Socialist Party. According to the Irish Constitution of 1937 the Irish language is the first official language and English is recognised as a second official language.

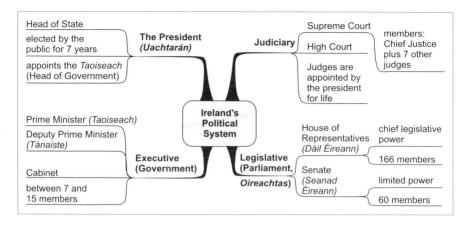

Invasions of Ireland

Most of the Irish people are descended from peoples who **invaded** Ireland and settled there in the course of more than 7,000 years. These peoples included Celts, Vikings, Danes, Normans, and the British. Each group influenced Irish civilization and helped shape the character of the Irish people. Around 600 BC the **Celts** arrived from central Europe in Britain and Ireland, spreading their culture across the entire island. Up to the late 8th century, Ireland was divided into five kingdoms inhabited by Celtic and pre-Celtic tribes. The next invaders were the Norsemen, **Danes** and **Vikings**, two groups from modern-day Denmark and Norway, who came across the water in their longboats towards the end of the 8th century. The Vikings began to raid various places in Ireland and Britain. They attacked and ransacked monasteries along the coast, among them the great monastery at Lindisfarne in Northumberland, which was founded by an Irish monk in the 7th century to bring Christianity. The Norsemen landed in 793, burnt the settlement and killed many monks. After fifty years of sporadic plundering the Vikings eventually picked a convenient place for their raids on the Irish Sea at the mouth of the River Liffey. Their naval base of wooden houses later developed into the city of Dublin. The Danish Vikings came to Ireland from about 849 AD and fought the Norse Vikings. In 1014, Brian Boru defeated the Danes at Clontarf, and for the next 150 years Ireland was free from invasion but subject to clan warfare.

In 1169 the Anglo-Normans invaded the country and made Dublin the centre of their conquest. Henry II of England (and Duke of Normandy), who held court in Dublin in 1172, established English control, and became Lord of Ireland. Henry VII (1457–1509) was the first monarch to send English settlers to the island to secure control of the conquered territory. This measure became known as **Plantations of Ireland** and was intensified by King Henry VIII (1491–1547), his daughter Queen Elizabeth (1533–1603) and James I (1566–1625). It was applied on a larger scale in the provinces of Munster and Ulster after a rebellion of Irish tribal chiefs. Over half a million acres of the northern county were taken from the Irish earls and given to English and Scottish settlers. The Irish, in their majority Catholics, saw these Protestant newcomers as invaders and occupiers. This colonisation marks the beginning of the **Ulster conflict** – three hundred years of bloody and bitter hostility between the Irish and the British.

Struggle for independence
Oliver Cromwell thwarted the **Irish rebellion** of 1641 against the English administration in Ireland. During the Glorious Revolution (1688/89), Irish Catholics supported James II, while Ulster Protestants backed William of Orange, who became William III. After James' defeat at the "Battle of the Boyne" (1690, cf. "Conflict in Northern Ireland", page B 20), the English-controlled Irish Parliament passed a series of laws against Catholics. The period of independent legislation ended with the Act of Union in 1800, passed by the government of William Pitt. It abolished the Irish Assembly and created the United Kingdom of Great Britain and Ireland. In 1829, largely due to the efforts of the Irish political leader Daniel O'Connell, the Roman Catholic Relief Act was passed, which secured **Irish representation in the British Parliament** in Westminster. In spite of this, demands for self-government (**Home Rule**) within the British Empire intensified. As Ulster Protestants (Unionists) opposed the Irish Home Rule movement, a new political party, **Sinn Féin** (Irish for "ourselves" or "we ourselves"), was founded in 1905. Its policy involved passive resistance to the British, withholding of taxes, and establishing an Irish ruling council. In 1914 Home Rule was agreed, but with the "temporary" exclusion of the six counties of Ulster that would become Northern Ireland. However, implementation of Home Rule was suspended during World War I. In the **Easter Rising** (April 1916) Irish nationalists announced the creation of the Republic of Ireland. Led by Patrick Pearse and Tom Clarke, some 1,560 Irish Volunteers and 200 members of the Irish Citizen Army seized the Dublin General Post Office and other strategic points in Dublin. After five days of fighting, British troops put down the rebellion, and 15 of its leaders were tried and executed. Though the uprising itself had been unpopular with most of the Irish, the executions caused revulsion against the British authorities and led to a landslide victory for Sinn Féin in the Irish elections of 1918. The party won 73 out of 105 seats. In this way, the Easter Rising heralded the end of British power in Ireland.

Between 1919 and 1921 the **Irish Republican Army** (IRA), founded by Michael Collins, fought a guerrilla war against British forces. In 1920, a new Home Rule Bill established separate parliaments for Ulster and Catholic Ireland. In December 1921 an agreement, the **Anglo-Irish Treaty**, was signed by the British government and the provisional Irish Republican government, by which Ireland was divided into two parts: the Irish Free State in the south, which became a dominion within the Commonwealth, and the province of Ulster in the north, which remained part of the United Kingdom. Diverging opinions among the IRA about the treaty led to the **Irish Civil War** (1922/23) between a faction led by Michael Collins which supported the treaty and a group under Eamon de Valera opposing it. After heavy fighting pro-treaty government forces gained the upper hand. A ceasefire was called and in May 1923 the war ended. However, no surrender was called and no formal end to the war was ever negotiated. The Civil War exposed the rifts among Irish nationalists and left bitter memories, which have influenced Irish party politics until today (cf. "Conflict in Northern Ireland", page B 20). In 1937, under the presidency of de Valera, the Irish Free State established a new constitution which created the sovereign state of "Eire" (the Gaelic name for Ireland), but still kept some ties to Britain. In 1949 the country left the Commonwealth and became fully independent as the Republic of Ireland. Since 1973 Ireland has been a member of the European Union.

Social and economic developments

Ireland's outlying position in the far north-western corner of Europe and its separation from Great Britain by the Irish Sea and the St George's Channel have, for a long time, been the reasons for the island's **geographical marginalisation**. Long under English or British rule, nearly all Irish people made their living from farming, and many who could not find employment were forced to leave their homes to make a new start in England, the USA or other parts of the world. Following the Great Famine of the 1840s Ireland lost half its population and fell further into neglect. The turning point came in the 1920s when Ireland gained independence and in the 1970s when it joined the European Community. Not only did the exodus of Irish people come to a halt, migrants from other European and 'non-European' countries arrived in great numbers, transforming the island's demographic and cultural landscape. Ireland, which for centuries had been an exporter of labour, now became a receiver and was thus now longer regarded as the "poor man on the outskirts of Europe".

Economy and waves of emigration

The waves of emigration and immigration which Ireland experienced in the course of time are a reflection of the country's **economic struggles**. People in Ireland were never rich, least of all the small farmers who grew just about enough to feed their families. At the beginning of the 19th century Ireland's rural population began to grow rapidly as a result of the Industrial Revolution. Generally speaking, living standards and health care improved and mechanisation generated jobs and made goods cheaper. People earned more and were younger when they could afford to marry and start a family. Consequently, Ireland's population increased from 3 million people in 1700 to 8.2 million in 1841. However, a catastrophe in the mid-1840s brought about a dramatic **demographic shift**. For several years running the entire potato crop failed due to a fungus with disastrous consequences. One million Irish people died of starvation during the **Great Famine** and over one million fled across the Atlantic. There is evidence that prevailing ideologies in the late 1840s among the British ruling classes prevented the government in London from helping the Irish in their desperate situation and supplying food. The political élite and the middle classes were still deeply prejudiced against the Catholic Irish and many also believed the famine was a divine judgment on the inefficient Irish agricultural system. By the end of the decade, half of all **immigration to the United States** was from Ireland. The descendants of Irish immigrants made their marks in politics in America (Kennedy, Nixon, Reagan) and Canada (Claude Ryan, Brian Mulroney). Many Irish **emigrated to Britain** where they found work on the railways or in the construction industry. The exodus of Irish people continued because the social conditions in Ireland did not improve. Working class people in Dublin's slums lived in dreadful poverty and many died of hunger, fever, typhoid, whooping cough *(= Keuchhusten)*, pneumonia *(= Lungenentzündung)* and consumption *(= Schwindsucht)*. Millions turned their backs on their homeland to escape from a cold and pitiless world where unemployment, alcoholism, crime and violence thrived. As a result of this **mass emigration** the Irish population fell to 4.5 million in 1900 and continued to fall until the mid-20th century. In 1961 it reached its lowest point in modern history, 2.8 million people, less than half its pre-famine tally of 6 million.

The turning point for Ireland's economy came under the guidance of the Secretary of the Department of Finance, T. K. Whitaker, who replaced the Irish economic policy of protectionism with a liberal, wide-open economy. It took decades for Ireland to change **from a closed and rural society to an urban, tourist-centred land**, but eventually the country came out of its depression, economic growth accelerated and unemployment figures fell. A great boost came in 1973, when Ireland joined what was then the European Economic Community (EEC), later European Union (EU). As a result, Irish citizens stopped flooding out of the country, thus reducing emigration to an all-time low. Better still, a **reverse trend** began. Many people started coming home as there were now job opportunities for all. It is estimated that from 1995 to 2000 a quarter of a million people immigrated to Ireland, only half of them were returning Irish. The population rose to 3.7 million, transforming Ireland into a "country of net immigration". For the first time in its history, Ireland experienced a significant inflow of migrants – both workers and asylum seekers – from outside the European Union. The population has continued growing and reached almost 4.5 million in 2011.

To describe the boom years of the late 1990s the term '**Celtic Tiger**' was coined. The average growth rate of the Irish economy in those years was between 6 and 9.5 per cent and mainly due to foreign investors (many of them tech firms such as Microsoft or Siemens) who set up production plants because of Ireland's favourable tax rates. The rise in the Gross Domestic Product per head illustrates Ireland's enormous progress: In 1973 the GDP amounted to $ 2,351 and shot up to $ 25,680 in 1999.

The boom ended with the bursting of the internet bubble in 2001, when Internet sites which had suddenly risen and attracted bankers and shareholders, went out of business, causing substantial losses for many investors. In spite of this, a second boom for the Irish economy began in 2004, when the EU was enlarged and Ireland (like Britain and Sweden) allowed residents from ten **new EU member nations** (among them the Czech Republic, Estonia, Hungary, Latvia, Lithuania and Poland) to move in and work right away. In hardly more than a year, 85,000 Eastern Europeans arrived to work, fuelling a new '**Celtic Tiger II**' boom. However, the tides turned again, when the world economy was hit by the financial crisis of 2008, which also triggered an economic crisis in Ireland. After 24 years of continuous growth a recession set in and the problem which Ireland had thought to have got rid of returned. In order to deal with the country's enormous fiscal deficit and the instability of the banking sector the Irish government applied for help from the EU, the euro area Member States and the **International Monetary Fund** (IMF) in November

2010. Credits of 85 billion Euros were granted to cover the costs of the most expensive **banking crisis** in an advanced economy since the 1970s. Following the demands of the European money lenders the Irish government introduced an **austerity programme**, raising taxes and cutting benefits and services. Many young people were forced to leave the country to escape from rising living costs, unaffordable house prices and bleak job opportunities. The unemployment rate rose from 5.8 in 1999 to 13.5 per cent in 2011.

Employment chances today are primarily in the production (pharmaceuticals, food, computer and electronics) and service industries. Agriculture, once Ireland's most important sector, plays a minor role, although Irish farmers benefited greatly from the country's membership of the **European Union** which provided grants for the modernization of farming. Agriculture employs only a small percentage of Ireland's workforce; the overwhelming majority are employed in the service industries, such as education, health care, insurance, real estate, and the operation of restaurants and hotels. Irish **tourism** has increased steadily in importance in recent years, especially in view of the fact that the major drivers of growth since 2002 – construction, financial services and the retail sector – have slowed dramatically. By the late 1980s, some 2.7 million tourists annually visited the country, today more than 8 million come, adding considerably to Ireland's income. Despite this overall positive development, the Irish tourism industry is going through a difficult phase. In 2010 there were over two million fewer visitors coming to Ireland, compared to 2007. The downturn in overseas visitors to Ireland is due to the global recession of 2008 and 2009 and the perception that for many foreign visitors Ireland is a very expensive destination.

Society
Wealth has never been evenly distributed in Ireland and the disparity has often resulted in **social clashes**. A study by the Bank of Ireland of 2007 highlighted the extent of inequality in wealth distribution in Ireland today. The top 1 per cent of the Irish population controlled 34 per cent of all wealth. Even during the times of the financial crises of 2008/9 the rich got richer, whereas the working class suffered, many losing their jobs, savings and houses. Inequality and discrimination are not phenomena of the present, they have a long tradition. In the days of the Plantation of Ireland in the 16th and 17th centuries the English monarchs seized the most fertile stretches of land from the Irish and gave it to English and Scottish settlers. The fact that the new masters from Britain were Protestants and the dispossessed Irish were Catholics added a religious dimension to the hostility between these two groups and became the root of a **religious and economic struggle** that was to last for more than four centuries. Especially Ireland's northern province Ulster became the stage for the sectarian conflict.

Conflict in Northern Ireland
Constant revolts in all Ireland against the often brutal British rule ignited in the 1916 Easter Rising in Dublin, which caused a chain of events that led to Ireland's independence from Britain in 1921. Since the Protestants in Ulster did not want to be part of a Catholic-dominated Ireland, the country was divided (cf. "Struggle for independence", page B 17). The 26 counties in the south formed a separate state, **the free**

Republic of Ireland, whereas the six counties in the north maintained the union with Great Britain. Tensions in Northern Ireland between the Protestant majority, referred to as "**Unionists**" or "**Loyalists**", and the Catholic minority, known as "**Nationalists**" or "**Republicans**", intensified. Not only did both groups fight for different political aims, they were also bitterly opposed in everyday life, because the Catholics felt discriminated over housing and jobs, which fuelled bitter resentment and led to violent protests. In order to avoid a civil war the British government decided to deploy troops in Northern Ireland in 1969 and handle Northern Irish affairs from Westminster (**Direct Rule**). This marks the beginning of a period of bombings and killings which came to be known as "**The Troubles**". The month of July was always a month of extreme violence, because the Protestant Unionists traditionally marched through predominantly Catholic areas in Belfast and Londonderry in commemoration of the **Battle of the Boyne** in 1690. Then the forces of the King James II and the Irish Catholics were defeated by **William of Orange** and the Ulster Protestants. Catholic protestors usually attempted to stop the marching Protestant Orangemen and as a precaution the police and army were called in to keep the opposing groups apart. But the same sad scene repeated itself year after year: Masked men throwing stones, bottles, petrol and paint bombs, setting cars on fire and attacking police officers with cudgels. On Sunday, January 30, 1972 British soldiers shot into a crowd of unarmed civil-rights protesters in Derry in Northern Ireland, killing 13 people. The massacre went down in history as "**Bloody Sunday**" and is often referred to as an example of the absurdity and futility of war. One of the most famous songs of the Irish band U2 centres on the incident. In 2010, the British government released a report calling the British Army's actions on Bloody Sunday "unjustified".

Over the years numerous **attempts to overcome the conflicts** were made by governments of Britain and Ireland or independent mediators (e. g. US Senator George Mitchell) to come to a peaceful agreement between the **Green** (Catholics) and the **Orange** (Protestants). More than 3,500 people lost their lives as a result of political violence in Northern Ireland. After many ups and downs, the two governments and the Northern Ireland political parties began peace talks and finally came to an agreement on April 10, 1998. They signed the **Good Friday Agreement**, which called for the transfer of power from London back to Belfast (the return of **Home Rule**) and the establishment of a Northern Ireland Assembly and Executive Committee in which unionist and nationalist parties would share power. However, hopes that the agreement would bring an end to 30 years of bitter civil and sectarian conflict were not fulfilled, because the IRA refused to hand in arms ('**decommissioning**') and committed repeated terrorist acts in protest against the agreement. Consequently, in October 2002 the devolved government was suspended again – for almost five years. In 2007 Home Rule returned to Northern Ireland, elections were held and former enemies joined forces: the leader of the Democratic Unionist Party (DUP), Ian Paisley, was elected First Minister (2007/08) and his year-long opponent of **Sinn Féin**, Martin McGuinness, took office as Deputy First Minister (2007–2011). The success of the Northern Ireland peace process also made the first visit of a reigning British monarch to the Irish Republic possible. Queen Elizabeth paid a **state visit** in May

2011, the **first by a British monarch since independence**. Her grandfather King George V was the last to visit the country in 1911 when it was then part of the United Kingdom.

Timeline Northern Ireland Conflict

1603–1660: Plantation of Ulster	Scottish and English farmers, mainly Protestants are sent to Ireland by James I. They settle in Ulster. Confessional division and discrimination of the Catholics
1690	Battle of the Boyne
1801: Act of Union	"Home Rule" = limited self-government; autonomy under British sovereignty
1916: Easter Rising	In Dublin Irish Republicans rebel; rebellion crushed by British Forces
1921: Partition of Ireland	As a result of the Anglo-Irish War (1919–1921) Ireland is divided into Republic of Ireland and Northern Ireland (Ulster).
14/08/1969: Deployment of British troops	The British government sends troops to Ulster to avoid a civil war. The IRA heightens its campaign of terrorist acts.
1972: Bloody Sunday	13 Catholics are killed by British troops during a protest march. End of "Home Rule": The British government rules over Ulster from London.
1985: *Anglo-Irish Accord*	The Irish government in Dublin is given a consultative role as far as the interests of the Catholics in Northern Ireland are concerned.
During the 1990s	Repeated efforts to solve the problem in Northern Ireland in peace talks. Sinn Féin (Irish = *wir selbst*), the political wing of the IRA is included
1998: *Good Friday Agreement*	Agreement between Britain, Ireland and the conflicting parties in Northern Ireland; elections are held to form a new Northern Irish Assembly.
Dec.1999	Creation of *Northern Ireland Assembly*
Feb. 2000	Row over weapons decommissioning results in a four-month suspension of the Assembly
Sep. 2001	After the terrorist attacks on America, the IRA promises to decommission its weapons; the Ulster Unionists return to the Assembly.
2005	Decommissioning completed: an independent commission confirms that the IRA has decommissioned its weapons.

2007	Home Rule restored
2010	British government apologises for army's actions on Bloody Sunday.
June/July 2011	Riots in Belfast, spreading to other parts of Northern Ireland
2012	Queen Elizabeth II shakes hands with former IRA commander Martin McGuinness.

Cultural developments

Ireland's **cultural roots** lie in the traditions of the native Gaelic population and the diverse ethnic groups that settled in the country over centuries. Celts, Vikings, Anglo-Normans (English and French) have left their marks and created a rich cultural heritage. After the decline and collapse of the Roman Empire Ireland was the centre of Christian civilisation in Northern Europe. The **Irish monasteries** – with those in Clonmacnoise and Clonard among the most famous – became notable centres of learning. From the 6th century to the Middle Ages, Irish bishops, monks and missionaries (St Patrick, St Columba) played a prominent role in **spreading Christianity** and establishing monasteries in Great Britain (Lindisfarne in Northumberland) and continental Europe (Luxeuil Abbey in France and Bobbio Abbey in Italy). St Patrick's Day (17 March) and other Irish festivals such as Halloween (31 October) are observed and celebrated all over the world. Ireland's contributions to the world of music and literature are recognised worldwide and Irish authors have influenced modern writers in all countries.

Catholic religion – importance today

The **Roman Catholic Church** has long played a major role in Irish social life, although the number of believers attending mass has been declining in both parts of the island. In the south 84 per cent of the population regard themselves as Catholic, whereas the percentage in the north amounts to 48 per cent. The Roman Catholic Church has always held **strong opinions on ethical issues** such as abortion and divorce. It was regarded as a sensation when in 1995, after a bitter campaign of the Irish Government against the Roman Catholic hierarchy, a slight majority in Ireland voted to remove its constitutional ban on **divorce and remarriage**. However, abortion still remains a controversial issue and several national referendums have been unsuccessful, which means that **abortion** in the Republic of Ireland is illegal unless it occurs as the result of a medical intervention performed to save the life of the mother. Recently, the reputation of the Catholic Church has been badly tarnished by investigations revealing widespread **abuse of children** as well as **illicit sexual relationships** (homosexuality and priests breaking their celibacy vows) among the clergy. In 2010, Pope Benedict apologized to the children of Ireland ("You have suffered grievously and I am truly sorry.") and severely reprimanded Irish bishops.

Literature

The earliest **Irish literature** was preserved orally by the Gaelic poets and was later written down by Irish monks. When the English conquered Ireland, Gaelic literature became forgotten, and was only revived towards the end of the 19th century by William Butler Yeats (1865–1939), who wrote in English, but showed a deep love for **Gaelic tradition** and folklore. Yeats was awarded the Nobel Prize for literature in 1923.

Among the most well-known Irish writers are the satirist Jonathan Swift (1667–1745), the dramatists Oliver Goldsmith (1728–1774) and Richard Brinsley Sheridan (1751–1816). In the 20th century Oscar Wilde (1854–1900) and George Bernard Shaw (1856–1950) made Irish writing famous on the London stage. Shaw won the Nobel Prize for Literature in 1925. James Joyce (1882–1941) is regarded as the founder of the modern psychological novel. His first major work was *Dubliners* (1914), a collection of stories about lower middle class people of his hometown. His novel *Ulysses* (1922) had an enormous impact on modern world literature because of the technique of narration *(stream of consciousness)* which Joyce used to present the thoughts, sensations, and memories of the main character. Another Nobel Prize winner was Samuel Beckett (1906–1989), whose play *Waiting for Godot* (1953) has become a modern classic of absurd theatre. The latest Irishman to win a Nobel Prize is the poet Seamus Heaney (born 1939). In Germany, interest in Irish literature and Ireland as a country was especially stimulated by the writer Heinrich Böll, who spent time on Achill Island off the west coast of Ireland and recorded some of his experiences in his book *Irisches Tagebuch* (1957).

Irish history provides the backdrop in many works of Irish writers. The "Easter Rising" of 1916, for example, is an important event in Michael McLaverty's (1904–1992) first novel *Call My Brother Back* written in 1939. The book became a bestseller only later when it was re-issued in the 1970s because of its relevance to incidents of the "Troubles". In *Cal* (1983) Bernard MacLaverty (born 1942) describes the psychological conflicts of a young man who participates in a murder planned and carried out by the IRA. Roddy Doyle (born 1958) also uses the Irish national rebellion in Dublin in 1916 as a decisive incident in the life of Henry Smart, the protagonist in Doyle's novel *A Star Called Henry* (1999). Frank McCourt (1930–2009) gained fame for his memoir *Angela's Ashes* (1996), in which he retells his miserable childhood in the slums of Limerick, where he grew up in extreme poverty because his father rarely worked, and when he did drank his wages.

Irish artists have always found a way of combining tradition and modernity. This is not only true for Irish bands and musicians like Bono of U2 or Enya, but also writers who took up topical issues such as violence and alcoholism or modern man's insecurity, his search for identity and his place in the world. The Irish artists Joyce, Becket and Brendan Behan (1923–1964) were at the forefront of those who re-interpreted traditional values in a new modern urban context.

Music

Irish traditional music and **Irish folk songs** are heard all over the world. Tourists flock to the "singing pubs" in Ireland to enjoy an evening out, listening to Irish tunes performed by artists on instruments such as **harp** (one of the Irish national symols), bagpipes, banjoy, bodhran (a wooden percussion instrument with goat skin), guitar, Irish Bouzouki, tin whistle and, of course, fiddle and accordion. Most folk songs have been written in English and Irish and are less than two hundred years old. The list of world-famous Irish musicians is almost endless. The most popular include the folk band The Dubliners, singers Sinéad O'Connor, Enya, Chris de Burgh, Ronan Keating, Declan O'Rourke and the rock band U2.

Food and Drink

A pub visit is not complete without having tasted typical Irish food. One of the most frequently used ingredients is the potato, which came to Ireland in the second half of the 16th century and has heavily influenced Ireland's cuisine. Representative Irish dishes are **Irish mutton stew**, bacon and cabbage, boxty (a type of bread made using grated raw potatoes and flour), coddle (consisting of layers of roughly sliced pork sausages and bacon with sliced potatoes and onions) and colcannon (cabbage and potatoes boiled and mashed together).

As to drinks, **Irish coffee** consisting of hot coffee, **Irish whiskey** (with an "e"), sugar and topped with thick cream and Irish beer are known in all bars and restaurants of the world. Brewing in Ireland has a long history, and one of the traditional breweries is **Guinness** in Dublin. The types of beer that Guinness make are called stout (very dark brown and bitter) and porter (a sweeter stout).

Abiturähnliche Übungsaufgaben und Originalprüfungen

Schleswig-Holstein – Englisch
Abiturähnliche Übungsaufgabe 1 *(Canada)*

Mediation

20 % Gesamtleistung

In einem Chatroom unterhalten Sie sich mit der Amerikanerin Roisin über das Phänomen „Sexting". Sie ist eine High School-Schülerin im letzten Jahr und arbeitet an einem Projekt, mit dem sie ihre Mitschüler über mögliche Gefahren aufklären möchte. Sie haben vor Kurzem einen Artikel dazu gelesen. Roisin wird neugierig, als sie hört, dass das Phänomen sich auch in Deutschland ausbreitet. Sie bittet Sie, ihr eine kurze Zusammenfassung des Textes zu schicken.

Fassen Sie zusammen, wie sich das Problem in Deutschland äußert, welche Probleme dadurch verursacht werden und wie Eltern, Pädagogen und Wissenschaftler darauf reagieren.

Nacktfotos als Tauschobjekt: Lehrer warnen vor „Sexting"-Trend

Das „Sexting"-Problem ist den Schulleitern so wichtig, dass sie keine Zeit verlieren. „Wir ... stehen vor einem Problem", schreiben die fünf Pädagogen aus dem niedersächsischen Cloppenburg gleich im ersten Satz ihres Briefes an die Eltern.

Berlin. Immer häufiger berichteten Schülerinnen und Schüler von Nacktbildern, die über Soziale Netzwerke und Smartphones verbreitet würden. Auf diesen Bildern seien auch eigene Schüler zu sehen, berichten die Schulleiter in dem Elternbrief, den der NDR auf seiner Webseite veröffentlichte. Der Schulleiter des Cloppenburger Clemens-
5 August-Gymnasiums, Günter Kannen, sagte dem Sender, dass oft 13- bis 14-jährige Mädchen auf den Bildern zu sehen seien. Die Fotos würden schnell weitergereicht, „so dass alle Handys voll von Nacktfotos sind", sagte er dem NDR. „Ich finde es sehr erschreckend, vor allen Dingen wenn ich bedenke, dass wir Lehrer ebenso wie die Eltern von diesen Dingen tatsächlich nichts wissen."
10 Kannen und seine Kollegen sind auf ein Phänomen gestoßen, das aus den USA nach Deutschland herüberschwappt: das „Sexting". Das Kunstwort setzt sich aus „Sex" und dem englischen „texting" zusammen, was „SMS schreiben" bedeutet. Vor allem Jugendliche schießen anzügliche oder nackte Fotos von sich und anderen und stellen sie ins Internet oder verschicken sie mit dem Handy. Denn ihre Smartphones
15 benutzen Teenager schon lange nicht mehr vorrangig zum Telefonieren, wie es die Eltern vielleicht erwarten. Stattdessen kommunizieren sie über Apps wie WhatsApp, Snapchat oder Facebook. Auf Facebook sind 81 Prozent der 12- bis 19-Jährigen aus Deutschland aktiv, zeigen Zahlen der JIM-Studie über Jugendliche im Netz. Mit der App Snapchat können Nutzer Bilder verschicken, die sich innerhalb weniger Sekun-
20 den selbst zerstören. Der Anschein der Vergänglichkeit sorgte für einen Nutzeransturm, über 200 Millionen Bildchen werden inzwischen nach Angaben der Firma pro Tag verschickt.

Jugendliche nutzten auch die Frage-Webseite Ask.fm, um erotische Bilder hochzuladen, berichtet Stefanie Rack von der Initiative klicksafe. Sie hat Material zum Thema für Lehrer entwickelt. Teenager machten sich oft wenig Gedanken darüber, wie sich die Bilder im Internet verbreiten können, sagt sie. „Sie glauben immer noch, dass das nur ein eingeschränkter Kreis sehen kann." Weil die Apps ständig verfügbar sind, landeten Fotos schnell im Netz. Das sollten Eltern beim Smartphone-Kauf bedenken, warnen die Schulleiter. „Sie kaufen ein Gerät mit unbeschränktem Zugang zum Internet."

Zu überprüfen, was Kinder und Jugendliche damit anstellen, ist gar nicht so einfach. „Viele dieser Gespräche zwischen Jugendlichen laufen inzwischen versteckt", sagt der US-Forscher Justin Patchin von der Universität von Wisconsin. Früher führten Jugendliche etwa Telefonate vom gemeinsamen Familienapparat in der Küche, SMS und WhatsApp-Nachrichten dagegen sind für Eltern eben meist uneinsehbar.

Patchin forscht zu digitalem Mobbing, neben Nacktbildern ein weiteres Problem. Doch er warnt davor, die Verantwortung auf die Technik zu schieben: Dieses Schikanieren habe es lange gegeben, „bevor es diese Technologie gab", sagte er kürzlich bei einem Kongress gegen Cybermobbing in Berlin. Er rät Eltern, sich über Technik-Trends zu informieren, um ihren Kindern Rat geben zu können. Eltern sollten mit Kindern und Jugendlichen über ihren Umgang mit Technologie sprechen, meinen die Experten. Denn die Verbreitung von Pornobildern könne auch rechtliche Folgen haben: „Die machen sich strafbar, wenn sie das anderen Jugendlichen zugänglich machen", warnt Rack von klicksafe. Sie rät Teenagern dazu, die Selbstdarstellung privat auszutesten – mit dem eigenen Partner, nicht dem Smartphone. (531 Wörter)

dpa, 31.10.2013

Textaufgabe 80 % Gesamtleistung

Excerpt from *Death by Landscape* by Margaret Atwood

Lucy was her best friend at camp. Lois had other friends in winter, when there was school and itchy woolen clothing and darkness in the afternoons, but Lucy was her summer friend.

She turned up the second year, when Lois was ten, and a Bluejay. (Chickadees,
5 Bluejays, Ravens, and Kingfishers – these were the names Camp Manitou assigned to the different age groups, a sort of totemic clan system. […])

Lois helped Lucy to unpack her tin trunk and place the folded clothes on the wooden shelves, and to make up her bed. She put her in the top bunk right above her, where she could keep an eye on her. Already she knew that Lucy was an exception,
10 to a good many rules; already she felt proprietorial.

Lucy was from the United States, where the comic books came from, and the movies. […] The only reason Lucy was being sent to *this* camp (she cast a look of minor scorn around the cabin, diminishing it and also offending Lois, while at the same time daunting her) was that her mother had been a camper here. […]
15 "My father plays golf," [Lois] ventured at last.

"*Everyone* plays golf," said Lucy. "My *mother* plays golf."

Lois's mother did not. Lois took Lucy to see the outhouses and the swimming dock and the dining hall […], knowing in advance they would not measure up.

This was a bad beginning; but Lucy was good-natured, and accepted Camp Mani-
20 tou with the same casual shrug with which she seemed to accept everything. She would make the best of it, without letting Lois forget that this was what she was doing.

However, there were things Lois knew that Lucy did not. Lucy scratched the tops off all her mosquito bites and had to be taken to the infirmary to be daubed with
25 Ozonol. She took her T-shirt off while sailing, and although the counsellor spotted her after a while and made her put it back on, she burnt spectacularly, bright red, with the X of her bathing-suit straps standing out in alarming white; she let Lois peel the sheets of whispery-thin burned skin off her shoulders. When they sang "Alouette" around the campfire, she did not know any of the French words. The difference was
30 that Lucy did not care about the things she didn't know, whereas Lois did.

During the next winter, and subsequent winters, Lucy and Lois wrote to each other. They were both only children, at a time when this was thought to be a disadvantage, so in their letters they pretended to be sisters, or even twins. Lois had to strain a little over this, because Lucy was so blonde, with translucent skin and large
35 blue eyes like a doll's, and Lois was nothing out of the ordinary – just a tallish, thinnish, brownish person with freckles. They signed their letters LL, with the L's entwined together like the monograms on a towel. […]

They were more effusive in their letters than they ever were in person. They bordered their pages with X's and O's, but when they met again in the summers it was

3

always a shock. They had changed so much, or Lucy had. It was like watching someone grow up in jolts. At first it would be hard to think up things to say.

But Lucy always had a surprise or two, something to show, some marvel to reveal. The first year she had a picture of herself in a tutu, her hair in a ballerina's knot on the top of her head; she pirouetted around the swimming dock, to show Lois how it was done, and almost fell off. The next year she had given that up and was taking horseback riding. (Camp Manitou did not have horses.) The next year her mother and father had been divorced, and she had a new stepfather [...] and a new house, although the maid was the same. The next year, when they had graduated from Bluejays and entered Ravens, she got her period, right in the first week of camp. The two of them snitched some matches from their counsellor, who smoked illegally, and made a small fire out behind the farthest outhouse, at dusk, using their flashlights. They could set all kinds of fires by now; they had learned how in Campcraft. On this fire they burned one of Lucy's used sanitary napkins. Lois is not sure why they did this, or whose idea it was. But she can remember the feeling of deep satisfaction it gave her as the white fluff singed and the blood sizzled, as if some wordless ritual had been fulfilled.

They did not get caught, but then they rarely got caught at any of their camp transgressions. Lucy had such large eyes, and was such an accomplished liar.

This year Lucy is different again: slower, more languorous. [...] She hates her private school. She has a boyfriend, who is sixteen and works as a gardener's assistant. This is how she met him: in the garden. She describes to Lois what it is like when he kisses her – rubbery at first, but then your knees go limp. She has been forbidden to see him, and threatened with boarding school. She wants to run away from home.

Lois has little to offer in return. Her own life is placid and satisfactory, but there is nothing much that can be said about happiness. "You're so lucky," Lucy tells her, a little smugly. She might as well say *boring* because this is how it makes Lois feel.

(931 words)

© *Margaret Atwood 1991, Wilderness Tips, Bloomsbury Publishing Plc.*

Assignments

1. Lois' aunt, who used to be a camper at Camp Manitou as well, has asked her niece what life at camp is like nowadays. Write Lois' letter. *(20 %)*

2. Analyse how the girls' relationship is presented. *(45 %)*

3. Conceive of an ending to the story. *(35 %)*

Lösungsvorschläge

Mediation

- Keep in mind that you are writing the summary for someone who is about your age.
- You may use colloquial language, but since Roisin needs the information for a school project, you should not use slang. The aspects which are directly asked for in the task (What happens in Germany? Which problems arise? Reaction of scientists, parents and teachers?) may help you to structure your text. Do not neglect any of them.

Hi Roisin,

Here is the information from the article: "sexting" is a real problem at our schools here in Germany, which is underestimated especially by young students. More and more photos of 13- to 14-year-old girls are being shared via smart phone or the Internet.

The problem is that it is difficult to control what children and teenagers do on the Internet. Teenagers decide themselves what they put on the Internet and usually neither parents nor teachers know about it. By posting a picture the girls and boys give away the ability to control what happens with their images. Most of them do not think about the consequences at all and thus involuntarily destroy their or their friends' reputations with one click. Another problem caused by this phenomenon is bullying, which is the reason why more parents and teachers are becoming aware of what their children and pupils are doing, and are calling for prevention.

Scientists say that the problem does not only have a technical side but that awareness is the key. Since children have direct access to the Internet at any time and almost everywhere thanks to smart phones, it is easy to communicate secretly. To keep phenomena like "sexting" from happening, parents and teachers must talk to the children. Stefanie Rack from klicksafe has rather plain advice – get naked if you want but do not do it on the Internet.

So you can see that we are aware of the problem here in Germany and that prevention is the first line of defence against it. Let me know your results at the end of your project …

Bye,
Anne   *(272 words)*

Textaufgabe

1. *This assignment is basically meant to test your reading skills, so make sure you get all the facts right and do not invent anything. On another level, it also tests your ability to write a letter. Therefore, you ought to pay attention to the question of which facts are interesting to the recipient, or which ones Lois would reveal. Naturally, you must also fulfil the formal requirements of a letter.*

21st July

Dear Aunt Sally,

Thank you for your letter about your experiences here at camp. I've been here for two weeks already, and I'm enjoying myself very much.

This is my sixth year at camp, so I'm a Raven now. We still live in groups in the cabins, like you said, and eat together in the dining hall. The swimming dock is pretty much the same too, I would guess. Everything seems to be getting a bit old, but I like it! Only I could do without the mosquitoes ... They're especially bad when we sit around the campfires in the evening. Did you sing "Alouette" all the time, too? Speaking of campfires – I learned how to make a fire in Campcraft. That's really useful.

But the best thing about camp is probably my best friend Lucy, who is from America. I call her my "summer friend" because we only ever meet at camp. The rest of the year we just write letters. That's pretty strange, because when we see each other again after almost a year, we have a lot of catching up to do. Lucy always has something new to tell. When we first met we were still Bluejays, and she was totally into dancing. Then she turned to riding horses. Right now she doesn't do sports, because she has a boyfriend. Her parents are acting up about him, though, because he's just their gardener's assistant. Poor Lucy! She says she'll run away if they don't stop. I hope she won't ... she's so much fun!

I have to go now, because we want to go swimming in the lake. I'll write again soon!

Love,
Lois

(280 words)

2. *In this assignment you need to take a closer look at the relationship between Lois and Lucy. You should start by characterising their relationship and then go on to analyse the way the author describes it. Find out what is said between the lines from the author's allusions and choice of words.*

Lois and Lucy have a very special relationship. At camp they are best friends. According to Lois, Lucy is her "summer friend" (l. 3). She distinguishes her from her "other friends in winter" (l. 1) by associating them with winter clothes, winter weather, and having to go to school. Therefore, Lucy is indirectly endowed with all the good qualities usually connected with "summer", such as light, warmth and leisure.

As the person from whose perspective the story is narrated, Lois takes the more active part in the relationship, at least at the beginning. When Lucy arrives, for instance, Lois helps her to find her way around Camp Manitou, thus giving her an advantage over Lucy at first. Lucy is unfamiliar with traditional Canadian songs, for example, despite her being half Canadian ("When they sang 'Alouette' around the campfire, she did not know any of the French words", ll. 28 f.). She even makes very obvious mistakes because she does not know how to behave in the wilderness ("Lucy scratched the tops off all her mosquito bites [...]. She took her T-shirt off while sailing, and [...] burnt spectacularly", ll. 23 ff.). In contrast to Lois, however, she does not seem to be bothered by this ("Lucy did not care about the things she didn't know", l. 30). Lois' interest seems to be more than that of a fellow camper. She admits to feeling "proprietorial" (l. 10) about Lucy from the start. This feeling of possessiveness is increased by the narrator's description of how Lois practically treats Lucy like an object: "She put her in the top bunk right above her, where she could keep an eye on her" (ll. 8 f.), and culminates in her characterisation of Lucy as a toy ("large blue eyes like a doll's", ll. 34 f.).

Their friendship is surprising to the reader because they have very different personalities. This becomes clear in their attitudes towards Camp Manitou, for example. Lois, on the one hand, identifies with the camp ("Lois was ten, and a Bluejay", l. 4). She is affronted by her friend's frank disapproval (cf. ll. 17 f.). Lucy, on the other hand, tries to provoke Lois by disdaining Camp Manitou, as we can see in ll. 12 ff.: "she cast a look of minor scorn around the cabin, diminishing it [...] while at the same time daunting her". Lucy's behaviour makes Lois feel inferior. According to Lois, Lucy is satisfied that Lois' life is less interesting than hers ("'You're so lucky,' Lucy tells her, a little smugly. She might as well say *boring* because this is how it makes Lois feel", ll. 64 f.).

Nevertheless, there are signs of intimate friendship between them. When Lucy has sunburn, she lets "Lois peel the sheets of whispery-thin burned skin off her shoulders" (ll. 27 f.). Their relationship is even stronger on a fictional level when they write letters to each other over the winter and imagine they are twins in order to overcome the disadvantage that they have no siblings (cf. ll. 31 f.).

When they meet in person, they have to get used to each other again. This is where Lucy takes the initiative: every year she has something new to tell to break the ice (cf. l. 42). What is more, she becomes the instigator of a great deal of mischief they get up to together, like burning "one of Lucy's used sanitary napkins" (l. 53) on an illegally built fire. Lucy is also the reason why they are never found out or punished because she looks so innocent (cf. l. 57).

All in all, the relationship between Lois and Lucy leaves the reader slightly uneasy and with a sense of foreboding, as if the "wordless ritual" (l. 55) they perform together might have serious consequences. *(633 words)*

3. *Before you start writing, you should remind yourself of the different elements of the plot. Which ones seem promising for the further development of the story? Choose one or two and then start planning your ending. When writing, you should attempt to match the style of the author as closely as possible. Make sure you find a smooth transition from the ending of the extract to your first sentence. It is important, for instance, that the narrator switches from past tense to present tense – this might be a signal for the action to begin.*
Possible plot elements:
– boyfriend
– puberty
– parents
– running away
– jealousy
– letters in winter

The next campfire night, when they were all supposed to sit round the fire and sing songs to the counsellor's guitar, Lucy lags behind when all the others leave the cabin. Lois looks at her inquiringly. "Do we really have to?" Lucy sighs. "If I have to stand another chorus of 'Alouette', I'll scream." "Come on, it won't be that bad. Didn't you say you liked singing round the fire?" "I'd rather sit on the swimming-dock and watch the sunset. Are you coming?"
Lois follows her reluctantly. She has half promised to help with the singing, but she doesn't want to let Lucy down either, so they sit on the dock and throw small pebbles into the water. Lucy smokes a cigarette she has pilfered from one of the group leaders. She offers it to Lois. "No, thanks," Lois refuses. "I tend to feel sick afterwards." "Don't be ridiculous!" says Lucy. "You're starting to be really boring, just like all the others!" "And you're always complaining. You're behaving like a spoiled princess!" shouts Lois.
Lucy throws her cigarette into the lake. "Fine. Go sit by the fire and have a sing-song. I'm going to bed." And she storms off in the direction of the cabin. Lois hears a door slam. After a minute, she gets up and joins the others. But she isn't in the mood for singing anymore. Murmuring an apology, she leaves the campfire and walks to their cabin.
"Are you awake?" Lucy doesn't react. Lois is used to that – when Lucy sleeps, she sleeps like a log. She hears absolutely nothing. Lois gets undressed quickly and climbs into her bunk.
The next morning, she is woken by one of the girls shaking her. Bewildered, Lois sits up in bed. "What's up? What happened?" Lisa, who also sleeps in the cabin with them, is standing in front of Lucy's bed. Her body is screening most of it from Lois' view. "Lisa, what's the matter?" Lisa steps aside. "She's gone!" "We have to get the counsellor!"
The counsellor arrives. The girls report that Lucy is missing. The camp leader calls all the staff and organises a search of the area. Without success. Lucy remains lost. Phone calls are made. The police arrive. Search parties comb through the woods. There's no sign of Lucy. Finally, parents' cars begin to arrive and take

girls with them. Lois is among the last to be picked up. She begins to feel that something might have gone badly wrong.

The days are getting shorter. Lois has put away her shorts and her summer dresses. School will start soon. One morning, a letter arrives. Lois recognises the handwriting at once.

5th September 1991

Dearest Lois,

How are you? I'm fine. Although I miss you sooooo much! I'm with Steve right now. I'm so sorry about disappearing, but it was the only way to escape my dreadful life. You weren't worried about me, were you? No, you know all about me, you would've guessed what we were up to ...

Steve waited for me on the highway in his mother's car. We're going to start a new life together. When we've settled a bit, you simply must come and visit us. I can't give you my address now because my parents will probably pester your parents and make them supervise your mail or something. But I'm going to send you word real soon, and then we can talk everything over.

Lots of love and kisses,
LL *(580 words)*

Schleswig-Holstein – Englisch
Abiturähnliche Übungsaufgabe 2 *(Canada)*

Mediation 20 % Gesamtleistung

Sie nehmen an einem kulturellen Austauschprojekt mit einer High School in Arizona teil. Da es an der Schule viele Schüler mit Migrationshintergrund gibt (vor allem Schüler aus Mexico), wird an der Schule viel Spanisch gesprochen. Der Direktor möchte dies jetzt verbieten. Aus diesem aktuellen Anlass bittet Sie ein Lehrer zu berichten, ob es auch in Deutschland solche Probleme gibt. Sie haben von der Herbert Hoover Schule in Berlin gehört.

Berichten Sie, mit welchen Problemen die Schule und ihre Schüler zu kämpfen haben, mit welchem Projekt die Schule diesen begegnet, welche Kritik in der Presse laut wurde und warum das Projekt dennoch ein Erfolg ist.

Man spricht Deutsch

Eine Realschule in Berlin bemüht sich um Integration. Nun ist die Empörung groß

Jutta Steinkamp hätte nie gedacht, dass sie plötzlich einmal zu den Bösen rechnen würde. Die resolute weißhaarige Leiterin einer Realschule im Berliner Problemkiez Wedding taugt eigentlich ziemlich schlecht für die Rolle des Gottseibeiuns der Integrationspolitik. Sie führt eine Schule, in der 90 Prozent der Schüler „nichtdeutscher
5 Herkunft" sind, wie es im Amtsjargon heißt. Jutta Steinkamp arbeitet Tag für Tag mitten in der Parallelgesellschaft, und sie arbeitet tapfer gegen die Dynamik zunehmender Abschottung und Segregation. So jedenfalls hat sie es selbst immer gesehen.

Doch dann wurde in der vergangenen Woche bekannt, dass an der Herbert-Hoover-Schule Deutschsprechen Pflicht ist – und zwar nicht nur im Unterricht, son-
10 dern auch auf dem Schulhof und bei sonstigen schulischen Aktivitäten. Jutta Steinkamp muss sich seither eine Menge böser Vorwürfe gefallen lassen. Die Regelung an der Schule „schüre Ressentiments in der Mehrheitsgesellschaft", sagt Eren Unsal, die Sprecherin des Türkischen Bundes Berlin-Brandenburg. Das „Sprachverbot provoziert die Jugendlichen", warnt die PDS-Politikerin Evrim Baba. Der Grünen-Abge-
15 ordnete Özcan Mutlu hält die Deutschpflicht gar für den Ausdruck einer „Kultur der Ablehnung". Und Marianne Demmer vom Bundesvorstand der Lehrergewerkschaft GEW findet die Regelung „mindestens so kontraproduktiv wie den Einbürgerungsleitfaden aus Baden-Württemberg".

Jutta Steinkamp kann sich auf diese Kampagne gegen ihre Schule keinen Reim
20 machen: „Warum greifen mich ausgerechnet diejenigen an, die mich unterstützen müssten, weil sie doch angeblich ein Interesse an besserer Integration haben?"

Die türkischen Zeitungen, vor allem Hürriyet und Türkiye, spielen dabei eine unrühmliche Rolle. Sie stellen die Deutschpflicht an der Hoover-Schule in den Zusammenhang angeblich europaweit zunehmender Schikanen gegen Migranten und ihre kulturellen Eigenheiten. Als jüngste Beispiele für diese Tendenz gelten der Gesprächsleitfaden und die Pläne der niederländischen Integrationsministerin Rita Verdonk, die Ausländer verpflichten will, überall in der Öffentlichkeit nur noch Holländisch zu reden. Die türkische Presse nimmt all dies als Indiz einer neuerdings grassierenden Fremdenfeindlichkeit. Und nun, so wird suggeriert, kommt auch noch Frau Steinkamp daher!

Es mag gute Gründe geben, gegen den Leitfaden und gegen die niederländischen Kulturkampfmethoden zu sein – was jedoch im Wedding an der Hoover-Schule versucht wird, hat mit solchen obrigkeitsstaatlichen Regulierungsversuchen gerade nichts gemein. Die eifernde Empörungsroutine der Kritiker steht in auffallendem Kontrast zum Pragmatismus der Betroffenen. Die vermeintlich diskriminierende Regel ist nämlich in Wahrheit von den Schülern und Eltern der Hoover-Schule mitentwickelt worden. Und die Schulkonferenz, in der alle am Schulleben beteiligten Gruppen vertreten sind, hat sie bereits vor mehr als einem Jahr debattiert und abgesegnet.

Mit der Deutschpflicht hat man an der Schule gut gelebt, bis die mutwillig aufgepeitschten Wogen der Erregung über Jutta Steinkamp zusammenschlugen. „In vielen Klassen meiner Schule ist es völlig normal, dass Kinder mit acht verschiedenen Muttersprachen zusammensitzen", erklärt die Direktorin. „Die allermeisten von ihnen sprechen zu Hause nicht Deutsch, sehen kein deutsches Fernsehen, lesen keine deutsche Zeitung." Ihr sei es darum gegangen, den Raum, in dem die Kinder dem Deutschen ausgesetzt sind, möglichst auszuweiten. Die Deutschpflicht an der Hoover-Schule sei keine Alibipolitik, sondern Teil der pädagogischen Schwerpunktbildung Deutsch. An der Hoover-Schule gibt es mehr Deutschstunden als an anderen Schulen, und, wo immer möglich, sogar in kleinen Gruppen. Die kontinuierlich steigenden Anmeldezahlen zeigen, dass die Migrantenfamilien diese Anstrengungen honorieren.

(525 Wörter)

Lau, Jörg: „Man spricht Deutsch". In: Die Zeit (05/2006)

JA - ZUM LEISTUNGSPRINZIP

Leistungsbereitschaft ist eine Voraussetzung zum Erreichen eines Schulabschlusses. Wir unterstützen euch in Stärken und Schwächen, damit ihr in jedem Fach eure Fähigkeiten und Kenntnisse ausbauen könnt.
Die deutsche Sprache spielt dabei eine wichtige Rolle, denn:

Deutsch ist Bildungssprache.

JA - ZUR INDIVIDUALITÄT

In Wahlpflichtkursen, Projekten und Arbeitsgemeinschaften könnt ihr euch ausprobieren und ganz neue Erfahrungen sammeln.
Die Individualität der Einzelnen braucht als verbindendes Element für unterschiedlichste Nationalitäten die deutsche Sprache, denn:

Deutsch ist Integrationssprache

JA - ZUM MITEINANDER

Freundlichkeit und Toleranz und klare Regeln prägen unseren Schulalltag. Dabei werdet ihr begleitet von Konfliktlotsen, Sozialarbeitern und zahlreichen Kooperationspartnern, die euch beim Lernen, dem Weg in den Beruf und auch bei allgemeinen Problemen unterstützen.
Auch in diesem Bereich ist es wichtig, dass alle diesel- be Sprache sprechen, denn:

Deutsch ist Kommunikationssprache.

© *Herbert-Hoover-Schule Berlin-Mitte*

Textaufgabe 80 % Gesamtleistung

Canada – a linguistic battleground between the US and Britain

As a Canadian living in London, I am caught between ancient British roots and the new American order laid down by Webster in his dictionary. Where should my loyalties lie?

A few years ago I moved to the United Kingdom from the Canadian prairies. This
5 was a luxury I was afforded via two grandparents who were born in Britain, ensuring my access to the elusive ancestry visa.

Many Canadians still feel a greater allegiance to our colonial British roots than to our neighbours to the south; the monarchy is still represented on our money and most Canadians are well versed in singing "God Save the Queen". We even toast Her Maj-
10 esty at most fancy public events.

Despite these and other symbols of allegiance, however, Canadians continue to hold on to some ambivalence over our British roots through our generally inconsistent use of language. While gazing at our commemorative Princess Diana spoons and watching the Queen's Christmas Message every December, we are still uncommitted
15 when it comes to our geopolitical allegiance to language. Just as we often straddle international conflicts by playing the peacekeeper, most Canadians sit on the fence, moving interchangeably between American and British spellings. If there's anything notable about our use of language, it's that we are pretty lackadaisical about it.

Before the American Revolution, everyone in North America was formally gov-
20 erned by the United Kingdom, except for a region in eastern Canada that was held by France. Following America's independence, there was a movement towards differentiating its unique culture from that of Britain. This was a major inspiration for Noah Webster, the man behind the dictionary that decisively set out a new order in American spelling and style. Some of the most noticeable differences Webster introduced
25 to the language include the replacement of words ending in -*our* in Britain (honour, favour) with the American spelling of -*or* (color, harbor); and his replacement of -*ise* word endings (capitalise, familiarise) with the American usage of -*ize* (dramatize, visualize). His most comprehensive dictionary, *An American Dictionary of the English Language*, also contained 12,000 new words native to America.

30 If politics propelled Webster to adapt the English language as one way of carving out a unique American identity, why do Canadians tend to treat linguistic choices with such ambivalence?

The question doesn't have a simple answer. Though Canada is still part of the Commonwealth, our unique history of colonisation and the sheer geographic range of the
35 country make the enforcement of consistent language rules difficult from coast to coast. Just as the United Kingdom has a variety of dialects, accents and even native languages, Canada has the languages of its aboriginal peoples, our physical proximity to the United States and a strong history of French culture as a result of a long occupation by France. Though our love affair with the United Kingdom continues, our lan-

guage is surprisingly fluid, reflecting, perhaps, our comparative youth as a nation and our typical international position as mediator.

Recently I was asked to write a comprehensive style guide for a UK-based company. The grammar nerd in me loved the task, yet I was surprised to find that even in Britain, where English language conventions are sacrosanct, there is still a great deal of flexibility in style. Beyond the basic rules of proper use, there is a great sphere of ambiguity.

Decisions about language are actually very politically charged and the impact of embracing, rejecting or creating new conventions should not be underestimated. Webster's dictionary changed the culture of America. As a Canadian living in London I have felt my own relationship with culture change as I adapt my flighty linguistic allegiances to better align with those of my new country of residence.

(617 words)

Thibodeau, Amy: "Canada – a linguistic battleground between the US and Britain." In: Guardian.co.uk, 9 June 2010.

Cartoon

A Pertinent Question

MRS. BRITANNIA: Is it possible, my dear, that you have ever given your cousin Jonathan any encouragement?
MISS CANADA: Encouragement! Certainly not, Mama. I have told him we can *never* be united.

Cartoon by John Wilson Bengough, 1886

Assignments

1. Outline the influences on and the development of language on the North American continent as presented in the text. *(25 %)*

2. Starting from the text, analyse the cartoon in the context of the relationship between Canada, Great Britain and America. Take your background knowledge into account. *(40 %)*

3. You have come across this article on the Internet. Explain your point of view concerning this topic in the comment section of the page. *(35 %)*

Lösungsvorschläge

Mediation

"Herbert Hoover Schule" is a school in a suburb of Berlin, 90% of whose pupils are immigrant children from all over the world who do not automatically share a common language. Most of them do not speak German at home and do not have much access to German mainstream culture either, so that they hardly have any chance to acquire a high proficiency in German. That is why it was mutually decided by teachers, pupils and parents to use German as a study language during lessons as well as a means of communication outside the classroom and to finally acknowledge it as a common language that everybody who wants to live in Germany has to learn in order to have the chance to integrate more easily into German society.

Everything was fine until politicians from a Turkish background heard about this, scented discrimination and spoke up for the supposedly oppressed students. Then two major Turkish newspapers picked the topic up and made the debate a national issue. Additionally, a German teachers' union jumped aboard and denounced the programme as "counterproductive" for the integration of immigrants. However, the criticism was not justified because the decision to use only German as a working language was made voluntarily and democratically, as mentioned above, by a large majority of the school community.

Actually, the programme has proven to be a success, as can be seen by the continually rising number of students from immigrant families enrolling at "Herbert Hoover Schule". *(247 words)*

Textaufgabe

1. *Basically your task is to give a simple summary of the aspect given in the task. You need to scan the text for information given in the text on the topic of language development. Use your own words to sum up briefly what you have found.*

In the text "Canada – a linguistic battleground between the US and Britain", the author describes why Canadians alternate between British and American spellings. Until the American Revolution, most parts of North America were ruled by Britain, and so most people spoke English. After it, Americans obviously wished to be somewhat different from their old mother country and this was expressed in Webster's dictionary, which was the first dictionary of American English. Through this dictionary many new spellings and quite a number of Native American words were introduced. The most popular examples were the replacement of the British word-ending *-our* with the American *-or* and the altered spelling of *-ise,* which became *-ize* in American English.

While in the U.S. the development was clear from then on, in Canada it was not. Canada remains part of the Commonwealth, but it shares its borders with the

USA. Since it has quite a large French-speaking community and the languages of its aboriginal peoples play an important role, different languages have always been a part of the Canadian culture. Therefore, in Canada there is a mixture of British and American English rules and spellings. *(190 words)*

2. Look at the relationship between Canada, Great Britain and the U.S., starting from the text and then using your background knowledge. Then explain what message the cartoon is intended to convey. Start by describing what you see and what you think it represents. Make sure that your interpretation makes sense and is understandable to people who do not know anything about the topic. Quote from the text when it makes sense to do so.

The Canadian author of the text claims that "[m]any Canadians still feel a greater allegiance to [their] colonial British roots than to [their] neighbours to the south" (ll. 7 f.) and explains this by the fact that Queen Elizabeth II is still the official representative head of state in Canada (together with the vice-regal Governor General of Canada). That Canada is still connected to the monarchy is visible not only on Canadian money but is also revealed by Canadian behaviour. At important public events many Canadians still toast Her Majesty the Queen of Canada, and the lyrics of "God Save the Queen" (ll. 9 f.), the British national anthem, are very well known to them. According to the author of the text, it is also common for many Canadians to keep memorabilia of the Royal Family and to love to watch the Queen's Christmas Message every year (cf. ll. 13 f.).
That is a major difference from the U.S., of course, which cut all cords with Britain after the War of Independence and even fought against it in the British-American War at the beginning of the 19th century. In the war the Americans tried to incorporate the British colonies to the north into the Union, which failed. The outcome of this war is today seen by many Canadians as the successful defence against an American invasion and it also proved the loyalty of the colonists to the British crown.
The scene in the political cartoon may hint at this attempt. It shows three people: two women sitting on a bench and one man leaning with his back against a column. They are dressed in 19th century fashion and are outside in a garden or a park. The two women are sitting on a park bench talking to each other while the man is smoking a cigarette and is obviously trying to impress the ladies with his laid-back style as he leans against the column. One of the women is depicted as Mrs Britannia while the other symbolises Canada (she is called "Miss Canada"). The man, who looks like Uncle Sam, represents the United States of America of course. Mrs Britannia asks the frightened Miss Canada, "is it possible, my dear, that you have ever given your cousin Jonathan any encouragement?" This shows that Canada is obviously looking for help to keep away Cousin Jonathan (a figure which represented the United States just as the more popular Uncle Sam does nowadays). Miss Canada replies indignantly to Mrs Britannia that she certainly has not and declares that she has told him that they would never be united. The union which is

spoken of as a marriage between Cousin Jonathan and Miss Canada clearly represents the wish of the United States to incorporate the Canadian provinces into the North American Union of States known as the United States of America. There were several attempts to accomplish this union, but neither the British-American War – after which the Canadian-American border was codified – nor any later diplomatic approaches proved successful from the American point of view. The Canadian provinces kept close to Britain. The cartoon shows the American-Canadian relations as they were in the late 19th century and as they still are today, as the last agreements (e. g. NAFTA) have shown, although today Canada makes sure that its national identity and independence remain intact. *(559 words)*

3. *This last task allows you the freedom to write what you think about this topic. You write this text for the online section of* The Guardian. *To be convincing you should stick to the rules of writing a comment. Since* The Guardian *is a quality newspaper, your language should be neutral or formal. Remember your own Internet reading habits and don't make the text too long – stick to the important facts.*

I think we should stop this American-British rivalry when it comes to the English language! Does it make sense? Not in my opinion. There is one world and we need one world language – English is widespread and probably has a very good chance of being that language. But does every English-speaking nation need its own spelling and grammar rules?
Everybody talks about globalisation, but the one language that might unite us is separated by grammarians and English teachers, who differentiate between British and American English. Here we have Webster's dictionary and there the Oxford English Dictionary – and honestly, what's next? Should there be an official standard for Canadian English, Australian English, a New Zealand English and Indian English as well …? The list could go on and on. Of course, each region has its own dialect and it's true that they also have words which are specific to that region. But that's true for different regions within a country as well. Just compare New York and Texas! Don't they speak a different language, too? But they still don't need different spelling rules!
British and American spellings are very similar already so why should there be any differences in spelling at all? Exaggerated nationalism, probably. What else could be the reason? The Americans, for instance, claim to speak American ENGLISH – so you already have "English" in the terminology. There is no such language as AMERICAN. Of course, you can argue that it differs from British English, but seriously – it derived from British English and it is still very similar.
So in the sense of globalisation, PLEASE let's try to only use one set of grammar and spelling rules that are not only accepted worldwide but are also valid for all native speakers of English and for all those who learn it as a foreign language as well. That won't stop all the regional dialects in the world and it will still allow everybody to feel special and individual – but when we turn official we would have one common set of rules we could stick to. Doesn't that sound tempting?

(349 words)

Schleswig-Holstein – Englisch
Abiturähnliche Übungsaufgabe 3 *(Ireland)*

Mediation
20 % Gesamtleistung

Die Eltern Ihres 15-jährigen amerikanischen Austauschpartners sind besorgt, dass ihr Sohn in Deutschland zu leicht an Alkohol käme. Um sie zu beruhigen, erläutern Sie ihnen in einer E-Mail, wie die Situation in Deutschland gehandhabt wird.
Berichten Sie Ihnen von den aktuellen Maßnahmen, die in den folgenden beiden Artikeln dargestellt werden. Gehen Sie hierbei auch auf Einwände ein, die von Gegnern gemacht werden.

Alkoholtestkäufe: Jugendliche dürfen losziehen

Kommunen in Schleswig-Holstein mit mehr als 20 000 Einwohnern dürfen künftig mit Alkohol-Testkäufen durch Jugendliche die Einhaltung des Jugendschutzes kontrollieren. Ein neuer Erlass von Gesundheitsministerin Kristin Alheit liefert Alkohol- oder Tabaktestkäufen von Jugendlichen die notwendige Rechtssicherheit.

Kiel. Die kommunalen Ordnungsbehörden können unter bestimmten Voraussetzungen Minderjährige zu Testkäufen in Geschäften losschicken. Diese müssen mindestens 16 Jahre alt und Lehrling oder Beamtenanwärter der Stadtverwaltung sein. Die Testkäufer müssen vorher geschult und beim Kauf von einem Erwachsenen begleitet
5 werden. Der solle erfolgreiche Käufe rückgängig machen und Beweismittel sichern. Auch ist eine pädagogische Nachbereitung Pflicht. Alkoholtestkäufe seien ein wirksames Mittel, um die Einhaltung des Jugendschutzes zu überprüfen und zu verbessern, sagte Alheit.
   Auch die CDU bezeichnete Testkäufe als notwendig. „Viel zu häufig wird Jugend-
10 lichen Alkohol verkauft. Dem kann nur durch jugendliche Testkäufer ein Riegel vorgeschoben werden", sagte deren sozialpolitische Sprecherin Katja Rathje-Hoffmann. FDP-Fraktionsvize Christopher Vogt bezeichnete die Legalisierung von Alkoholtestkäufen dagegen als „völlig daneben". (154 Wörter)

dpa, 30.10.2013

Kein Alkohol mehr an der Tanke?

Auf dem Weg zur Disco erst einmal zur Tanke und mit Alkohol ordentlich vorglühen. Auch in Schleswig-Holstein praktizieren das Jugendliche jedes Wochenende. Gekauft wird Hochprozentiges meist von Volljährigen – getrunken aber auch von Jüngeren. Immer wieder landen dabei Komasäufer in der Notaufnahme. Experten fordern deshalb: Abends und nachts dürfen Tankstellen, Supermärkte und Kioske keinen Alkohol mehr außer Haus verkaufen.

Kiel. Das Sozialministerium in Kiel setzt im Kampf gegen das Komasaufen auf Testkäufe durch Jugendliche. Für Prof. Reiner Hanewinkel reicht das nicht. Auch der Außer-Hausverkauf von Alkohol in den Abend- und Nachtstunden müsse auf den Prüfstand, fordert der Leiter des Kieler Instituts für Therapie- und Gesundheitsforschung (IFT-Nord). Treffen würde solch ein Verbot vor allem Tankstellen, aber auch Kioske, Supermärkte und Pizzadienste.

Prof. Hanewinkel begründet seine Forderung mit neuen Ergebnissen einer Langzeitstudie im Auftrag der DAK an 1 128 Schülern in Schleswig-Holstein, Hamburg und Brandenburg. Danach erhöht ein leichter Zugang zu Alkohol das Risiko für das Komasaufen deutlich: Bei denjenigen, die leicht an Alkohol herankommen konnten, erlebte fast jeder Zweite innerhalb von zwei Jahren sein erstes Rauschtrinken. „Damit ist ihr Risiko 26 Prozent höher als bei jenen, die angaben, nur schwer oder gar nicht an Alkohol zu gelangen." Für Studienleiter Hanewinkel gibt es damit „einen klaren Zusammenhang zwischen dem ersten Rauschtrinken und der wahrgenommenen Verfügbarkeit von Alkohol".

2011 mussten in Schleswig-Holstein 938 Kinder und Jugendliche wegen Rauschtrinkens im Krankenhaus behandelt werden – 23 Prozent mehr als im Vorjahr. Um den anhaltenden Trend beim Komasaufen zu stoppen, müsse von allen Seiten der Zugang erschwert werden, sagt Hanewinkel. Es sei zwar gut und notwendig, zu prüfen, ob sich das Verkaufspersonal ans Gesetz halte und etwa einem 17-Jährigen keinen Wodka verkaufe. „Das nutzt aber nichts, wenn dieser 17-Jährige einen Älteren vorschickt und Hochprozentiges kaufen lässt. Und genau das passiert." Tatsächlich berichten Jugendliche, dass es am Kieler Bahnhof und an einigen Tankstellen kein Problem sei, einen Erwachsenen zu finden, der für einen den gewünschten Alkohol kauft. „Wir wissen, dass sich Jugendliche zum Vorglühen am Bahnhof oder an Tankstellen treffen und dann in die Disko ziehen", bestätigt Bernd Triphahn von der Kieler Polizei.

In Baden-Württemberg ist deshalb seit 2010 der Außerhaus-Verkauf von Alkohol zwischen 22 und 5 Uhr nur noch Gaststätten erlaubt. „Wir haben damit gute Erfahrungen gemacht, hätten allerdings aus fachlicher Sicht lieber ein Verbot ab 20 Uhr. Das war politisch aber bisher nicht durchsetzbar", sagt Günter Loos vom badenwürttembergischen Innenministerium. Auch für die Kieler Polizei würde ein Verkaufsverbot nur ab 20 Uhr Sinn machen: Dann wäre das „Nachttanken" deutlich schwieriger, wenn der mitgebrachte Alkohol aufgebraucht sei.

Doch die Politik hält sich bedeckt. Der Verband des Kfz-Gewerbes Schleswig-Holstein, der rund 300 Tankstellen vertritt, lehnt ein Verkaufsverbot grundsätzlich ab. Bei mindestens 70 Prozent aller Tankstellen würden moderne Kassen- und Warenwirtschaftssysteme dafür sorgen, dass beim Kauf von Waren, die einer Altersbeschränkung unterliegen, das Personal automatisch darauf hingewiesen werde.

Ohnehin würden nur zwei Prozent der Alkoholika über Tankstellen verkauft. Ein Verbot bedeute Umsatzverluste, kürzere Öffnungszeiten und Arbeitsplatzabbau.

(492 Wörter)

Stüben, Heike: „Kein Alkohol mehr an der Tanke?"
In: Kieler Nachrichten (31.10.2013).

Textaufgabe 80 % Gesamtleistung

Excerpt from *The Snapper* by Roddy Doyle

Sharon Rabbitte, 20 years old, lives in Dublin with her family (her parents, Veronica and Jimmy Rabbitte Sr, as well as three brothers and two sisters). She is pregnant, but she has so far refused to reveal the identity of the baby's father, although most people correctly suspect it to be Mr. Burgess, the father of Sharon's friend Yvonne. He made Sharon have sex with him when she was drunk. Sharon's parents are not happy with the situation. Sharon plans to tell her father that she is going to move into a flat with her friend Jackie.

Jimmy Sr didn't go to bed these days until Sharon got in.
– Hiyeh, said Sharon.
Jimmy Sr didn't answer. He kept his eyes on *Curiosity Killed the Cat.*
– I said Hiyeh, Daddy, said Sharon.
5 – I heard yeh.
– Then why didn't yeh answer me?
– Wait a –
– An' why haven't yeh answered for the last – weeks?
She got the pouffe and sat in front of him.
10 – You're in me way, look it, he said.
She said it louder.
– Why haven't yeh answered me?
– Get lost, will yeh; I have.
Jimmy Sr'd been taken by surprise. He tried to look around Sharon. She leaned back
15 – it wasn't easy – and turned off the telly.
– Yeh haven't, she said. – Yeh haven't said hello to me properly in ages.
Jimmy Sr was never going to admit anything like that.
– You're imaginin' things, he said.
– No, I'm not.
20 She looked straight at him. There wasn't any shaking in her voice. She just spoke. She was a bit frightening.
[...] Jimmy Sr wondered if he'd be able to get past her and up to bed. He thought she was capable of trying to stop him.
– Are yeh goin' to tell me why? Sharon asked him.
25 He looked as if he was going to get up. She didn't know what she'd do if he did that. She'd follow him.
– There's nothin' to tell, for fuck sake, said Jimmy Sr.
– It's me, isn't it?
– Go up to bed, will yeh.
30 – It is, said Sharon. – I can tell.

21

Sharon nearly had to stop herself from grinning as she asked the next question.
- Did I do somethin' to yeh?

Jesus, she was asking him had she done something: had she done something! She could sit there and –
- You've done nothin', Sharon.
- I'll tell yeh what I've done.

Her voice had softened. The bitch; he couldn't have a proper row with her that way.
- I'm pregnant. – I saw yeh lookin' at me.

Jimmy Sr said nothing yet.
- I've disgraced the family.
- No.
- Don't bother denyin' it, Daddy. I'm not givin' out.

The look on his face gave her the sick for a minute.
- I've been stupid, she said. – An' selfish. I should've known. An' I know tha' you still think it was Mister Burgess an' that makes it worse.
- I don't think it was –
- Ah ah! she very gently gave out to him. – You were great. Yeh did your best to hide it.
- Ah, Sharon –
- If I leave it'll be the best for everyone. Yeh can get back to normal.
- Leave.
- Yeah. Leave. Go. Yeh know what I mean.

She stopped herself from getting too cheeky.
- I'm only bringin' trouble for you an' Mammy, so I'm – Me an' Jackie are goin' to get a flat. Okay?
- You're not goin'?
- I am. I want to. It's the best. Nigh' night.

She went upstairs.
- Ah Sharon, no.

Sharon got undressed. She wondered if it would work; what he was thinking; was he feeling guilty or what. The face on him when she was talking to him; butter wouldn't melt in his fuckin' mouth, the bastard. She got into bed. She wondered if she'd be here next week. God, she hoped so. She didn't want to move into a flat, even with Jackie. She'd seen some. She didn't want to be by herself, looking after herself and the baby. She wanted to stay here so the baby would have a proper family and the garden and the twins and her mammy to look after it so she could go out sometimes. She didn't want to leave. What was he thinking down there?

Jimmy Sr sat back and stretched.

Victory: he'd won. Without having to admit anything himself, he'd got her to admit that she was the one in the wrong. She was to blame for all this, and he'd been great. She'd said it herself.

Jimmy Sr stretched further and sank down in the couch. He punched his fists up into the air.
– Easy! Easy! he roared quietly.
He'd won. He'd got what he wanted.
– Here we go, here we go, here we go!
He stood up.
He could get back to normal now. He'd drive her all the way to work on Monday, right up to the door. He'd bring her out for a drink at tea-time on Sunday, up to the Hikers. He'd insist. [...]
He was glad it was over. He preferred being nice. It was easier.
Sharon had been great there, the way she'd taken the blame. Fair play to her. She was a great young one; the way she'd just sat there and said her bit, and none of the fuckin' water works that you usually got. Any husband of Sharon's would have his work cut out for him.
Tomorrow he'd tell her not to leave. (892 words)

From: Roddy Doyle: The Snapper. Martin Secker & Warburg Ltd, 1990.

Assignments

1. As Sharon's mother and Jimmy's wife you witness the scene in the living room. Outline the situation and the problems in your family in a diary entry. *(20 %)*

2. Analyse how Sharon sees her future against the background of the Irish reality of the 1990s. *(40 %)*

3. "Tomorrow he'd tell her not to leave."
   Speculate on Sharon's reaction when Jimmy Sr puts his words into action and continue the story. *(40 %)*

Lösungsvorschläge

Mediation

Dear Martha and Frank,

Jamie told us about your worries concerning the accessibility of alcohol in Germany. My parents asked me to sum up two articles on that topic for you showing that the German authorities are doing everything they can to prevent underage teenagers from drinking.

First of all, the authorities now have the right to send minors to shops or gas stations as test buyers in order to check if the law to protect young people is being properly enforced. Besides the possibility of convicting those who sell alcohol to minors, this also offers the opportunity to force sales clerks to check their customers' age because they might be test buyers.

Now you might say that kids could give the money to older pals to buy the alcohol for them. This problem is presently being discussed by politicians, law enforcement officers and researchers. They argue that limiting the time during which alcohol can be bought will help to stop teenagers' binge drinking. If alcohol can only be bought during the daytime (the models discussed range from banning alcohol from being sold after 8 pm or 10 pm), it would be harder for partygoers to stock up when they run out of booze before they hit the clubs.

The plans are still opposed by those who have an obvious interest in going on selling alcohol at night, e.g. gas-station owners who claim that they check their customers' age well and sell alcohol responsibly. They warn that the new regulations would lead to shorter opening times and sales staff losing their jobs, but in some parts of Germany this law is already in force.

So you can see that the German authorities care about us teenagers, too, and that Jamie will be safe with our family.

Regards

Johannes *(299 words)*

Textaufgabe

1. *There is a lot of dialogue in this extract, but you should avoid paraphrasing it. Instead, you are supposed to scan the text for information on the Rabbitte family and their living situation. Do not interpret or guess at this point, but stick to the facts you can find in the text. Make sure you fulfil the formal requirements of a diary entry, namely a first-person perspective and an idiosyncratic (= characteristic) style. Don't forget to put the date.*

April 22nd, 1990

Jimmy's still making a fool of himself. He's been giving Sharon the cold treatment for weeks now because she still won't say who got her pregnant. She must be the most stubborn person in the world. Peas in a pod, the two of them.
But last night, I think Sharon got the better of him. She confronted Jimmy in the living-room. He was still sitting in front of the TV, probably the better to ignore her when she came home. He's been doing that for days now. When I heard them talking, I went downstairs and listened at the door.
Of course, Jimmy denied everything. At least he tried to, but she didn't take any excuses from him. She never raised her voice though. Clever, so he had no way of getting angry. Then she put on a real show of apologising for what she'd put us through, and that we'd be better off without her (and right she was!) and finally she offered to move out (move into a flat with her friend Jackie – honestly!) to spare us the neighbours' silly remarks and the rumours. I have to admit, she is a cunning little thing. Somehow she managed to turn the argument around and manipulate her father into pacifying *her*! Instead of giving her a piece of his mind, he actually stopped her apology halfway through. When she told him she'd be moving out, he was totally taken by surprise. He didn't know what to say, which is not something that happens regularly. I really wish I could've seen his face. Then he tried to make her change her mind, but Sharon stuck to her guns and went to bed, still the dutiful, repentant daughter.
I'm curious about his next move – how he intends to clean this mess up. I don't think she really wants to move out – how will she raise the child, all by herself? But somehow he'll have to stop her before she really feels forced to put her money where her mouth is. I wouldn't put it past her to go through with it just to prove her point – in that way she's just like him.
If he doesn't do it, I'll have to talk to her tomorrow ... *(377 words)*

2. *For this assignment, you have to examine Sharon's wishes for her future. You should then explain these wishes by outlining the situation she finds herself in. Refer to your background knowledge of Ireland, especially the conditions young people are facing, be they social, economic or demographic.*

Since abortion is illegal in the Republic of Ireland, now that she is pregnant, Sharon has to give birth to the child. Afterwards she can decide if she wants to keep the baby or give it up for adoption. Since Sharon is a very strong character, she plans to raise the child herself together with the help of her family.

In the given extract, it seems that Sharon has already come to terms with her situation. She does not appear to have a problem with the idea of being a single mother, but she does not want to live alone (cf. ll. 64 ff.). Her notion of a "proper family" is quite different from the traditional concept: for her, it is living with her parents, because then her mother and sisters could help her to care for her child (cf. ll. 65 f.). The child's father does not feature in her plans, most likely because the child is not the product of a (however secret) relationship, but of a one-night stand or possibly even a sexual assault. Thus, her parents are the only people who can provide the elements of family life Sharon is used to, namely a house with a garden and someone to take a share in caring for the baby (cf. ll. 65 f.). Moving to a flat with her friend Jackie is not a real option for Sharon.

Sharon tells her father she plans to share a flat with her friend – because of her financial situation, she would not be able to afford a decent flat alone. If she were able to afford it, she would probably have moved out a good while before this scene, considering that she shares the house not only with her parents but also her five siblings. Sharon's situation reflects that of a large number of young Irish people from the middle and lower classes.

A large family like this is characteristic of a Catholic country like Ireland, at least at the time the novel was written. Since then, family size has been slowly declining, reflecting the decreasing influence of the Roman Catholic Church with its negative attitude towards contraception and birth control. However, a lower or lower middle class family in Ireland would still be more likely to have a large number of children than its counterparts in many other countries in the EU.

However, Sharon's disapproval of living in a flat (cf. ll. 63 f.) might also be rooted in the fact that in Ireland living in your own house is rather the rule than the exception. This is true of other anglophone countries like Great Britain and the USA as well, because their governments usually encourage home ownership and support it through tax exemptions, for example. This is the result of the belief that both individual homeowners and society in general will benefit from the economic and social side-effects that saving for and living in your own house will produce. The global financial crisis, however, with its crash in real estate prices, has reduced the enthusiasm of potential home buyers.

Finally, Sharon's intention to stay within her stable family might also arise from an apprehension of ending up as a typical single mother. Statistically speaking, the poverty risk of single parents is significantly higher than that of married parents, especially if they are young. As a single mother, she will have problems finding work to support herself and her child and will be more likely to become dependent on social benefits. Hence, her decision to stay with her parents might be quite a reasonable and realistic choice. *(599 words)*

3. *In this assignment you are required to use the knowledge about the protagonists and their relationship in order to speculate on the further development of events. Jimmy Sr's assessment of his daughter as somebody whose husband "would have his work cut out for him" (ll. 84 f.) suggests that simply telling her "not to leave" (l. 86) will not be that easy.*
What is equally important is that you manage to imitate the author's style. He uses a lot of dialogue, including Irish slang. You should make sure that your versions of Sharon and Jimmy talk in a similar manner. Additionally, you could have the perspective shift between Jimmy Sr and Sharon, as in the original scene.

The next day, Jimmy Sr waited for the others to be gone before he approached Sharon in the kitchen. She was just making herself some breakfast.
– Listen, Sharon. You're not leaving. That's a stupid idea. You're stayin' here, where yeh belong.

Sharon's heart was beating faster. One part of her wanted to shout with joy and hug her dad, but she checked herself. She wouldn't give in that easily.
– Daddy, that's rubbish. I've talked to Jackie about it. It's for the best – for the baby, for me, an' for you an' Mammy as well. I'll just be in your way.
– Ah, nonsense! I'm not allowin' it!
– I'm 20, Daddy. Yeh can't forbid me to do anythin'. My decision is made.
– Now listen here, Sharon.

Jimmy Sr was getting decidedly nervous now. She meant it. He would have to tackle this from a different angle.
– Sharon, look it. What are we goin' to do without yeh? The twins look up to yeh. Yeh can't just leave them alone. Plus, the baby needs a father figure, and it doesn't look like you've got one comin' along just now, does it?

Sharon looked hurt. And angry. Jimmy Sr realised this wasn't going according to plan. He silently cursed himself.
– For fuck sake, Sharon, I mean, sorry, excuse me, that was not wha' I meant. I just wanted to say tha' the little snapper will need his granddaddy, won't he?

Inside, Sharon was cheering. But there was still something she'd have to check.
– And wha' about the dad?
– I don't care about the dad, Sharon. I ... we just care about you. It's not important who's the dad. I was actin' stupid. Please forgive me, said Jimmy Sr

Now where had that come from, he wondered. Hadn't she apologised? Why did he ask her for forgiveness? But never mind, it seemed to be doing the trick. Sharon was smiling, a bit at least, he thought. He went on:
– Yeh can't raise a little one in a flat. Yeh belong here with us. With your family.

Sharon felt her eyes water. She hugged her father.
– Thanks, Daddy. Tha' feels really good.
– That's OK, love. C'mon, I'll take you to work, righ'? *(366 words)*

Schleswig-Holstein – Englisch
Abiturähnliche Übungsaufgabe 4 *(Ireland)*

Mediation   20 % Gesamtleistung

Wohnen für Hilfe

Wohn-Partnerschaften von Familien oder älteren Menschen mit Studierenden

Kontakt:
www.studentenwerk-s-h.de
0431-8816-314

STUDENTENWERK SCHLESWIG HOLSTEIN

Ihre englische Freundin möchte gerne in Kiel studieren. Sie hat bei ihrem letzten Besuch dieses Plakat gesehen und möchte jetzt mehr über das Projekt wissen.

Verwenden Sie den folgenden Artikel und erklären Sie ihr in einer E-Mail, welchen Hintergrund das Projekt hat und welche Bedingungen der Kandidat erfüllen muss.

Gehen Sie auch auf die Vor- und Nachteile ein, die sich für die Untermieter ergeben könnten.

Studentenwerk Schleswig-Holstein

Wohnprojekt für Studenten: Zimmer gegen Hilfe

[...] Die Idee ist so simpel wie einleuchtend: Menschen mit überflüssigem Wohnraum bieten Studenten eine Bleibe an, die Miete begleichen die jungen Leute, indem sie im Haushalt helfen, den Rasen mähen oder Einkäufe erledigen – ein Gewinn für beide Seiten. Seit Anfang Oktober wohnt Sergei bei Familie Kaczenski. „Es fühlt
5 sich schon so an, als sei Mister Sergei schon seit einem Jahr hier", sagt die Heilpraktikerin lächelnd und legt einen Arm um die Schultern des jungen Mannes. Sie führt ihn ins Esszimmer, wo belegte Brötchen und Kekse auf einer Servierplatte auf dem sorgfältig gedeckten Tisch liegen. „Nimm dir bitte Kaffee!" Christiane Kaczenski hat lange in der Krankenpflege gearbeitet, musste aber 2007 mit 46 Jahren aus gesund-
10 heitlichen Gründen aufhören. [...] Da kommt die Hilfe des jungen Studenten gerade richtig. Seine Aufgaben im Haushalt sind überschaubar: das Treppenhaus und die Böden einmal die Woche feudeln, draußen Blätter zusammenfegen, im Winter beim Schneeschippen helfen, dem 13-jährigen Sohn Englisch-Nachhilfe geben – und was sonst noch so anfällt.

Die Faustregel des Projektes: Pro Quadratmeter Wohnraum leisten die Studenten eine Arbeitsstunde im Monat ab. Darüber hinaus beteiligen sie sich an den Nebenkosten. In Sergejs Fall sind das pauschal 50 Euro im Monat, Telefon und Internet kosten extra. „Für einen solchen Preis kriegt man ja nirgendwo ein Zimmer, und ich greife Frau Kaczenski gerne unter die Arme", sagt Sergei und schenkt seiner Gastgeberin ein Glas Wasser ein. „25 Stunden gehen schneller 'rum, als man denkt," meint Kaczenski. Sergei nickt zustimmend: „Die merkt man gar nicht." Es ist eine sehr familiäre Atmosphäre, und es wird deutlich, dass das partnerschaftliche Wohnen beiden Seiten gut tut. Trotzdem ist es wichtig, die Privatsphäre zu wahren. Da sind sich Vermieterin und Mieter einig. [...]

Viele Ehepaare haben leerstehende Räume in ihren Häusern, nachdem die Kinder ausgezogen sind. Auch ältere und alleinstehende Menschen können meist ein Zimmer entbehren – und in den meisten Fällen wünschen sie sich ein wenig Gesellschaft und Hilfe im Alltag. Dem stehen viele Studenten gegenüber, die händeringend eine Unterkunft suchen. Genau da soll das Projekt ansetzen. „Es ist ein innovativer Ansatz, um zusätzlichen Wohnraum für Studierende zu mobilisieren", sagt Bildungsministerin Waltraud „Wara" Wende. Doch darüber hinaus stiften die Wohnpartnerschaften auch zu mehr menschlichem Miteinander an. „So wird ein wichtiger Schritt getan raus aus der sozialen Isolierung hin zu generationenübergreifendem Wohnen, von der vereinzelnden Abgrenzung hin zur gegenseitigen Ergänzung", so Wende. Für Sergei ist das Projekt ein Erfolg. „Ich habe gerade gestern gehört, dass schon 40 Studenten so eine Unterkunft bekommen haben", erzählt er begeistert, „und es werden noch mehr!"

Sergei trinkt den Kaffee aus, verabschiedet sich bei seiner Gastgeberin und läuft über den verregneten Hof zurück zu seinem neuen Heim. Als er 2011 aus dem estnischen Tallinn nach Kiel kam, war die Wohnungsnot in der Landeshauptstadt schon sehr groß. Wegfall der Wehrpflicht und gebührenfreies Studieren ließen Schleswig-Holstein auf den Favoritenlisten vieler Studenten nach ganz oben wandern – und die Mietpreise ebenso.

Bis heute hat sich die Situation nicht viel verändert: Es mangelt an Wohnraum, und wenn was gefunden wird, ist es für die meisten Studenten nicht bezahlbar. Sergei kennt das Problem aus seinem Umfeld.

„Viele Bekannte fanden hier in Kiel kein Zimmer", erzählt der junge Este, „sie mussten dann in Städte gehen, in denen sie eine Wohnung gefunden haben – und nicht dorthin, wo sie eigentlich hinwollten." [...] Die Frage, ob er lieber in einer eigenen Wohnung wohnen würde, verneint er: „Hier habe ich eine Art Familienersatz und fühle mich wirklich sehr wohl. Wenn ich eine Freundin hätte, dann würde ich vielleicht lieber alleine wohnen", sagt er lächelnd während er seine Tür aufschließt, „aber das ist zur Zeit nicht der Fall." (600 Wörter)

Bahtijarevic, Maja: „Wohnprojekt für Studenten: Zimmer gegen Hilfe."
Quelle: http://www.ndr.de/nachrichten/schleswig-holstein/studium117.html (13.10.2013).

38 years after Bloody Sunday a report was published that came to the conclusion that the shooting was unjustified.

Bloody Sunday report: 38 years on, justice at last

[…] Fourteen unarmed civilians were shot dead by the Parachute Regiment which had been sent into Derry's Bogside on 30 January 1972. The deaths propelled a generation of nationalists into the Provisional IRA.

Saville's conclusion that none of the 14 dead was carrying a gun, no warnings were given, no soldiers were under threat and the troops were the first to open fire, marked a final declaration of innocence for the victims of the biggest British military killing of civilians on UK soil since the Peterloo massacre in 1819.

Northern Ireland's director of public prosecutions confirmed tonight that he was considering whether prosecutions for murder, perjury or perverting the course of justice could arise from the report.

Sir Alasdair Fraser QC will be asked to assess the report to decide whether there is sufficient evidence for "a reasonable prospect for conviction" of paratroopers found to have participated in the killings.

Lord Gifford QC, who represented the family of civil rights marcher Jim Wray, who died on Bloody Sunday, said: "There are a number of possible charges arising from this report, which has been thorough and even-handed. Murder is of course the obvious one. But the report also found that soldiers deliberately attempted to mislead the inquiry."

As David Cameron announced the findings and apologised on behalf of the British state, a crowd of up to 10,000 people watching his statement on a television screen in Derry's Guildhall Square cheered wildly.

"I never want to call into question the behaviour of our soldiers and our army, who I believe to be the finest in the world," Cameron told the Commons.

"But the conclusions of this report are absolutely clear. There is no doubt, there is nothing equivocal, there are no ambiguities. What happened on Bloody Sunday was both unjustified and unjustifiable. It was wrong." […]

In a measured and dispassionate report Saville, a supreme court judge, concluded there was no justification for shooting at any of those killed or wounded on the banned civil rights march.

"None of the firing by the Support Company (Paratroopers) was aimed at people posing a threat or causing death or serious injury," he said. "Despite the contrary evidence given by the soldiers, we have concluded that none of them fired in response to attacks or threatened attacks by nail or petrol bombers. No one threw or threatened to throw a nail or petrol bomb at the soldiers on Bloody Sunday."

A copy of the discredited 1972 report by Lord Widgery, which accused the victims of firing weapons or handling bombs, was torn apart by one of the families' representatives in Derry. "My brother was running away from the soldiers when he was shot," Joe Duddy said of his brother, Jackie. "He was posing no threat. [The Widgery report] destroyed our loved ones' good names. Today we clear them. I'm delighted to say that Jackie was innocent."

Saville's 10-volume report also found that some of the paratroopers who gave evidence to the tribunal had lied to it.

It said these soldiers had "knowingly put forward false accounts in order to seek to justify their firing".

But the report did not find any conspiracy in the government or in the higher echelons of the army to use lethal force against either rioters or demonstrators in Derry. The shootings "were not the result of any plan to shoot selected ringleaders", the report said.

During the 12-year tribunal a number of players in the peace process testified including Martin McGuinness, who admitted that at the time of Bloody Sunday he was the IRA's second-in-command in Derry. McGuinness "was probably armed with a Thompson sub-machine gun" but it was insufficient evidence that he actually fired the weapon, Saville said.

Although Republican gunmen from the Official IRA took up firing positions, the report said, it was the soldiers who fired first and the paramilitaries' presence provided no justification for them doing so.

The report appeared to exonerate the army's then commander of land forces in Northern Ireland, General Robert Ford, of any blame. He had agreed to deploy the Parachute Regiment in the city against the advice of a senior police officer in Derry.

The report concluded that Ford "neither knew nor had reason to know at any stage that his decision would or was likely to result in soldiers firing unjustifiably on that day".

There was strong criticism of Lt Colonel Derek Wilford, the officer directly in charge of the paratroopers. Wilford ignored orders from his brigadier that he should not order troops beyond a barrier deeper into the Bogside, the report said.

The operation was "not a justifiable response to a lethal attack by republican paramilitaries but instead soldiers opening fire unjustifiably," the report said.

Kate Allen, Amnesty's UK director, said: "The right to redress of the victims and their families is only partly met by establishing the facts about what happened that day; full accountability for any unlawful actions by state agents will also need to be ensured." But Stephen Pollard, a solicitor representing soldiers who gave evidence to the inquiry, said Saville did not have any justification for his findings and said he would fight any moves to prosecute the soldiers. "The evidence has been cherry-picked. I think Lord Saville felt under considerable pressure to give very clear findings even when the evidence did not support it," Pollard said.   (890 words)

Bowcott, Owen and Henry McDonald: "Bloody Sunday report: 38 years on, justice at last."
In: The Guardian, 15 June 2010.

Assignments

1. Sketch the incidents mentioned in the text that led to the Bloody Sunday massacre. *(20 %)*
2. Relate to what extent Bloody Sunday marked a turning point in Northern Ireland's history. *(45 %)*
3. Take on the perspective of somebody who played an active role in the Northern Ireland conflict. Write a letter to the editor assessing this article. *(35 %)*

Lösungsvorschläge

Mediation

Re: Hand gegen Koje an Land?!
Dear Julie,
So you wanted to know how "Hand gegen Koje an Land" works. I have read an article about it and, frankly speaking, it's quite simple. It's a programme that was set up because there weren't enough flats for students available for several reasons. Rents were soaring, so students needed a cheap alternative, especially those who didn't have much money.
Many people who have extra living space available, for instance after their kids have moved out, rent it to students and expect them to help in the household in exchange. As a rule, the amount of work that the students have to put in per month equals the number of square metres they rent. The nature of the work has to be discussed with the landlord and may include chores like gardening, cleaning the floor, or helping the kids with their homework and so on. As a lodger, you would also have to pay your share of the running costs, like heating, water, electricity and the Internet.
The advantages that the student in the article mentions are that firstly, it is not expensive (in his case, €50 a month) and secondly, that it is nice to have a sort of host family to talk to and to help you get organised in your new environment, especially for a foreigner who has just started university.
Of course, there are also some disadvantages, because naturally you have to be considerate of the people you live with. Having a boyfriend or girlfriend over all the time would be difficult.
If you need to know more, don't hesitate to ask.
Hope to see you soon,
Peter

(280 words)

Textaufgabe

1. *First of all you should read the text carefully and then explain the chain of events that led to Bloody Sunday. Use your own words and do not quote from the text in this task. Make sure that anyone who has not read the text would be able to understand what happened.*

On 30th January 1972 there was an unauthorised demonstration in the Bogside, a part of Londonderry in Northern Ireland – or Derry, as the Irish Republicans call it – mainly inhabited by Irish Republicans. The civil rights march through the city was stopped by British soldiers reinforced by the police. In spite of being warned by a high ranking Derry police officer about the risks of leading military into the town, the commander of land forces in Northern Ireland ordered his troops in together with the police. There was a certain point defined that was not to be passed by soldiers. The officer in command of the paratroopers that day did not follow that order and led his forces beyond this point towards the demonstrators. Among the crowd were some important members of the IRA who were probably armed, but until the clash between demonstrators and law enforcement forces everything had been peaceful. Neither the human rights activists nor the IRA members provoked the soldiers by throwing nail or petrol bombs or by shooting at them. Nevertheless, the military opened fire upon the demonstrators, which, according to the report, was unjustified. According to the relative of one victim, the soldiers even fired into the fleeing crowd, hitting his brother in the back. The Irish Republicans see the results of the Saville Report – which came to a different conclusion from the Widgery Report, which was published 38 years ago – as proof that justice has finally been done, while members of the military claim that not all evidence has been heard. *(257 words)*

2. *Now in this task you can show what you have learned about Northern Ireland. Bearing the information from the text in mind, you have to show to what extent Bloody Sunday marked a turning point in Northern Ireland's history. You could say a few words about what led to Bloody Sunday and what happened afterwards, decide if it was a turning point or not and give reasons for your opinion. The approach of the following solution is a little different though. It sums up the most important events and developments with regard to the conflict. By describing the long history of the conflict and by showing that Bloody Sunday was not the end of it, the solution proves that despite being a terrible event, Bloody Sunday was of minor importance to the conflict.*
It is also possible to argue that Bloody Sunday was a turning point in the history of Northern Ireland. Do not forget that this task is worth 45 % of this part of the exam – so make sure you fulfil the task thoroughly.

As with many other trouble spots in the world today, the conflict in Northern Ireland has its origins in the times of colonialism and imperialism. During the Ulster Plantation, which started in 1606, English and Scottish Protestant settlers drove the native Catholic Irish inhabitants off their land and deprived them of their rights. The formerly unplanted area of Ulster – the Irish province that is now known as Northern Ireland – was settled by Protestant Royalists. Uprisings against these unjust measures led to suppression and further repression of the native Catholic people.

Religious confession has always been at the root of the conflict, since both the settlers and those who ruled Ireland were Protestant, while those suppressed were mainly Irish Catholic. Catholics were suppressed by the British until the beginning of the 20th century, when a limited self-government was discussed. This idea was opposed by the Protestants, who feared being ruled by a Catholic majority in Ire-

land. In the area of Ulster, where the Protestant settlers were concentrated, this led to the forming of paramilitary organisations on both sides.
After the Easter Rising, the Irish War of Independence and the Irish Civil War, Ireland became divided into the Irish Free State, which was still part of the Commonwealth but widely independent, and Northern Ireland, which was under Unionist rule. The idea was to have the areas mainly inhabited by Irish Catholic people stay with the Free State, and those mainly inhabited by British Protestants form a Northern Ireland, which stayed part of the United Kingdom. In fact the situation turned out differently, since the actual partition of the population was approximately 50/50. With the pro-British half holding all key positions of civil life in Northern Ireland, there was the Irish Catholic half of the population that felt – and actually was – underrepresented and suppressed.
This led to the development of a powerful civil rights campaign in Northern Ireland in the 1960s. It was also a time when many paramilitary organisations formed, reformed or were re-installed. The existence of these paramilitary organisations led to first acts of violence, such as the 1966 bombing of a Catholic-owned pub in Belfast by the Ulster Volunteer Force (UVF), which declared war against the IRA and all its splinter groups. This and other violent acts led to an aggravation of the situation on both sides. The civil rights marches were opposed by loyalist protests and officially banned by the Northern Ireland government whenever possible. Film documentation showed police violence against peaceful protesters on a banned civil rights march and this culminated in the Battle of the Bogside. During these riots between the police and the Irish nationalists, a Catholic boy was shot. This incident eventually led to the radicalisation of the IRA and turned Northern Ireland into a country in a state of civil war, which had its most terrible phase in the early 1970s. It ended with the British Army re-conquering the areas controlled by armed Irish nationalists as well as the suspension of the unionist government of Northern Ireland in favour of direct rule from London. During this period of time many people were killed in Northern Ireland. Afterwards, the IRA took their war into the world (e. g. bombings in London). Violence on both sides did not come to a halt until April 10th, 1998, when the Good Friday Agreement was made. It cleared the status of Northern Ireland towards Great Britain and the Republic of Ireland, with all three sides guaranteeing civil and cultural rights to the people of Northern Ireland. Part of the agreement was the decommissioning of all armed paramilitary forces. The agreement paved the way towards the comparatively peaceful life as we know it today with equal rights for both Catholics and Protestants. Concluding this agreement obviously sets an end to an almost 400-year long history of injustice, suppression and violence and can therefore be seen as the turning point in Northern Irish history that incidentally also made the Saville report possible.
As you can see, Bloody Sunday only marked one climax of violence in a line of such events. The history of the conflict started more than 350 years before Bloody Sunday and afterwards it took another 20 years to end it. Although it probably led to further radicalisation among Irish nationalists, it cannot be seen as a turning point in Northern Irish history. *(725 words)*

3. In this task you are free to choose the perspective from which you are writing. You might want to write as a protester in the Bloody Sunday crowd, a soldier from the parachute regiment, an IRA member, an inhabitant who saw the incidents from his/her window, a member of the press covering the incidents, or any other person involved in the conflict. Make sure that you refer to the article, that your point of view is realistic and that it is to the point, i.e. not too long.

Dear Sir or Madam,

I would like to refer to your article "Bloody Sunday report: 38 years on, justice at last" in yesterday's edition of *The Guardian*. As an SAS Falklands war veteran who has also been stationed in Northern Ireland, I follow the whole peace process over there with great interest and would like to take this opportunity to share a soldier's point of view of the matter.

When I was stationed in NI in the late seventies, the situation was very unstable to put it mildly. We patrolled the whole territory, especially the rural areas where we suspected the existence of IRA hideouts and weapon depots, we set up road blocks, searched people and locations that seemed suspect and followed the rule of "forcing down any kind of resistance" – no matter where it came from, because in those days radical measures could have saved our lives. It sounds very harsh, and it was very harsh, especially for those people who had to endure our procedures. We were no angels by any means BUT, and I cannot stress that enough, in the given situation the Irish opposition, mainly the IRA, forced us to act in this way. We did not have a choice, although I am sure they, from their point of view, would say the same. However, it is time to forgive and move on. So let me say that I am glad that the Saville Report exonerated the victims and concluded that the shootings were unjustified, but from a veteran's point of view I can understand those soldiers who were in the situation and say that their voices were not heard by the commission. It is unbelievable what goes through your head when you are standing in the line of fire, which they did, as is also proven by the Saville report. BUT – and it is a big BUT – as a trained soldier you should be professional enough to follow your orders and not to endanger your men, even when provoked. To conclude, I would like to say that the only thing I hope for is that in this report – unlike the Widgery Report, which was clearly politically motivated – Lord Saville was able to judge freely. Let Northern Ireland be at peace and let us hope that we will all be able to visit this beautiful part of the world without any awkward thoughts so that the wounds from the past will be able to heal completely.

A. Smith, Sheffield *(413 words)*

Abitur 2011 Schleswig-Holstein – Englisch (Kernfach)
Aufgabe 1: London – Life in a Changing Metropolis

Excerpt from: *A Great Deliverance* by Elizabeth George (1989)

Introductory note:
In the 19th and 20th century Acton was an industrial area. Today it is mainly residential with the largest housing estate in the west of London and with a mixed population.
In this excerpt from George's novel the reader is introduced to the social and familial background of the female protagonist Barbara Havers, who works as a constable at Scotland Yard. Despite the fact that she is in her late twenties and financially independent, she still lives with her parents.

In Acton there were two potential areas of residence, simply called by inhabitants the right and wrong streets. It was as if a dividing line split the suburb arbitrarily, condemning one set of residents while it elevated others. In the right streets of Acton, pristine brick houses boasted woodwork which always sparkled admirably in the
5 morning sun in a multiplicity of colours. Roses grew in abundance there. Fuchsias flourished in hanging pots. Children played games on unlittered pavements and in patchwork gardens. Snow kissed gabled roofs in peaks of meringue in the winter, while in summer tall elms made green tunnels through which families strolled in the perfumed evening light. There was never an argument in the right streets of Acton,
10 never loud music, the smell of cooking fish, or fists raised in a fight. It was sheer perfection, the single ocean on which every family's boat of dreams sailed placidly forward. But things were much different as close as a single street away. People liked to say that the wrong streets of Acton got the heat of the day and that's why things were so different there. It was as if an enormous hand had swept down from the sky and
15 jumbled up houses and avenues and people so that everything was always just a bit out of sorts. No one worked quite so hard on appearances: houses sagged moodily into decay. Gardens once planted were soon ignored, then forgotten altogether and left to fend for themselves. Children played noisily on the dirty pavements, disruptive games that frequently brought mothers to doorways, shrieking for peace from the din. The
20 winter wind spat through poorly sealed windows and summer brought rain that leaked through the roofs. People in the wrong streets didn't think much about being anywhere else, for to think of being elsewhere was to think of hope. And hope was dead in the wrong part of Acton.
 Barbara drove there now, turning the Mini in on a street lined with cars that were
25 rusting like her own. Neither garden nor fence fronted her own house but, rather, a pavement-hard patch of dirt on which she parked her little car.
 Next door, Mrs Gustafson was watching BBC 1. Since she was nearly deaf, the entire neighbourhood was nightly regaled with the doings of her favourite television heroes. Across the street, the Kirbys were engaging in their usual preintercourse argu-

ment while their four children ignored them as best as they could by throwing dirt clods at an indifferent cat that watched from a nearby first-floor window-sill.

Barbara sighed, groped for her front-door key, and went into her house. It was chicken and peas. She could smell it at once, like a gust of foul breath.

'That you, lovey?' her mother's voice called. 'Bit late, aren't you dear? Out with some friends?'

What a laugh! 'Working, Mum. I'm back on CID.'[1]

Her mother shuffled to the door of the sitting-room. Like Barbara, she was short, but terribly thin, as if a long illness had ravaged her body and taken it sinew by sinew on a march towards the grave. 'CID?' she asked, her voice growing querulous. 'Oh, must you, Barbara? You know how I feel about that, my lovey.' As she spoke, she raised a skeletal hand to her thin hair in a characteristic nervous gesture. Her overlarge eyes were puffy and rimmed with red, as if she had spent the day weeping.

'Brought you some peaches,' Barbara responded gesturing with the bag. [...]

Diverted from the thought of CID, Mrs Havers' face changed, lighting with a dusty glow. She caught at the fabric of her shabby housedress and held it bunched in one hand, as if containing excitement. 'Oh, that doesn't matter at all. *Wait* till you see. Go in the kitchen and I'll be right there. Your dinner's still warm.'

Barbara walked past the sitting-room, wincing at the chatter of the television and the fusty smell of a chamber too long kept closed. The kitchen, fetid with the odour of tough broiled chicken and anaemic peas, was little better. She looked gloomily at the plate on the table, touched her finger to the withered flesh of the fowl. It was stone cold, as slippery and puckered as something kept preserved in formaldehyde for forensic examination. Fat had congealed round its edges and a single rancid dab of butter had failed to melt on peas that looked as if they had had their last warming in a former decade.

Wonderful, she thought. [...] She looked for the daily paper and found it, as always, on the seat of one of the wobbly kitchen chairs. She grabbed the front section, opened it to the middle, and deposited her dinner on the smiling face of the Duchess of Kent.

'Lovey, you've not thrown away your nice dinner!'

Damn! Barbara turned to see her mother's stricken face, lips working in rejection, lines drawn in deep grooves down to her chin, pale blue eyes filled with tears. She clutched an artificial leather album to her bony chest.

'Caught me, Mum.' Barbara forced a smile, putting an arm round the woman's bird-like shoulders and leading her to the table. 'I had a bite at the Yard[2], so I wasn't hungry. Should I have saved it for you or Dad?' (966 words)

From a GREAT DELIVERANCE by Elizabeth George, © 1988 by Susan Elizabeth George.
Used by permission of Bantam Books, a division of Random House, Inc.

1 *CID:* Criminal Investigation Department
2 *the Yard:* Scotland Yard

Assignments

1. Write a paper to brief the new mayor of the London borough of Ealing, to which Acton belongs, on Acton's special urban and social structure. *(15 %)*

2. Analyse how Elizabeth George depicts Acton. *(25 %)*

3. "And hope was dead in the wrong part of Acton" (ll. 22/23).
   Explain in what sense this applies to the life of the two protagonists. *(25 %)*

4. Conceive of yourself as the new mayor of Ealing. He is an expert in urban development. In Acton he would like to concentrate on bridging the gap between the two parts of Acton and on improving social conditions in general.
   Write a speech, which you are going to deliver in front of Acton residents. *(35 %)*

Lösungsvorschläge

1. *Here you are supposed to write a briefing paper. So you have to make sure that you make it look like one. Choose formal language and include the important information from the text in a short, objective note. The intention behind this task is to check whether you have understood the text and you are basically required to reproduce information. If, however, you have any other information about Acton, add it. Since it is a briefing paper you do not have to address the mayor or anybody else personally.*

London Borough of Ealing
Acton District
Acton
Department of Urban and Social Structure

Briefing paper on the social and urban structure of Acton (status as of Feb. 2011)

Acton, part of Greater London as part of the London Borough of Ealing since 1965, is home to approximately 50,000 inhabitants. A wide variety of different nationalities and social classes, and the change from a former industrial suburb to a now mainly residential area have led to the present problems in social structure and urban development.

While approximately half of the city is in a very representative state with its well-tended houses, clean pavements and cultivated gardens, the other half needs remodelling. The line dividing the two parts can clearly be seen and different streets are referred to by the population as being "right" or "wrong".

The social structure of the area can be described as well situated on the "right" side and poor on the "wrong" side. The poor wage and social welfare situation on the wrong side displays a lack of education and care for the children that are brought up here. This also makes a general change in living conditions, starting with the renovation of the houses and cleaning up of gardens that have seen better times, highly unlikely, which is why the Borough and District must take measures to improve the situation. *(224 words)*

2. *In this task you have to analyse how Elizabeth George describes Acton, mainly in the first paragraph of this text. When you work on this task, do not only look at the content but also at the language the author has used, working out contrasts, metaphors etc. Bear in mind that this task is worth a little more than the last one.*

Elizabeth George describes Acton as a city with two faces – a prosperous one and a not very promising, disadvantageous one. She supports her description by her use of language to illustrate the contrast.

This becomes evident at the very beginning of the text when she speaks of "the right and [the] wrong" streets in the city (l. 2). Of course, nobody wants to be among those condemned (cf. ll. 2 f.) to live in the wrong streets, not far from those that are described as elevated (ibid.), yet more than unlikely to be ever able to join the "right" part of Acton. The reader is influenced by this use of language throughout the text. Other examples that show this contrast are: the children in the right part of town play on "unlittered pavements" (l. 6) and in "patchwork gardens" (l. 7) while the others play "disruptive games" (l. 18) on "dirty pavements" (ibid.). The good side of town is metaphorically described as "every family's boat of dreams" (l. 11), while in the other one hope is personified as being dead (cf. l. 22). In a similar way, the snow kissing the gabled roofs (cf. l. 7), the "green tunnels through which families strolled" (l. 8) and the "perfumed evening light" (l. 9) in the prosperous part of Acton are contrasted with the "smell of cooking fish" (l. 10) and the houses and avenues that are "jumbled up" (l. 15). The words "kiss", "green" and "perfumed" awaken warm feelings, whereas "smell" and "jumbled up" have negative connotations in this context. In particular, the metaphorical "hand" (l. 14) that did the jumbling up clarifies the brute force that has to be imagined and the desolate state these streets are left in afterwards. While there is "never an argument in the right streets" (l. 9), in the wrong streets there are "fists raised in a fight" (l. 10) and mothers "shrieking for peace" (l. 19). By using alliteration and imagery the author heightens the effect of this contrast on the reader. Similarly, the alliteration "winter wind" (l. 20) together with the personification "spat through poorly sealed windows" (l. 20) makes the reader shiver and see a picture of a very uncomfortable environment.

In conclusion, one can say that Elizabeth George plants a certain image in her readers' minds, not only by the sheer facts she mentions but also the language and the words she uses to transport them. *(405 words)*

3. *Now you have to leave the level of describing the city and environment and show how it affects the lives of the inhabitants – here Barbara Havers and her mother – in the wrong part of Acton. Referring to the text, show how hopeless their lives are by giving examples:*
   – *tedious daily routine*
   – *dreary situation in the house: bad smell, disgusting food*
   – *hopeless state of Barbara's mother, Barbara's lack of energy to change her life*

The two protagonists' routine clearly shows that hope is dead in their lives. Everything seems to be the same things repeating themselves over and over again. It starts with Barbara coming home in her rusty car that she parks in front of her house, which does not have a fence or a garden but a chunk of hard dirt in front of it instead (cf. ll. 24 ff.). Stepping into the house she has to listen to a cacophony that seems to be the same every day, too. Her old, nearly deaf next-door neighbour is listening to her favourite TV programme, and the neighbours on the opposite side of the road are quarrelling as usual while their children are throwing mud at a cat in an attempt to ignore their parents (cf. ll. 27 ff.).

The drab situation continues when Barbara opens the door and enters the house that she inhabits with her parents and is welcomed by the odour of the meal that

her mother has fixed for her (cf. ll. 32 f.). Throughout the place there is a fetor (cf. ll. 48 ff.) because her mum obviously does not let enough air in during the day.
In the kitchen Barbara is disgusted by the cold chicken and peas that her mum has left for her (cf. ll. 50 ff.) and is about to throw it away (cf. ll. 56 ff.) when her mother, who is very thin and doesn't look very healthy, comes in.

There is not much information about Barbara's outward appearance in the text except for the fact that she is "short" (l. 37) like her mother, who is described as "terribly thin, as if a long illness had ravaged her body and taken it sinew by sinew on a march towards the grave" (ll. 38 f.). When Barbara is walking towards the kitchen, her mother raises "a skeletal hand to her thin hair in a characteristic nervous gesture. Her overlarge eyes were puffy and rimmed with red, as if she had spent the day weeping" (ll. 41 f.). She wears a "shabby housedress" (l. 45) and shuffles (cf. l. 37) from one room to the next. All these descriptions show that the mother has already given up on herself. Lines 48/49 suggest that she doesn't do much more than watch television all day.

The fact that Barbara still lives with her parents although she has a good job with Scotland Yard shows that she obviously does not have the energy to change her life, maybe because of her workload and the fact that she hasn't got a lot of time to herself (ll. 34 ff.) and also perhaps because she cannot bring herself to leave her parents on their own.

The conversation between mother and daughter only seems to be tender in a practical way, i.e. the mother asking her daughter why she is home so late (l. 34) and not welcoming her warmly, asking how her day was, or indicating to her daughter that there is some dinner sitting in the kitchen (ll. 46/47) instead of having a proper conversation.

All this shows clearly how desperate life in the wrong streets obviously has to be.

(534 words)

4. *This task offers plenty of room to express the thoughts and ideas that you might have gathered while working on the first two tasks. Just remember that a speech needs addressees, a logical structure and an aim. What can you do to improve the situation? Give examples. Can you do it alone or do you need help? The right use of figures of speech will make your speech more convincing.*

Fellow citizens,

I am proud that you placed your trust in me when you voted for me as mayor of Ealing. Of course, many of you came here today for the answers that I promised during the election campaign.

Let me quickly outline the situation as it is before I introduce you to our ideas.

We all live in a great city that lies in the heart of England. As you know, equality is my highest aim – the socially deprived parts of our lovely area of Acton need to be elevated to social equality. The deep trench that runs through the heart of our district needs to be overcome. But what can we do?

In order to improve the situation we need to find funds to do the necessary reconstruction and we have to create jobs to make sure our improvements last, but we also need a great deal of will and idealism. We can't just sit and wait for something to happen. We must take this matter into our own hands. But what can we do?

Well, everybody can start by keeping their house and garden in an attractive state because nice attracts nice. I know it is going to be a tough start, but if all of us shoulder our part of the burden, we will eventually reach our goals. Now you are going to say, "That's all us! What is the mayor or the borough going to do to help us?" Of course you are right to ask those questions but as I already pointed out during my election campaign, the borough cannot do it alone. So I proudly stand in front of you and ask you for your help. But what can we do? What can your borough do for you?

We have done a lot of thinking on this matter. I do not believe there is a master plan but we are going to march forward and start by improving the infrastructure. The roads, the pavements and the parks will be returned to their original state using funds from the London 2012 Olympic Renovation Fund that have already been filed for. There will also be capital for renovating façade that you can apply for with the district council or online.

Public transport in town will be reorganized. Some old lines will go out of service and new ones will be introduced connecting both parts of Acton efficiently.

The schools, nursery schools and social institutions will be enhanced according to the law the government passed last autumn. By increasing the number of nursery schools, teachers and social workers we will create jobs for qualified citizens and brighten the future for our children and old age pensioners and thereby for ourselves, too.

In order to guarantee progress, we will also enforce the law to make our lovely area a safe place to live in. More police officers and modern technology will provide security. We can also improve our economic situation because a clean, safe, modern and well-structured community will attract new businesses that will also provide the financial support for further investments. So what can we do? We can all stand together and make Acton a wonderful home for all!

Thank you! *(535 words)*

> Abitur 2011 Schleswig-Holstein – Englisch (Kernfach)
> Aufgabe 2: London – Life in a Changing Metropolis

How I Lost My Faith in London
by Balaji Ravichandran

There is a gut-wrenching scene in Michael Haneke's "Code Inconnu"[1], where Juliette Binoche[2] is verbally abused on a Parisian metro train by a Turkish youth, and no one seems to notice. Just as things look set to get out of hand, however, an older Turkish passenger intervenes.

I wasn't so lucky. Last Saturday, I took a night bus from Marble Arch. At the next stop, four young men about 16 to 20 years of age, all white, boarded the bus, looked around, and within a few minutes sat down surrounding me. I don't know why I caught their attention, but I cursed myself for reading Walden[3] on a late-night bus. Then the abuse began.

"Hey Paki? Did you not listen to Prince Harry? Get the fuck out of this country, you brown monkey!" "Fairer than other Pakis? Maybe his mum was a slut." "You stink, like the rest of them do! Soaked in curry, did ya?" "Mowgli, you get paid in bananas or tikka masalas?"

Several other passengers boarded the bus at the next few stops. The young men, however, continued undaunted, imitating the behaviour of monkeys, playing with my book, and continuing the verbal assault. I didn't have the nerve to confront them, fearing further aggravation. Two black men, standing on the concertina area of the bendy bus, laughed initially and then egged the gang on. Two other men of south Asian origin sitting further along stared helplessly at what was happening. At least 20 other passengers were on the bus, most of them older than the four youths. I shifted my eyes in every possible direction to ask for support. None was forthcoming. Near King's Cross, after 15 minutes of torment, things became physical, as the relatively sober gang began to prod, pull and pinch me.

I swiftly got out of the bus and climbed into the nearest taxi. Behind me, I saw that the gang had followed me. Did I call the police? No, I didn't see the point. Besides, as someone who wants to stay in this country? Yes, as an immigrant? I didn't want to risk getting my name on any legal record, lest it cause problems in the future.

Are these incidents rare? To be sure. Yet I have never identified myself through my race; never belonged to any Indian or Asian groups or societies; do not even frequent curry houses. I've never been to Club Kali[4] nor, for that matter, Brick Lane[5].

Race is a superficial identification that society forces upon me, be it through dating sites, where men (more than women) expressly specify a racial preference, often unkind towards south Asians, or through equality monitoring, or when confronting prejudices or racial abuse. Even if I accepted an identification that is so meaningless to me, it wouldn't have been of much help.

Those two Asian men in the bus were unwilling or unable to do anything. Fear, or indifference, was the uniting factor in the bus. Not race. Just look at the behaviour of

the black men who egged the gang on. Could it be that they were just as sick of other ethnic minorities as these disaffected youths were? And what of tolerance? Was what
40 I witnessed yesterday a measure of tolerance in a multicultural London, or one of willed, self-protective indifference? Do we just misread the latter as the former? Would things have been different in a different bus, at a different time, with a different crowd?

The nobler or the baser attributes of humanity unite and divide us more than race,
45 religion or sexuality ever could. Racism is out there, and we know it. But the worrying trends that this incident reveals have little to do with it. They reveal an alarming coldness that runs through the veins of an otherwise vibrant, multicultural city. They show the strained relations between different races, not just white people and "ethnic minorities". They hint at disaffected youth, clueless political parties, and a media base
50 that exploits the former for money. People often say that we use the word "racism" a bit too much these days, and that we have made a hobby out of taking "offence." I don't feel offended. I feel hurt. Let down. Attitudes such as these, and the accumulation of small doses of indifference towards intolerance and prejudice, are what bring about systematic discrimination.

55 Schopenhauer[6] said of humanity that the more he loves it, the less he admires individual human beings. For me, the inverse has long been closer to the truth. The experience of 15 minutes reinforced that conviction and lost me my faith in London.

(794 words)

From: Balaji Ravinchandran, "How I Lost My Faith In London"
In: The Guardian, 22 February 2010
http://www.guardian.co.uk/commentisfree/2010/feb/22/london-racist-attack-indifference-discrimination

1 *Haneke's "Code Inconnu":* film that shows the interaction of several different nationalities in search of a language code. Haneke was the director.
2 *Juliette Binoche:* famous French actress
3 *Walden:* title of the book by H. D. Thoreau, 1854, also known as *Life in the Woods*
4 *Club Kali:* popular meeting point for people of Asian origin in London
5 *Brick Lane:* a street in the East of London, today the heart of the city's Bangladeshi community, known to some as Banglatown
6 *Schopenhauer:* German philosopher (1788–1860), known for his pessimistic view of the world, which according to him cannot be ruled by reason.

Assignments

1. Portray the facets of London as they become evident. *(25 %)*

2. Using your knowledge about London, evaluate the "worrying trends" the author refers to in lines 45/46. *(40 %)*

3. The incident on the bus has been reported to the police. During their enquiries they have identified some of the eye-witnesses. You are one of them and have been asked to write a testimony and to justify why you did not interfere. *(35 %)*

Lösungsvorschläge

1. *The intention behind this task is to check whether you have understood the text and are able to render the facts given in the text that show London as a city with different faces: the positive one we all know and the darker side that the author experiences.*

London is the multicultural, multi-ethnic, cosmopolitan and tolerant capital of Great Britain. It is a pulsating metropolis. However, this picture has certain cracks as the author of "How I lost my faith in London", Balaji Ravichandran, a Pakistani immigrant who lives in London, points out after he has experienced racism on a bus.

As the title suggests, Balaji Ravichandran loses his faith in London and completely changes the image of the city that he had had before. The reason for this is the fact that during the incident on the bus nobody seemed willing to help him. Most people showed indifference and some black people even encouraged the white youths that were tormenting him. He escaped the situation physically unhurt but emotionally damaged by a cruelty that he had not expected to meet in 21st century London. His new image of London shows resentful youths, political parties that have no idea what they are doing and media that just use people.

According to Balaji, calling on official institutions like the police that are supposed to help the victims doesn't seem very promising, because an entry in any kind of legal record could spoil the immigrant's chance of a future in the country. So it seems as if verbal and physical harassment are normal and part of present-day London.
(218 words)

2. *In this task you have to examine the "worrying trends" the author mentions in lines 45/46. Keep in mind what he says about London and see how this corresponds to what you have learned about the British capital. Judge the statements here and give reasons for your verdict.*

As I have already pointed out, London is known as a multicultural, multi-ethnic, cosmopolitan, tolerant and pulsating metropolis. Balaji Ravichandran's text, however, reveals a different reality. On the bus the Pakistani immigrant experiences psychological and physical harassment by a group of 16 to 20-year-old white youths that can only be called racist. To him the situation gets even worse when all the other people on the bus are afraid to interfere with the injustice that is happening or even show great indifference towards a person who is desperately looking for help. Instead of helping him, members of a different ethnic group even encourage the youths by laughing about what is happening and show that the different ethnic minorities, people that one would think would take a stand for each other, have different interests nowadays.

This example shows that the situation is the same all over the world. Even in New York, which the Americans call "The Melting Pot" because all races and cultures are supposed to have mixed there, people are disillusioned by the fact that this theory was more wishful thinking than reality. In London the situation is a little different though, since the former British colonies supply the capital with a constant flow of immigrants. Approximately 50 different ethnic groups live together in London and about 40 % of Londoners are members of an ethnic minority. This has made many British citizens leave the capital over the last few years. Some of the reasons for this development might be the conflicts with immigrants or media coverage about incidents such as Balaji Ravichandran's experience. This story is an example of the problems existing both between different ethnic groups and between immigrants and white English citizens.

However, it is not as simple as that, because neither every Englishman nor every black person is a racist. Of course, the media report on racism all the time, so it is evidently there, but is the racism the result of the media coverage or is it the other way around? Who profits from this sort of racism? I believe that this is the core of what Balaji Ravichandran meant by worrying trends. Today's mass media need catchy headlines to keep the consumers interested and by reporting on all sorts of cruel incidents they indirectly promote them. This trend is picked up by a disaffected youth that basically has everything but a goal and so starts looking for weaker victims to fill their lives with some sense of purpose. In this case the victim did not necessarily have to be a foreigner; he could just as well have been a Scottish or English geek wearing unusual glasses or clothes. The only difference would have been that in cases like that we do not talk about racism but about bullying. Balaji Ravichandran also talks about clueless political parties, but is the situation really that easily explained? I do not believe it is, because when a new Prime Minister is introduced after an election, his or her party has a clear strategy of what they want to achieve in the following years. This strategy is of course sabotaged by reality because every day numerous news items force them to react in a certain way, so that they sometimes can't keep track of their actions. To a normal citizen this behaviour might seem clueless, but it is obviously not.

So is London an intolerant city ruled by clueless parties and inhabited by a disaffected youth? To sum up, I do not think so. I would rather say that you can experience the same incidents of intolerance, the same discrimination and the same prejudices all over the world, whether you are in London, Berlin, Moscow, Tokyo or Los Angeles. Even young people, the media and politicians are pretty much alike. So London is no better but no worse than other cosmopolitan metropolises.

(644 words)

3. *This task gives you the opportunity to describe the whole situation as you would have seen it through your own eyes. So the text has to be written from your perspective as a witness. Do not forget to give your insights and justify your actions. The text form is a testimony – so it has to be logical and objective to a certain degree.*

Testimony

I, Kenneth Clark, hereby declare that the following report of the events of May 19th 2010 is the truth, the whole truth and nothing but the truth.

It was late, about 2 a.m. when I caught the night bus N 98 from Marble Arch to Stanmore at the Odeon. The bus was not overcrowded and there were still some free seats towards the back of the bus. So I went past a group of youths, who were obviously drunk, to the second to last row, put my backpack on the first seat and sat down by the window. I put my headphones into my ears and listened to some music while I was looking out of the window, watching the streets passing by. The lights in the back of the bus were not working properly so there was a rather dim atmosphere that seemed to suit the lovers behind me perfectly well. Those two people were completely involved with each other so that they didn't notice either me or anybody else on the bus.

A little further forward, in the middle of the bus, there were two black men who had obviously had a good night out and were in a very good mood, laughing and chatting away. The group of drunk youths – there were about five or six of them, I cannot exactly recall the number – looked like they were having fun, too. One of them, I believe he was the leader, was constantly talking to an Indian-looking guy who was sitting in the middle of them trying to ignore them by reading a book. Every now and then he turned around, looking at everyone else on the bus and at what they were doing. I noticed this behaviour by chance and thought it a little strange. Then there were a few other people sitting in front of those people, actually in the rows next to and in front of that chap, who were all chatting. At every stop some people got on or off.

Suddenly the Indian-looking guy jumped up from his seat, quickly pushed past the youths and left the bus at I believe it was Maida Vale, looking grimly at everybody else on the bus. He must have hit one of the youths on his way out because the boys followed him. Luckily for him they did not get a hold of him because he jumped into the next taxi and drove off. It was lucky because the boys obviously felt offended and seemed to want to take revenge for his rude behaviour on his way out.

All the other passengers acted normally until I got off the bus at Neasden.

(446 words)

> Abitur 2011 Schleswig-Holstein – Englisch (Kernfach)
> Aufgabe 3: India – Roots and Challenges

Samar and his Father
by Pankaj Mishra

My ancestors were Brahmins, originally from Kanauj, the capital of the great seventh-century Indian empire founded by Harshavardhana. We vaguely knew that after the sixteenth-century Mogul emperor, Akbar, had created a native aristocracy by awarding large grants of land to the Brahmins of the region, my an-
5 cestors had remained wealthy landowners in the flatlands of the western Himalayas.

With India's independence in 1947, their regulated life was unraveled with bewildering speed. My grandfather and his sons found themselves thrown into the new ruthless go-getting world of independent India with none of their old certainties intact.
10 Successive land reform legislation undermined the family's assets to the point where ancestral jewelry had to be sold off to pay for the education of my father and his brothers. There was a time when neither studentship nor marriage seemed a possibility.

My father grew up knowing both a kind of feudal grandeur and shameful penury. From a life of secluded leisure, he was catapulted into the ranks of desperate millions
15 seeking jobs under the new regime. I did not know until after my mother's death how deeply marked he was by that period of difficult transition.

In time, the years of struggle were left behind. He joined the Public Works Department (PWD); he worked his way to a kind of middle-class security and equilibrium. But he never spoke about his early years. Once, in an uncharacteristic burst of nos-
20 talgia, he mentioned the caparisoned[1] elephants he rode to his grandmother's village. On another occasion, he spoke of the time Pandit Nehru had come to the family house to borrow a horse from the stables. These memories alone came to represent for me the life he had known as a child.

For me, born in 1969, and growing up with cricket, the books of Enid Blyton[2], and
25 Tintin Comics[3], there could be no such memories. That past of my father – and also my mother, whose family had suffered a similar upheaval – was very far away from the series of PWD bungalows and mediocre Christian-run schools in which I had spent my childhood. The serenity of the old Brahmin world in which his family had lived for centuries was even more remote from me. [...] I could feel my own life had
30 drifted apart from them; it had attached itself to another constellation of desires and reverences.

I had the sharpest sense of this at the time of my mother's death. She had chosen to spend the last months of her life in an ashram in Benares, which was in line with an immemorial Hindu belief that to die there was to be released from the cycle of re-
35 births. [...]

I was very much on my own: this was what my father sought to convey to me in the days that followed my mother's death. Until then, I had never exchanged more than a few words at a time with my father. He had been the same with my mother. Practical matters were briefly discussed before both withdrew into their respective private worlds. He had been a less distant figure when I was still a child; I remember him reading me stories from the Mahabharata[4], and explaining to my young, uncomprehending mind their message of the illusoriness of love and attachment. But he was by nature a reticent man, and his reticence grew with time.

I remember one afternoon in the ashram my father and I were staying at in Benares. [...] He asked me if I would go with him on a walk through the ghats.

There, amid the crowd of late-evening bathers, my father explained to me his plans for the future. He had decided to wind down his present life. He wanted to retire and move to the Aurobindo Ashram in Pondicherry. It was where he had long wanted to go; if he didn't go now, he would never be able to leave. As for me, he would make all possible arrangements. He had built no house to pass on to me, and there wasn't much money. But he could set aside a small allowance that would see me through college. After that, it was up to me to make what I could of my life.

He then concluded these abrupt announcements with an even more uncharacteristic personal-philosophical statement. He said he had never wanted to get married; his marriage was a mistake from the very beginning, and both he and my mother had suffered for it. Another mistake lay in joining the PWD. But there was no choice for him. It wasn't anything he ever wanted to do, and he had ended up spending the best years of his life in joyless drudgery. But then, he didn't have too many regrets about all that anymore. Experience had taught him that of such mistakes were most lives compounded.

What he had always desired was freedom: freedom from all bonds that tie one down to the vanities of the world, freedom from all duties and responsibilities to other people. It had come to him at last in old age, with the death of his wife, when he could not take full advantage of it. He was going to make the most of it in the time left to him.

It took him a few more months to wind up his affairs. I was still in Allahabad[5] and didn't see him leave for Pondicherry. He wouldn't have liked that anyway: the sentimentality of goodbyes. He did ask me to visit him during my holidays. But I never went. I sensed the awkwardness of such a visit for both of us. I went instead to Kerala[6], Kashmir[7], Darjeeling[8], and Simla[9]; I stayed in cheap hotels and traveled on buses. I wrote to him about my journeys. He seemed to approve of them in his replies. I wrote to him from Allahabad; my letters grew more brisk and confident.　(985 words)

From: Pankaj Mishra, The Romantics: a Novel, *New York 2000, pp. 68 –74*

1　*caparisoned:* covered with a decorated cloth
2　*Enid Blyton:* Famous 20th century British authoress of children's adventure stories
3　*Tintin Comics:* English for the German *Tim und Struppi* Comics
4　*Mahabharata:* Ancient India's most important history and philosophy book of about 100,000 verses.
5　*Allahabad:* an old-fashioned university town where Samar was studying in the northern state of Uttar Pradesh.
6　*Kerala:* a state in the Southwest of India.
7　*Kashmir:* a larger area, divided into an Indian, a Pakistani and a Chinese part

8 *Darjeeling:* a mountainous district in the Northeast of India
9 *Simla:* the former summer capital of the British Raj in the Himalayas in the Northwest

Assignments

1. Delineate the effects of the historical development in India on the narrator and his family. *(20 %)*
2. Examine the relationship between the narrator and his father. *(25 %)*
3. Reflect on the father's attitude towards life and what it is based on. Take your background knowledge into consideration. *(25 %)*
4. Write one of the later letters that are mentioned in the last line of the text. *(30 %)*

Lösungsvorschläge

1. *In this assignment you are required to demonstrate how recent historical developments in India influenced the history of the narrator's family. You should explain the information given in the text by using your background knowledge about India. Examine the parents' life first, and then look at the development of the narrator's life. Be careful to use your own words.*

The lifestyle of the narrator's family underwent considerable changes in the past. His father is descended from a wealthy family that can be traced back to the 16th century. On the rare occasions that his father talks about his childhood, the narrator learns that the family must have been rich and influential (cf. ll. 4–6, 20–22). After India was granted independence in 1947, land reform legislation cost them their property, forcing them to sell out in order to ensure their sons' [among them the narrator's father] education (cf. ll. 11 f.) and leading to the loss of social status (cf. ll. 10–13). Their "old certainties" (l. 9) being destroyed, the family find themselves fighting for survival in times of high unemployment (cf. ll. 14 f.). The narrator's father finally manages to stop his descent, finding work with the Public Works Department and building a middle-class existence for his family. However, this outward stability veils the emotional distress that the loss of social status inflicts on him and his wife. As a consequence, at the end of their lives both the narrator's parents turn to religion, moving into ashrams as a release from their burdensome "duties and responsibilities" (l. 62) and the "joyless drudgery" (l. 58) their middle-class existence imposes upon them.

The narrator, on the other hand, is used to a westernised, modern lifestyle, much like any other young man in the second half of the 20th century (cf. ll. 24 f.). He feels that he does not have much in common with his parents because their expectations of life have "drifted apart" (l. 30) from him. He has become estranged from his ancestors and has difficulty understanding his father's attitude towards life,

2011-15

even more so since he does not communicate (cf. ll. 37 f.). In time he forms his own views and becomes increasingly distanced from his father (cf. ll. 42 f.).

(316 words)

2. *The central aspect to this assignment is the increasing chasm between father and son. You should aim for a concise account of the actual facts that relates to the text but shows your ability to extract the relevant information by your choice of words and structure.*

The relationship between father and son is distanced to start with and grows increasingly more so through the years. Their life is characterised by their inability to communicate, which is due to the fact that the social overturn in 20th century India has influenced their everyday lives in quite opposite ways. Thus, they belong to two generations which could not be more different. While the father secretly yearns for the feudal lifestyle of his past (cf. ll. 19 ff.), the son is used to the family's middle-class existence (cf. ll. 24 ff.). When his father decides to move to an ashram in his old age the narrator realises that, while they share a desire for independence, he tries to achieve it by travelling and having new experiences (cf. ll. 29 ff., 69 ff.), whereas to his father it means independence from the demands of society (cf. ll. 61 ff.). For all his life his father has tried to fulfil the role society has designated for him: as a son whose education was bought dearly by selling family heirlooms as well as a husband and father who has to provide for his wife and children (cf. ll. 54 ff.), although it was never what he would have chosen for himself. In the narrator's childhood, the father attempts to bond with his son, but even then the boy feels his father's growing emotional isolation (cf. ll. 42 f.). This is also expressed in his choice of words: throughout his story, the narrator avoids using names, so the narrative remains vague.

At the end of his life the father finally manages to achieve his freedom by moving into an ashram. After this final separation, the son's increasing independence manifests itself in his reluctance to visit his father and in his letters that grow "more brisk and confident" (l. 72). *(306 words)*

3. *This assignment requires you to elaborate on the father's character as it is presented by the narrator and to explain it with the help of your background knowledge of the history and culture of 20th century India. You should be careful not to let your thoughts run away with you, but make sure your text is structured and concise. In your reflections, you should review the father's past and evaluate it according to his unacknowledged goals and desires. The chasm between the needs of the individual and those of society as well as between secular life and religion should also feature in your answer.*

The narrator's father is descended from an old Brahmin family, the highest caste in India. The family can be traced back to the 16th century, when they were given landed property by the Mogul emperor Akbar, which they kept until the country's independence in 1947, when India became a secular democracy and the caste system was abolished. This constituted a turning point in the father's life, which changed from luxury as a member of one of the upper castes – the Brahmins were the caste of teachers and priests – to a life in poverty after the abolition of the caste system and finally to a middle-class existence.

After growing up in wealth, the father has to make a living by working for the Public Works Department. This depresses him since he still thinks back nostalgically to his life in luxury while he hates his job, which he perceives as "drudgery" (l. 58). Nevertheless, he feels that he has to fulfil his duties to his family. Since he feels indebted to his parents for paying for his education by selling the family jewels, he also feels obliged to comply with their wishes for his founding a family, although it is expressly against his own wishes. He admits that he never had the wish to marry (cf. l. 54), a statement which is supported by the fact that the stories he read to his young son were about the "illusoriness of love and attachment" (l. 42). His submission to his parents' wishes is in line with the Hindu belief in the concept of 'dharma' as one of the objectives of life, which means doing the right thing and fulfilling your personal duties.

Other objectives are wealth, sensual pleasure and freedom from the cycle of reincarnation. Since he is denied the first two, he aims for the third, freedom. But while his wife expressly joins an ashram in order to attain the ultimate goal in life, namely serenity and detachment from worldly desires, thus being released from the cycle of rebirths, he prefers to be released from the demands society imposes upon him (cf. ll. 61 ff.).

These demands have shaped his past considerably: as a rule, the life of a Hindu consists of different stages, which include the student stage, the householder's stage and finally the stages of retirement and detachment from secular life. Every stage brings with it its own set of duties towards the self as well as to the family and society. The father's sense of moral obligation has made him put his family above his own wishes, but his son has always felt the distance, not only between him and his parents, but also between his mother and father. This is also a phenomenon that could be considered characteristic of cultures in which arranged marriages are common, as they are in traditional India.

Thus, it seems, while the son is eager for new experiences, the father seems to be resigned to his fate, claiming that "of such mistakes were most lives compounded" (ll. 59 f.). Only at the end of his life does he find the energy to pursue his own goals in life. *(525 words)*

4. *When you write this letter, you should make sure you stay in character with regard to the son's aims in life. Remember his cultural values and the social context he grew up in. Obviously, your letter must fit in with the plot development delineated in the original. You could, for example, describe some experiences the narra-*

> tor has had during his travels and have him refer to his father's reactions. The narrator's increased self-confidence should also become evident in your choice of words and topics. The narrator might criticise his father's turning religious at the end of his life or his lifestyle in general, contrasting it with the lifestyle the narrator has chosen for himself.
> Finally, don't forget to stick to the formal requirements of a letter.

Allahabad, 12th September, 1981

Dear Father,

I hope this letter finds you well. I had a slight touch of flu last month after my visit to Darjeeling, but I recovered quickly after Dr Gupta prescribed me a new kind of antibiotics.

Thanks for the tip about Darjeeling, by the way. It was an amazing experience. I took the steam train up to the tea gardens and found a job filling sacks with dried tea leaves and loading them onto the train. My first intention had been to work as a tea picker, but they turned me down – said I didn't have the necessary experience. Anyway, I really enjoyed the company of my fellow workers; they were really down-to-earth, hospitable people. I lived with one of them, so I got an insight into his everyday life, too. I will never again complain about the food at the university canteen being dull!

We staged a protest about the food at the canteen last week, though. They insist on giving us curries three days out of five; I know they're cheap and healthy, but it would be nice to have something modern now and again. How complicated can it be to make some ordinary chips? Or some pasta? This is the twentieth century, after all.

Are you still fasting every other week? I hope you know what you're doing; personally I don't think it can be good for your health, at your age. Please be careful.

The new semester starts tomorrow; I'm sorry I couldn't come and visit you this summer. Maybe I will be able to make it next year, after my trip to Kerala. I would really like to see you again.

Yours affectionately,
your son Samar *(286 words)*

Abitur 2011 Schleswig-Holstein – Englisch (Kernfach)
Aufgabe 4: India – Roots and Challenges

Delhi Wedding for Runaway Romeo and Juliet
by Shekhar Bhatia

A Muslim teenager who fell in love with a Hindu student on the internet has fled her home in Britain against her parents' wishes and married him in India.
The clandestine affair between Subia Gaur, 18, and her boyfriend Ashwani Gupta, 22, has provoked intense media interest on the subcontinent and captured the imagination of the Indian public, who turned up in their hundreds to watch the ceremony.
The traditional Hindu wedding, which took place in Mr Gupta's home town of Ghaziabad, near Delhi, on Monday, was broadcast on television throughout India.
Miss Gaur, from Plaistow, east London, met her husband three years ago in an internet chatroom. They exchanged photographs, began talking secretly through the night and fell in love.
The relationship was conducted in secret for many months before Miss Gaur travelled to India to meet Mr Gupta for the first time, on the pretence of visiting her grandparents in Bombay.
"I knew the first time I met Ashwani in person that he was the one I was going to marry," she said from her new home in India. "It is hard for people to understand what we have been through. My family have put a lot of pressure on me and I didn't want to hurt them, but I had to be with the man that I love."
"Religion doesn't matter. I am Muslim and he is Hindu. I am not converting and he doesn't want me to. Ashwani and his family have accepted me for who I am."
When Miss Gaur's family discovered the relationship while she was studying for her A-Levels at a sixth-form college, she claims they pressed her into ending it. They had planned an arranged wedding for her with a Muslim. But Miss Gaur defied them and flew secretly last month to Delhi to marry Mr Gupta. Her mother, discovering she had gone, took a flight the next day to persuade her to return home. Miss Gaur claims that she and Mr Gupta, who is studying to become a financial analyst, were forced to go into hiding until they could marry.
They were given police protection after claiming that they received threats from her family, an allegation they have denied. In turn, Miss Gaur's family told police she had been abducted. After police interviewed the bride-to-be, officers were instructed to ensure that her family were prevented from hindering the marriage.
"I knew they would never accept Ashwani so I decided to go to India," she said. "We thought if we got married then they wouldn't be able to take me back."
"I was a normal 18-year-old Londoner before this. I never wanted the attention that I have received. I couldn't believe 1,000 people turned up uninvited to the wedding because they saw our story on the news. But if there is someone else in my position I hope my story gives them the courage to follow their heart."

Miss Gaur's father, Abdul, 46, a shop manager, fainted at his home in Newham, east London, when he was interviewed about his daughter's fate. He believed she had been "brainwashed". The first he knew of the wedding, he said, was when he and his wife, Fameeda, 37, turned on an Indian satellite television channel at their home.

"She is a Muslim above all and she has married a Hindu and that is the most shocking thing about this – not that she has lied to us and married against our wishes," he said, weeping.

"I have two daughters and a young boy and we keep a very close watch on them to protect them. Subia likes London and designer perfumes and clothes. But the girls are teenagers and were not allowed out after school or college and certainly not near any men. But we could do nothing to protect our daughter from the evil of the internet. While we slept at night, this evil came into our home and has led to our daughter marrying a Hindu boy. He is only interested in getting a British passport."

Mr Gaur denied he and his wife had made threats to kidnap Subia. "She is part of my body, my first-born child and it is madness to say that we could harm her."

Mr Ashwani's father, BB Gupta, admitted that he was concerned his daughter-in-law was too young to marry but said the couple were determined to go ahead and it was better to allow it than have them run away.

"We are reconciled to it and happy to have her in the household," he said. "It doesn't matter that she is a Muslim." (776 words)

Telegraph.co.uk 16 Sep 2006. http://www.telegraph.co.uk/news/worldnews/1529023/Delhi-wedding-for-runaway-romeo-and-juliet.html

Assignments

1. The couple's story has been made into a documentary.
   Outline the development of their relationship for a blurb in a TV guide. *(20 %)*

2. Analyse the different attitudes of the respective families towards the marriage.
   Use your background knowledge. *(25 %)*

3. Immediately after her wedding in India, Subia writes a letter to her parents trying to explain to them why – in comparison to them – she has developed such a different attitude to life and love and marriage in particular. *(30 %)*

4. "Indians in London – a city of parallel societies?" Starting out from the reported case, write a commentary for a London weekly newspaper. *(25 %)*

Lösungsvorschläge

1. *This assignment requires two different aspects of you: on the one hand, you have to collect all the information about Subia and Ashwani's relationship. On the other hand, you must not simply write a summary of its development, but you are required to turn this into an interesting blurb that would attract viewers but doesn't give too much away. If necessary, you can add additional information. Make sure to use your own words.*

Love conquers all ☆ ☆ ☆ ☆ ☆

In her new documentary, Samantha McGregor presents a story that sounds too romantic to be true. It is the story of two teenagers from opposite ends of the world finding true love against all odds.
When Subia Gaur from Plaistow first meets Ashwani Gupta, it isn't in her local youth club. It's in an internet chat room, where Ashwani from Ghaziabad, thousands of miles away, is looking for someone to help him with his homework. But instead of finding the answer to his problem, he finds the love of his life.
What begins as a simple conversation on photosynthesis soon turns into regular nightly chats, with the two teenagers talking for hours on end. Despite their religious differences (Subia is Muslim, Ashwani Hindu) they soon discover how much they have in common, and when the opportunity arises, Subia uses the pretext of a visit to her grandparents in India to meet Ashwani in person for the first time. By then they have already fallen irrevocably in love. When her parents discover their relationship and try to put a stop to it, Subia flees to India. Since they fear Subia's family might force her to come back to England, Subia and Ashwani receive police protection and go into hiding. Finally the lovers decide to get married in order to prevent Subia's family from abducting her. On their wedding day, they are in for a surprise ...
McGregor's documentary skilfully blends interviews with Subia and Ashwani as well as their parents and friends with re-enacted scenes from their past and impressions of their cultural backgrounds.
Definitely worth watching! Five stars out of five.   *(279 words)*

2. *The central point of your analysis here is the fact that the families have different religions: While Ashwani Gupta is a Hindu, Subia Gaur is a Muslim. Taking this as a starting point, you should then move on to explain why the Gaurs are against the marriage, while the Guptas seem happy with it or at least complaisant. Support your findings with quotations from the text.*

Subia and Ashwani's parents demonstrate quite different attitudes towards their children getting married.
Subia's parents, on the one hand, oppose the marriage for religious reasons: they're Muslims and want their daughter to act according to their traditions, which forbid her to marry a man who is not a Muslim, i. e. an unbeliever. They claim that this circumstance is especially aggravating, even more than the fact that "she has lied to

[them] and married against [their] wishes" (l. 42). Mr and Mrs Gaur also fear that Ashwani might only be interested in marrying their daughter in order to obtain British citizenship (cf. l. 49).

Although they live in London they have always tried to protect their traditional lifestyle against modern influences, e.g. their daughters are not allowed to have contact with men. Consequently, they regard the internet as an evil which has secretly invaded their home (cf. ll. 44–49). As traditional Muslims, they expect Subia to obey them and yield to the marriage they have arranged for her with a Muslim man. Putting their faith above everything else, they cannot understand how their daughter can disregard the rules of her faith and marry a non-Muslim. They are not ready to grant Subia the right to follow her heart and fulfil her dream.

Ashwani's parents, on the other hand, accept the young couple's wish to get married although they think Subia's young age could be a problem (cf. ll. 52 f.). Nevertheless, they prefer giving Ashwani and Subia the freedom to decide for themselves to losing all contact with them (cf. l. 54). In contrast to the Gaurs, the Guptas do not object to their son marrying a Muslim. Possibly the diversity of Hinduism makes it easier for them to accept a daughter-in-law who is not from their own religious community. They have soon become reconciled to the idea of the young couple's marriage and are "happy to have her in the household" (l. 55).

(326 words)

3. *This assignment is supposed to test your text production skills as well as your analytical skills and your ability to step into the shoes of a fictitious character. Assuming Subia's point of view, you should have her explain her attitude towards marriage and religion to her parents. The fact that she has been brought up as a modern Londoner should feature strongly in her argumentation. In spite of all the differences, though, you ought to make sure Subia still addresses her parents with respect and affection. Don't forget the rules of letter writing.*

Ghaziabad, 20th September 2006

Dear Mother and Father,

I know that you're mad at me, and you've every right to be, but I hope you will do me the favour of reading this letter.

I would like you to know that I'm terribly sorry for the distress I've caused you. I really love you and it pains me to know that I hurt you. When I decided to leave home and marry Ashwani, I was aware of the pain I would inflict on you. But please believe me that I didn't do it out of spite. I really love Ashwani, and I want to spend my whole life with him. Of course I know you meant well when you arranged the marriage with Naveen, and I'm sure he is a decent man, but I don't think I could ever be happy with him. We hardly know each other, after all. Forcing us to get married wouldn't be fair to either of us – what if we don't get along? I'm not made for the traditional role of housewife and mother, I've got other plans for my future; I want a career, I want to earn my own money. If you didn't want me to make my own decisions, why did you send me to sixth-form college?

You said what hurt you most was that Ashwani isn't a Muslim. But I assure you that you needn't worry – we have so many things in common, it doesn't matter to us that we belong to different faiths. It was probably different in your youth, but today religion really isn't all that important when it comes to love, believe me. People do not let religion dictate their decisions in life anymore. They choose for themselves! And I want to be allowed to choose somebody I can relate to, somebody who shares my dreams and treats me as an equal. I wish you could accept that.

You cannot imagine how much it would mean to me if you could finally become reconciled to our being married. After all, I'm still a Muslim; you can be certain I won't give up my faith.

I sincerely hope that you can forgive me someday and that you will receive us into your home. I miss you terribly.

Please send my love to my brother and sister.

Love,
Subia
(389 words)

4. *This task takes the topic to a more abstract level. You are required to comment on whether the Indian citizens of London are starting to form a parallel society. It is important that your own opinion on the subject becomes clear to the reader. In order to be convincing you should support your ideas with your knowledge on immigrant cultures in London.*

Indians in London – a city of parallel societies?

London is a multi-cultural metropolis, and proud of it. Londoners and tourists alike value boroughs like Newham for its Asian shopping centres, Harrow for its Indian flair, Golders Green, Stamford Hill and Edgware for their Jewish culture. Chinatown is a tourist magnet whose guests enjoy immersing in its exotic culture for a short period of time. These places give us a good feeling about ethnic communities, we like to shop in them or eat at their restaurants. As a result, when the story of a young Indian woman from London who fled from home in order to marry the man she loved was in all British and Indian newspapers, this triggered a virtual flood of responses – many of our readers couldn't believe that in a city like this, there could still be families who lived according to orthodox Islamic values, who arranged marriages and expected total obedience from their children. However, the case of Subia Gaur taught us otherwise: her parents tried to break up her relationship with her boyfriend because he is a Hindu.

This is no extraordinary event. While we look the other way, there are whole communities that function according to their own set of rules.

The most notorious example would be Tower Hamlets, dubbed "Islamic Republic" by some of its residents. Here, the sharia might supersede the law when it comes to solving conflicts or laying down rules of behaviour. Assaults on unveiled women or openly homosexual residents are common. As was the case with Subia Gaur, women are expected to marry the men their parents choose for them – usually someone from their own community or home country. They are not allowed to make their own decisions concerning their careers and they often do not earn their own money. At worst, they receive no proper education and thus do not even learn English.

Since our housing policy of the past promoted the development of ethnic quarters, people can move around in spaces where everybody speaks the language of their ethnic group instead of English. Thus, they cannot escape even if they wanted to because they possibly have no idea that life can be different.

How can we encounter these dangers? Teachers and researchers alike point out the importance of education. The more young people are encouraged to think on their own, the more they will be empowered to take their lives into their own hands. As the example of Subia Gaur shows, emulation is also an important factor. When girls see that their peers are allowed to make their own decisions on their clothes and their career, they want the same rights for themselves.

So, as a consequence, if we make sure that no child is allowed to drop out of school early, we will strengthen their resistance to extremism. If we provide for English classes for immigrants, especially women, we will support them in their search for independence. In short, there will be hope that London's ethnic quarters keep on adding to the diverse face of our city without turning into parallel societies sealing themselves off against modern influences from outside.

Nadine Taylor, *The Observer* (528 words)

Abitur 2012 Schleswig-Holstein – Englisch (Kernfach)
Aufgabe 1: London – Life in a Changing Metropolis

Sebastian Faulks, *A Week in December,* 2010 (excerpt)

Five o'clock and freezing. Piledrivers and jackhammers were blasting into the wasteland by the side of West Cross Route in Shepherd's Bush. With a bare ten months to the scheduled opening of Europe's largest urban shopping centre, the sand-covered site was showing only skeletal girders and joists under red cranes, though a peppermint facade had already been tacked on to the eastward side. This was not a retail park with trees and benches, but a compression of trade in a city centre, in which migrant labour was paid by foreign capital to squeeze out layers of profit from any Londoner with credit. At their new 'Emirates' Stadium, meanwhile, named for an Arab airline, Arsenal of North London were kicking off under floodlights against Chelsea from the West, while the goalkeepers – one Czech, one Spanish – jumped up and down and beat their ribs to keep warm. At nearby Upton Park, the supporters were leaving the ground after a home defeat; and only a few streets away from the Boleyn Ground, with its East End mixture of sentimentality and grievance, a solitary woman paid her respects to a grandfather – come from Lithuania some eighty years ago – as she stood by his grave in the overflowing cemetery of the East Ham Synagogue. Up the road in Victoria Park, the last of the dog-walkers dragged their mongrels back to flats in Hackney and Bow, grey high-rises marked with satellite dishes, like ears cupped to the outside world in the hope of gossip or escape; while in a minicab that nosed along Dalston Road on its way back to base, the dashboard thermometer touched minus two degrees.

In his small rooms in Chelsea, Gabriel Northwood, a barrister in his middle thirties, was reading the Koran, and shivering. He practised civil law, when he practised anything at all; this meant that he was not involved in 'getting criminals off', but in representing people in a dispute whose outcome would bring financial compensation to the claimants if they won. For a long time, and for reasons he didn't start to understand, Gabriel had received no instructions from solicitors – the branch of the legal profession he depended on for work. Then a case had landed in his lap. It was to do with a man who had thrown himself under a Tube train, and concerned the extent to which the transport provider might be deemed responsible for failing to provide adequate safety precautions. Almost immediately, a second brief had followed: from a local education authority being sued by the parents of a Muslim girl in Leicester for not allowing her to wear traditional dress to school. With little other preparatory work to do, Gabriel thought he might as well try to understand the faith whose demands he was about to encounter; and any educated person these days, he told himself, really ought to have read the Koran.

Some yards below where Gabriel sat reading was an Underground train; and in the driver's cab a young woman called Jenni Fortune switched off the interior light because she was distracted by her own reflection in the windscreen. She slowed the train

with her left hand on the traction brake control and, just before she drew level with
the signal, brought it to a halt. She pressed two red buttons to open the doors and fixed
her eyes on the wing mirror to watch the passengers behind her getting in and out.

She had been driving on the Circle and Metropolitan lines for three years and still
felt excited when she clocked in for her eight-hour shift at the Depot. She felt sorry
for the poor passengers who sat and swayed behind her. Sideways on, they saw only
bags and overcoats, hanging straps and worn plush under strip lights with suffocating
heaters locked on max. They endured the jostle and the boredom, with occasional
stabs of fear when drunken, swearing youths pushed on.

From her view, Jenni saw soothing darkness, points, a slither of crossing rails and
signals that glowed like red coals. She rattled the train through the tunnels at forty
miles per hour and sometimes half expected skeletons to loom out from the wall or
bats to brush her face. Head-on, she saw the miracles of London engineering that no
passenger would ever glimpse: the corbelled brickwork through which the tunnels had
been cut or the giant steel joist that held up a five-floor building above the entry to the
platform at Liverpool Street.

The week before Christmas was the worst time of year for people throwing themselves on the track. Nobody knew why. Perhaps the approaching festivity brought
back memories of family or friends who'd died, without whom the turkey and the
streamers seemed a gloomy echo of a world that had once been full. Or maybe the advertisements for digital cameras, aftershave and computer games reminded people
how much they were in debt, how few of 'this year's musthave' presents they could
afford. Guilt, thought Jenni: a sense of having failed in the competition for resources
– for DVDs and body lotions – could drive them to the rails.   (859 words)

From: Sebastian Faulks, A Week in December, *London: Random House UK, 2010, novel, excerpt, pp. 1–4*

Assignments

1. Portray London and its inhabitants as shown in the text.   *(30 %)*

2. Based on the text and your background knowledge examine the major reasons for London's multi-ethnic and social conditions.   *(40 %)*

3. The following statement by Chuck Prince, Chief Executive of the Citigroup investment bank in an interview with the Financial Times from July 9, 2007, was chosen by Faulks to precede his novel: "As long as the music is playing, you've got to get up and dance … We're still dancing."
Gabriel Northwood and Jenni Fortune have read Prince's quotation in the Financial Times. Adopt either Gabriel's or Jenni's perspective and comment in a letter to the editor on the relevance the quotation has for their lives.   *(30 %)*

Lösungsvorschläge

1. *Here you are supposed to show that you have read the text thoroughly and understood it well. Summarize how London and its inhabitants are described by the author. In an introductory sentence you should say what the basic idea is before you go on to explain in detail what the text reveals. It is useful to structure your text into two parts, first explaining what the text reveals about the city and then summarizing which information it contains about its inhabitants. You might add where in the text you found the information. Do not deliver an interpretation here. Stick to describing the plain information given in the text.*

In the text excerpt from *A Week in December* by Sebastian Faulks, London is described as an inhospitable city that is inhabited by a variety of different individuals from different countries.

London in December as such is depicted as a cold and inhospitable place. The keepers of the local football teams do exercises during the game to keep warm (ll. 10 f.) and people walking their dogs go home and watch satellite TV rather than staying out in the cold (ll. 16 ff.). The author also describes the city as crowded, monotonous and demanding (ll. 44 ff) and sometimes even threatening, which is shown in the fear spread by the drunken youths (l. 47) or in the high suicide rate in the Underground transportation system (ll. 27 f. and ll. 55 ff.). At the same time it is globalised and booming with international money invested in it and immigrant workers employed there (ll. 5 ff.). The face of the international capital is changing due to the erection of huge shopping malls or football stadiums, but these also stand for commercialized, profit-orientated business (ll. 8 f.).

According to the text, London's inhabitants are multinational and multi-ethnic. There are Jews from Lithuania (ll. 14 f.), Muslims (l. 31) and sportsmen from the Czech Republic or Spain (l. 10), for example, that show the diversity of London's population. This occasionally leads to problems, as in the case of the Muslim girl who is not allowed to wear her traditional dress to school (ll. 30 ff.). Many people struggle desperately with their problems in an isolated, anonymous society (ll. 55 ff.), which leads to a number of suicides committed on the Tube. *(277 words)*

2. *In this task you need to look through the text and find hints that explain why London is so multi-ethnic and what has led to the social conditions portrayed in the text. Take the hints that you find and explain them using your background knowledge. Mark the place in the text where you found the information you are referring to. It could be useful to outline the history of migration to London.*

London is *the* metropolis of the British Empire, people from all parts of the Commonwealth come to London and to try to make their fortune there.

There is certain information in the text concerning London's multi-ethnic and social conditions. It mentions Jewish people who originally came from Eastern Europe, in this case Lithuania, very likely having fled the Nazis and whose children and grandchildren now live in London (ll. 14 f.). There is also mention of foreign sportsmen who are in London to earn a living – in this case a Czech and a Spanish football goalkeeper (l. 10). This particular multi-ethnic phenomenon is common all over the world today. From the name of the Arsenal stadium, it would appear that the money for this London club comes from an Arab airline rather than a British source (ll. 8 f.). The entire sports sector could be seen as an example of the effects of globalization. There is also information in the text about a Muslim girl from Leicester, but her not being Christian is the only hint that she comes from an ethnic background (l. 31).

Concerning the social conditions, there is a contrast hinted at between rich and poor. What is to become 'Europe's largest urban shopping centre' (l. 3) is in stark contrast to the grey high-rise flats in poorer areas of London, where the inhabitants have nothing to do but watch TV, gossip and hope for a better life somewhere else (ll. 16 f.). Neither of the characters introduced in the excerpt is particularly well-off. Although Gabriel Northwood is a barrister, he is obviously not rich since his business does not seem to be going too well (ll. 21 f.). As a driver on the Underground working eight-hour shifts Jenni Fortune probably does not earn fortunes either (ll. 42 f.).

What are the main reasons behind the multi-ethnic and social conditions in London? Here it is important to mention certain waves of immigration to Britain, and especially to London. The first important wave in the 20th century was the one that came during the Third Reich Era and after World War II – not only from Germany but also from Eastern Europe. Most of these people were Jewish, represented in the text by the women at the "overflowing cemetery of the East Ham Synagogue" (l. 15). Another major group of immigrants arriving after World War II were those from Commonwealth countries plus quite a few from those countries that gained independence after World War II. These people wanted to stay British rather than be part of their new-formed countries. They brought the eastern beliefs to London, such as Islam, Hinduism, Buddhism and many other smaller ecclesial groups. This changed life in London to a great extent. In the text this is represented by local education authorities being sued because a Muslim girl has not been allowed to wear traditional dress to school, or by the fact that a British barrister is of the opinion that every educated person "ought to have read the Koran" (ll. 35 f.).

A second large group came to Britain from Eastern Europe after the end of the Cold War in 1989. Many tried to make their fortune and worked for the better salary in the west and finally decided to stay. These people are not referred to directly in the text, but "migrant labour" (l. 6) is mentioned, and they can be included in this group.

Needless to say, there are tensions between these groups of people from very different backgrounds. Some of these groups are not integrated into British society at all but live in parallel societies. They have agglomerated in certain areas and live together there, sticking to their own language and culture. Due to ethnic differences, these areas sometimes become the focus of tension, and are of special interest to law enforcement forces. This tension has been exacerbated since 9/11 and the bombings of 2005.

However, the riots of 2011 were not only the consequence of ethnic or religious differences in multi-cultural society, but also of social differences. After the financial crisis of 2008, many British people, particularly low-income families, were left with barely nothing. In the text the violence and dissatisfaction in the population is shown in the persons of the 'drunken, swearing youths' (l. 47), and the suggestion is also made that suicides may have taken their lives as a result of not being able to keep up with the capitalist system (ll. 58 ff.).

So far the Government hasn't found adequate solutions to these problems, so it seems fair to say that it will be the task of future generations to improve racial and social tensions to achieve a fair society for everyone. *(784 words)*

3. To comment on the statement you need to get an idea of its meaning first. To solve this task you have to show that you have learned how to write a letter. Make sure to stick to the requirements. Choose one of the two characters and write from his/her point of view using the background knowledge you have gained from the text. The perspective the character gives on Chuck Prince's statement should be convincing and in accordance with his/her background. Find reasons why he/she agrees or disagrees with the quote and explain the relevance it has for his/her life using examples from the text or your background knowledge. You may invent extra information about the character to stress his/her opinion.

Dear Editor,

As an occasional reader of your newspaper, I was upset by your interview with Chuck Prince of July 9th, 2007. I was particularly annoyed by Prince's statement, "As long as the music is playing, you've got to get up and dance ... We are still dancing."

I totally disagree with that idea. I am very well aware of the fact that the music keeps going on, but how can someone in Mr. Prince's position obviously see the disaster coming and just carry on as normal?

He should bear in mind that he is playing with money that his clients have entrusted him and his bank with and that they have put their livelihood in his hands. If just like me you have taken out a mortgage to pay for the dream of your own home and you are working hard each day to meet the strict and tight regulations of the contract to make this dream come true, I think it is irresponsible for someone like Mr. Prince to make it look like some fun night out. I have personally lost all trust in these people, who I thought were taking me seriously.

People like him destroy the basis of a happy family life because they look at the numbers and forget that it's people they are dealing with. They are the reason that so many of my colleagues have had to give up the job they love because they could not take the strain of desperate people throwing themselves in front of the train and getting killed – decent people like a family father who threw himself on the tracks seeing no other way out after having gone bankrupt because he couldn't pay his mortgage anymore that some irresponsible banker had talked him into.

We are not on a pleasure cruise here, this is not the Titanic – this is real, and it will definitely be more than 1,500 people whose lives will be destroyed if we face another bank crash like the one back in 1929. That time our society was at the brink. Do we have to go through that again, or worse, because the managers think that it's all a big game?

I can't express my disappointment enough. Until recently I thought it was fair for people who have jobs in responsible positions, e. g. managers of multi-billion dollar companies, to earn more money than I do. But after reading this interview I have been forced to reconsider – I am far more responsible than these people, so why don't I get their salary instead?

I suggest Mr. Prince should think hard about what he has said and come up with some serious solution to handle the situation as well as the problems that might occur in the future. I have been a Tube driver for three years now and if there is an obstacle in the way I hit the brakes and try to avoid an accident, bearing in mind how many passengers are sitting behind me who have entrusted me with their lives.

Jenni Fortune, London *(511 words)*

> Abitur 2012 Schleswig-Holstein – Englisch (Kernfach)
> Aufgabe 2: India – Roots and Challenges

Aravind Adiga, "The Fourth Night", in: *The White Tiger*, 2008

"The Fourth Night" is a chapter of the epistolary novel The White Tiger *by Aravind Adiga, which deals with Balram, a member of the Indian Darkness, who gets a job as driver to the wealthy Mr. Ashok and thus the chance of looking beyond his "small" world.*
In this excerpt of the chapter "The Fourth Night", Mr. Ashok, his wife Pinky Madam, and Balram are on their way home from a night out. Pinky Madam has interrupted the ride, spontaneously taken the driver's seat and driven away, leaving Balram behind. After a few meters she returns the car and comes to a halt next to him who, irritated, has not moved since.

Madam opened the door and popped her grinning face out.
"Thought I had really left you behind, Mr. Maharaja?"
"No, madam."
"You're not angry, are you?"
"Not at all." And then I added, to make it more believable, "Employers are like mother and father. How can one be angry with them?"
I got into the backseat. They did another U-turn across the middle of the avenue, and then drove off at top speed, racing through one red light after the other. The two of them were shrieking, and pinching each other, and making giggling noises, and, helpless to do anything, I was just watching the show from the backseat, when the small black thing jumped into our path, and we hit it and knocked it over and rolled the wheels of the car over it.
From the way the wheels crunched it completely, and from how there was no noise when she stopped the car, not even a whimper or a barking, I knew at once what had happened to the thing we had hit.
She was too drunk to brake at once – by the time she had, we had hurtled on another two or three hundred yards, and then we came to a complete stop. In the middle of the road. She had kept her hands on the wheel; her mouth was open.
"A dog?" Mr. Ashok asked me. "It was a dog, wasn't it?"
I nodded. The streetlights were too dim, and the object – a large black lump – was too far behind us already to be seen clearly. There was no other car in sight. No other living human being in sight.
As if in slow motion, her hands moved back from the wheel and covered her ears.
"It wasn't a dog! It wasn't a –"
Without a word between us, Mr. Ashok and I acted as a team. He grabbed her, put a hand on her mouth, and pulled her out of the driver's seat; I rushed out of the back. We slammed the doors together; I turned the ignition key and drove the car at full speed all the way back to Gurgaon.

Halfway through she quieted down, but then, as we got closer to the apartment block, she started up again. She said, "We have to go back."

"Don't be crazy, Pinky. Balram will get us back to the apartment block in a few minutes. It's all over."

"We hit something, Ashoky." She spoke in the softest of voices. "We have to take that thing to the hospital."

"No."

Her mouth opened again – she was going to scream again in a second. Before she could do that, Mr. Ashok gagged her with his palm – he reached for the box of facial tissues and stuffed the tissues into her mouth; while she tried to spit them out, he tore the scarf from around her neck, tied it tightly around her mouth, and shoved her face into his lap and held it down there.

When we got to the apartment, he dragged her to the elevator with the scarf still around her mouth.

I got a bucket and washed the car. I wiped it down thoroughly, and scrubbed out every bit of blood and flesh – there was a bit of both around the wheels.

When he came down, I was washing the tires for the fourth time.

"Well?" I showed him a piece of bloodied green fabric that had got stuck to the wheel.

"It's cheap stuff, sir, this green cloth," I said, rubbing the rough material between my fingers. "It's what they put on children."

"And do you think the child …" He couldn't say the word.

"There was no sound at all sir. No sound at all. And the body didn't move even a bit."

"God, Balram, what will we do now – what will we –" He slapped his hand to his thigh. "What are these children doing, walking about Delhi at one in the morning, with no one to look after them?"

When he had said this, his eyes lit up.

"Oh, she was one of those people."

"Who live under the flyovers and bridges, sir. That's my guess too."

"In that case, will anyone miss her …?"

"I don't think so, sir. You know how those people in the Darkness are: they have eight, nine, ten children – sometimes they don't know the names of their own children. Her parents – if they're even here in Delhi, if they even know where she is tonight – won't go to the police."

He put a hand on my shoulder, the way he had been touching Pinky Madam's shoulder earlier in the night.

Then he put a finger on his lips.

I nodded. "Of course, sir. Now sleep well – it's been a difficult night for you and Pinky Madam."

I removed the maharaja tunic, and then I went to sleep. I was tired as hell – but on my lips there was the big, contented smile that comes to one who has done his duty by his master even in the most difficult of moments. (872 words)

From: Aravind Adiga, "The Fourth Night", in: The White Tiger, *New York: Free Press 2008, novel, excerpt, pp. 138–140*

Assignments

1. As a European journalist you happened to witness the accident. You are asked by the police to write a detailed report. *(25 %)*
2. Explain the reactions of the three people to the accident also using your background knowledge. *(35 %)*
3. A few weeks later you [the journalist] find out that Balram has admitted having been the driver.
   You use this false confession and the hit-and-run accident as a peg for a critical essay on the Indian society.
   Write this essay for a cultural magazine. *(40 %)*

Lösungsvorschläge

1. *This is basically a reading comprehension task. After selecting those facts about the accident that a bystander would have been able to gather, you must write an objective report that contains neither interpretation nor quotations from the text. Keep in mind that a report refers to important facts such as time and place and add this information. Don't forget to change perspective!*

On August 24th, I was sitting in my car, parked on Dattani Park Avenue. I first noticed the car when it did a U-turn at the end of the street. That must have been around 0:30 a.m. The car raced past me, tyres screeching. The driver ignored at least two red lights. When they reached the park, a child appeared from between the trees and was run over by the car. It seemed to be dead, since it remained lying in an unnatural position and made no sound at all. At first the driver didn't seem to have noticed, as it was only after a few hundred metres that the car finally stopped. Then two people jumped out of the car. The one from the passenger seat made the driver get into the back seat with him, while the one from the back seat took over the wheel. They then drove off at high speed in the direction of Mahatma Gandhi Road. *(162 words)*

2. *This assignment requires you to give a detailed analysis of the factors that influence the behaviour of the three protagonists, e. g. social status and background. Find out how the characters react at different points in the story and try to explain their behaviour. What information does the text offer about their feelings? Put this information into the context of what you know about the caste system. Also consider the position of the dead child in this system. Refer to the text to prove what you have found out.*

Before the accident, the behaviour of Mr. Ashok and his wife demonstrates how superior they feel. As wealthy members of one of the higher castes, they think they are above the rules when they race through the city: "They […] drove off at top speed, racing through one red light after the other. The two of them were shrieking, and pinching each other, and making giggling noises," (ll. 7–9). After the car hits the child, the three people in the car react quite differently. While the men recover quickly and try to save the situation, Pinky Madam, who drove the car and caused the accident by her reckless behaviour, doesn't get over it as easily. At first she is paralysed by the shock ("She had kept her hands on the wheel; her mouth was open", l. 18), but then she has an emotional breakdown ("As if in slow motion, her hands moved back from the wheel and covered her ears. 'It wasn't a dog! It wasn't a –'", l. 24; "Her mouth opened again – she was going to scream again in a second", l. 36). After realising that she has hit a human being, she wants to go back to the scene of the accident (l. 30) and take the victim to the hospital, although she still refers to the child as "something" and "that thing" (ll. 33/34).

Mr. Ashok behaves according to the rules of the patriarchal society he grew up in. Since he is used to making the decisions in his family, it is his task to protect his wife from the consequences of her behaviour. He is the first to claim that the "thing" they hit was a "dog" (l. 19). When realisation dawns on him, he cooperates with his driver to leave the scene of the accident as quickly as possible ("He grabbed her, put a hand on her mouth, and pulled her out of the driver's seat; I rushed out of the back. We slammed the doors together; I turned the ignition key and drove the car at full speed all the way back to Gurgaon", ll. 25–28). He is also used to having his orders obeyed, so he reverts to physical violence in order to prevent his wife from going back to the scene of the accident: he gags her and carries her bodily into the apartment (ll. 37–42). His initial fear and bad conscience ("God, Balram, what will we do now – what will we – ", l. 53) give way to anger and denial ("What are these children doing, walking about Delhi at one in the morning, with no one to look after them?" ll. 54/55) and finally relief when he realises that the dead child was a member of the Dalit and that there will in all probability be no consequences for him and his wife ("When he had said this, his eyes lit up. 'Oh, she was one of those people'", ll. 56/57). Both he and his wife regard members of the lower castes as creatures of lesser value; it comes naturally to them to order Balram around as they please, and killing a child of the "Untouchables" does not count much more with them than killing a dog.

Balram, however, is a member of one of the lower castes himself: he comes from the Darkness, that is, from a lower-caste community in a rural part of India. Nevertheless, he does not side with the victim, but is loyal to Mr. Ashok. His reaction is even less emotional than that of Mr. Ashok. Although he knows immediately what has really happened ("From the way the wheels crunched it completely, and from how there was no noise when she stopped the car, not even a whimper or a barking, I knew at once what had happened to the thing we had hit", ll. 13–15), his priority is to protect his employer. When Pinky Madam has her breakdown, he reacts immediately, takes the driver's seat and drives home. From this moment on, when the two men act "as a team" (l. 25) despite their social differences, his loyalty is sealed. When they are finally home, Balram starts to wash all traces of the accident off the car without hesitation. By the time he finds shreds of the child's clothing it must be clear to him that they have injured or killed a human being, but he calms Mr. Ashok by telling him the child was a member of the Dalit and explaining that "[h]er parents – if they're even here in Delhi, if they even know where she is tonight – won't go to the police" (ll. 62/63). The victim, according to him, is one of too many ("You know how those people in the Darkness are: they have eight, nine, ten children – sometimes they don't know the names of their own children", ll. 60–62), is therefore expendable and will not be missed. He has no choice to act differently without compromising his own goals. Since he is also a member of the Darkness, being allowed to work for members of one of the upper castes is his only opportunity to rise in the social order as well. Therefore, he feels he owes his employers total commitment, as he explains to Pinky Madam when she taunts him, "Employers are like mother and father. How can one be angry with them?" (ll. 5/6). That is why when he goes to bed he is no longer bothered by the events of the day, but satisfied because he has proved his loyalty towards Mr. Ashok (ll. 69–71). *(944 words)*

3. *This task goes beyond the events of the text given in the assignment. Use it as a starting point to reflect critically on the social injustice created by the caste system in India as well as its effects on people's attitudes towards human dignity. Make sure you do not just discuss Balram's case, but adopt a wider scope.*
For this task you will have to remember the rules of essay writing. Before you start, you need to decide on a thesis that you will have to discuss in your text. It is advisable to collect the arguments to support your thesis and possible counter-arguments that you will have to dismiss. After that you can structure your ideas logically, e. g. according to their strength. Since you are writing your essay from the perspective of a fictitious character, make sure you do not quote from the text. Keep in mind that you witnessed the accident and know Balram was not the driver!

"It was only a dog, for God's sake"
By Nadine Taylor

They wouldn't have stopped for a dog. But they didn't stop for a little girl, either. According to his testimony Balram S. didn't stop to check what or who he might have hit when he ran over an eight-year-old girl while driving his employers home at night in New Delhi last month. Consoling himself that it was most likely a dog, his only concern was to get the couple in the back seat home safely. The little girl, who must have been dead instantly, remains unidentified – nobody has stepped forward to claim her body yet. It almost seems as if nobody is interested in her fate – neither her parents nor her killer. It seems this child was expendable, thus cruelly supporting Balram S.' defence that he mistook her for a dog. Am I the only one thinking that in a society that values some of its members no higher than animals, something must be terribly wrong?
What is most disturbing about Indian metropolises is the large chasm between rich and poor. Elegant parts of the city are mixed in apparent chaos with slums without a proper freshwater supply or sanitation. Slums come into existence when people migrate from rural areas to the cities in order to find jobs, then put up shelter somewhere near their workplace because they cannot afford real housing. Slum residents are faced with multiple prejudices in everyday life, for example they often have problems getting bank accounts or job interviews. As a result an increasing number of slum residents, especially those born there, find work inside the slum, which in time develops an internal economy independent of the outside world.
This extreme difference in wealth also becomes obvious in the way people treat their children. The children of the rich receive an education while the poor have to send their children to work in order to keep the family in food and shelter. Often boys from poor families cannot finish their education because they have to earn money in order to contribute to their sisters' dowries. The large cities abound with street children who have left home because of family problems or poverty. Because they are usually illiterate and live on the streets they cannot find jobs to ameliorate their situation and are prone to drug abuse, crime and violence. There-

fore, they are usually regarded as dangerous and impure by people from higher castes.

While poor boys are in danger of sinking to the bottom of society by becoming street children, girls are faced with even worse problems: their upbringing is much more costly, since their families usually have to give them a dowry in order to marry them off adequately, so in poor families this money must be saved elsewhere. This is why girls often receive even less education than their brothers, resulting in a higher illiteracy rate among women, impairing their chances of finding proper jobs. Many girls are married off as soon as possible, even before they reach the legal age for marriage – and they are the lucky ones. The systematic abortion of female fetuses is unfortunately not uncommon among Indian families who think they cannot afford to bring up a girl. So maybe it made it easier for the driver to keep on pretending he ran over a dog when he realised that it was in fact "only" a girl and not a boy? A daughter might in all probability be even less missed by her family than a son.

Well Balram S. might have had such thoughts, but he was probably not the driver anyway. As a bystander I was able to witness the accident and what I saw was that the driver who hit the girl was not at the wheel when they drove off. So finally, a frightening suspicion sneaks into the observer's mind: What if the upper class couple forced Balram S. to take the blame for one of them? As a member of the lowest caste, it is an honour for him to work for these people. They are his opportunity for upward social mobility; only if members of upper castes allow those below them to serve them, come near them or even touch them, does a rise in social status become possible. So Balram S. is probably just pretending he caused the accident on the orders of his employers, which it would be impossible for him to disobey.

In conclusion I would like to say that it is alarming to what extent Indian society is still influenced by caste rules and solidified power structures. In many cases, descent seems to be more important than character and skills. That is why the country seems to be caught between two extremes: a seemingly medieval social structure on the one hand and extremely advanced IT technology and scientific achievements on the other. This is a conflict which Indian society has to resolve if it aims to take its place among the leading economies of the world. *(838 words)*

Abitur 2012 Schleswig-Holstein – Englisch (Kernfach)
Aufgabe 3: London – Life in a Changing Metropolis

Jonathan Gili, *"Silver Jubilee", BBC History*, blog entry, 2002 (updated in 2011)

Jonathan Gili is the producer and director of the television film 'Jubilee Day'. On this day people came together in villages and cities to celebrate the Queen's Silver Jubilee in 1977. 25 years later, in 2002, Jonathan Gili reflects on how times have changed.

Silver Jubilee

As I watched the archive film of the events celebrating Queen Elizabeth II's Silver Jubilee, after 25 years on the throne, I felt as if I was entering another world. The BBC coverage showed street parties, wheelbarrow races, egg-and-spoon races, fancy dress
5 parades, floats – it all seemed more like a hundred years ago than a mere twenty-five. There was an ingenuousness about the festivities, an uncritical affection for the Royal Family and a strength of community, all of which have dissipated over the last quarter of a century. [...]
   Since 1977 we've had rocketing oil prices, galloping inflation, rising unemploy-
10 ment, the 'winter of discontent', and Margaret Thatcher's chilling suggestion that 'there's no such thing as society'. On the royal front, the increasing accessibility of some members of the Royal Family has made people realise that they're harassed by the same problems as normal human beings. It's significant that the one person, apart from the Queen herself, who managed to keep her aura intact throughout the period
15 was the Queen Mother, who always resolutely refused to be intimate with the media.
   Across Britain there seems to have been a consistent pattern in the break-up of communities – urban as well as rural. In the country, idyllic farming villages have become commuter paradises; in the cities, ordinary families can no longer afford to live in their parents' houses as the yuppies move in.

20 ### Changing times

Two places in particular encapsulate the changes: Rochford in Worcestershire and Orbain Road in Fulham, West London. Rochford, halfway between Kidderminster and Hereford, is a long village with spectacular views over low, lush green hills. 'It was only farms and farm cottages when we were brought up,' says John Wilding, who
25 kept sheep and Shire horses there. 'There were a couple of shops in the village, and a post office that used to sell cigarettes and tea and bread. And then of course people got better off and they had cars and they went further afield, and the shops had to close. It was a great shame. Within a few years they closed the school and the post office too, and of course that does away with village life really.' [...]
30   John gave up his cows in October 1977, soon after the Silver Jubilee celebrations, after 28 years without a break. 'I never liked milking,' he says. 'Sheep I've always loved – ever since my parents used to give me the tiddling[1] lambs to rear, the ones whose mother had died off. This is always recognised as the land of milk and honey really, and there used to be 12 milking farms in this village – now there's only one.

The average herd size then was about 14 or 15; now of course that's no good, you've got to have 80 at least to make any living at all. The chap does a good job but he's the only one in the village now.'

You can't get his milk in the village, though – it all goes away on a tanker.

In Fulham, West London, each street used to be like a little village. Terry and Esther Connor were both brought up in Orbain Road – that's how they met. They lived on different sides of the street: Terry's family were in odd numbers, Esther's in evens. Between their families, they accounted for a dozen houses in Orbain Road. It was a friendly street: people never used to lock their doors – you just pushed the door and walked in. Now you have to make an appointment. The character of the area has changed. Houses with no gardens that used to be worth £ 400 are now worth £ 400,000. Backyards have become patios. The cars parked in the street are Porsches and Mercedes, and at weekends they disappear when the residents of Orbain Road go off to the country. [...]

Guy Fawkes night

'There's no friendship any more,' says Vanessa's aunt, Hannelore Galvin, another Orbain Road resident who's been forced out of the street by rising rents. 'Hooray Henrys[2] live there now. When I lived there we used to sit on the wall and drink in the street. Not wine, gin – until I found out I got a little bit nasty so I switched over to vodka.'

Sometimes there were punch-ups. 'But at least it was only with hands', says Hannelore's husband, Bill. 'Nobody fought with knives. When I was a kid, I watched men having a fight with blood all over the show, and the next day they're in the pub together, drinking. It was a recognised thing – you had a punch-up and the next day it was all forgotten. Not now.'

On Guy Fawkes night there was always a bonfire in the middle of the road and everyone danced round it. People accumulated any unmanageable bits of rubbish in anticipation of the blaze. [...]

'Firework's night was brilliant', says Vanessa Philips. 'That's my favourite memory. Of course the fire brigade would come and put it out, but as soon as they'd gone the people brought out more timber and junk and old settees, and lit the fire again. They used to use petrol, and one year they even threw on part of an old car. This was right in the middle of the street! But I don't remember there ever being an accident. And the fireworks were quite well organised, I think, but I wasn't that interested in them – I'd rather have the fire than the fireworks any day.'

It's hard to imagine that sort of thing happening today – you'd need a licence, you'd need insurance, you'd need to fill in a health and safety form. And today's 24/7 lifestyle means that people are too busy to throw themselves into community activities any more. Twenty-five years on from Jubilee Day, we can look back at what seems a lost world of innocence.   (994 words)

From: Jonathan Gili, "Silver Jubilee", BBC History, *blog entry, 2002 (updated in 2011),*
http://www.bbc.co.uk/history/british/modern/jubilee_01.shtml (letztes Zugriffsdatum: 02. 12. 2011)

1   *tiddling:* a delicate child or weak young animal that needs and receives tender care
2   *Hooray Henry:* a loud-mouthed but ineffectual upper class fool

Assignments

1. Sketch Gili's position on the changes and their causes that took place between 1977 and 2002. *(25 %)*

2. Analyse how the author tries to gain support for his critical view on modern London. *(35 %)*

3. Choose between: *(40 %)*

3.1 So far BBC-online has only published this view on modern London. BBC-online now appeals to send in counter-positions referring to the post-Jubilee period. You decide to send in your ideas.
Based on your background knowledge write the blog entry.

or

3.2 In 2011 J. Gili adds another chapter: Celebration of the 21st century. Write the blog entry.

Lösungsvorschläge

1. *In this task you are supposed to structure and summarize the given text without interpretation or judgment. Your text should be clearly structured, logical and easy to understand – be careful to avoid repetitions. You should also write a short introductory sentence. Make sure to show that the author not only portrays the loss of community in the city but also in rural areas.*

In his blog entry "Silver Jubilee", Jonathan Gili describes the changes that have taken place in London and the rest of the country during the 25 years since the Queen's Silver Jubilee in 1977.
Gili deplores the loss of community (ll. 16 ff.) and the consequent change in lifestyle. He suggests that the strength of community has dissolved (l. 7), the ingeniousness about festivities has gone (l. 6) and the social gap between yuppies and ordinary families has become larger (ll. 18 f.). This is a result of the increased mobility that has turned idyllic farming villages into commuter paradises (l. 18) due to real estate prices that are more affordable than those in metropolitan areas (ll. 45 f.). Another result of the increased mobility is that people in rural areas can travel by car to bigger places to go shopping, for example, which has led to small shops and post offices in villages having to close (ll. 25 ff.).
According to Gili, on the one hand people have been able to acquire certain things, such as cars (l. 27) while on the other they have had to struggle economically in terms of housing (ll. 45 f.), soaring oil prices (l. 9), inflation and unemployment (ll. 9 f.).
All this is flanked by the shifting of boundaries between the private and public life of the Royal Family (ll. 11 ff.). *(231 words)*

2. *Here you have to show how the author supports his opinion of modern London. You can do this by showing how he uses stylistic devices in terms of language, structure and content. Make sure that you use your observations to write a coherent text that answers the question rather than just to make a list of stylistic devices. Remember to indicate where in the text you found a particular piece of information.*

In contextual terms, Jonathan Gili contrasts a nostalgic view of the living conditions in London and Britain in 1977 with the situation today. For the Queen's Silver Jubilee in 1977 there was what the author calls "ingenuousness about the festivities" (l. 6) which was shown not only by an "uncritical affection for the Royal Family" (ll. 6 f.) but also by the kinds of activities that were shown in BBC coverage of the event: "street parties, wheelbarrow races, egg-and-spoon races, fancy dress parades [and] floats" (ll. 3 f.).
The situation has changed since then, as he describes the Royal Family as being ordinary people tackling the same problems as you and me (ll. 11 ff.) – this "increasing accessibility" (l. 11) might feel like a loss to those English people who used to see the Royal Family as something special.

2012-17

However, the word "uncritical" (l. 6) also carries a note of criticism for the old days – criticism that people did not notice or care about what was really happening. The change that has since happened in public opinion concerning the Royal Family has also happened with regard to all the other types of public behaviour he mentions or which the interviewees describe. This behaviour disappears for something that is not as good as it was in the old days. The interesting thing here is that the people he quotes are not what one would call the "winners" of the past 25 years and they are all people who prefer the old days to modern times of course. One is a former dairy farmer who gave up his cows because he didn't like milking them (ll. 23 ff.), another a man who used to get into fistfights (ll. 55 ff.), another a woman who used to drink gin in the streets but has now switched to vodka (ll. 50 ff.) and finally a woman who used to like the bonfires on the streets back in the old days (ll. 63 ff.). Gili himself criticizes the administrative regulations that would make such things almost impossible today (ll. 70 ff.). The credibility of these people is lower than that of the people who moved to the areas or districts mentioned in the text. They of course would have had a completely different view on the matter. You might also say that Gili tries to support his stance by limited views of the situation, because of course not everything has taken a turn for the worse.

In terms of language, Jonathan Gili uses stylistic devices to make his intention clear. He supports the criticism of modern times by making generalizations, for instance, when he says that communities are breaking up in a consistent pattern "across Britain" (l. 16) or that "in the cities" (l. 18) "ordinary families" (l. 18) can no longer afford their houses as "yuppies" (l. 19) move in. According to Gili, in Fulham "each street" (l. 39) was like a small village where people "never" (l. 43) locked their doors. These generalizations are of course exaggerated and draw a picture of a nostalgic era. A similar picture is drawn of the former "idyllic farming villages" (l. 17) which have now been turned into "commuter paradises" (l. 18). This metaphor shows the development of an area. What was once an idyllic village has now become a paradise – but only for those who have moved there. This metaphor is the first in this text to introduce the idea of paradise. Another is to be found when John Wilding speaks of his hometown of Rochford as "the land of milk and honey" (l. 33). This description is obviously to be taken more in a literal sense, since Rochford was a dairy farming village back in the 1970s, but it also shows how Wilding misses the old days, even though he "never liked milking" (l. 31). The last metaphorical allusion to paradise is in the final words of the blog entry, when the author calls the past "a lost world of innocence" (l. 74).

So all in all you can say that Jonathan Gili uses many stylistic devices to show how we tend to view with nostalgia an era that has passed by. *(697 words)*

3.1 *In this task you have to write a blog entry in which you as a fictional person can write about your point of view on the situation. The phrase "counter-position" implies that you disagree with Gili's thesis, so you should outline the positive changes London and the villages in Britain have undergone in the past. Still you may agree with some of the things Gili says. Here you can show that you have learned and understood many things about modern London. Put in all the information you have and use stylistic devices to make your text more convincing. The example given refers to the changes that have taken place in general. You could also contradict Gili's ideas in a more immediate way by explaining why the developments he condemns are actually positive.*

Post-Jubilee London
After reading Jonathan Gili's blog on Silver Jubilee London I have to say that I believe we live in a metropolis that is already a modern classic today. Of course many things have changed, but most developments are positive and will therefore last. When I walk through the city, I see not only hundreds of tourists that bring new ideas with them but also many people from all over the world who now live in London. Living in a multi-ethnic society brings influences that offer good opportunities for creating a better, multicultural society one day. Why not go to an Indian Restaurant with Jin from Hong Kong or Peter from Germany? Why not celebrate Europe's largest festival with Tina from the West Indies at the Notting Hill Carnival? Why not live on the same street as all these people, too? Will we lose our British identity? Is going from the local to the global and from the individual to the institutional bad for London? I don't think so ... On the one hand, our cultural heritage will always preserve what it means to be traditionally British while on the other hand we are offered the great opportunity here to establish a form of community that could be labeled "modern British".
Of course it is not only the people but also the improved infrastructure that lays the cornerstone for a possible bright future. During the pre-Olympic building boom 33,000 new homes and 32 million sq. ft. of commercial floor space were created that leave London residents with new affordable opportunities. Why not move out to a station along the East London Line Extension? Why not find a flat on Wood Wharf? Sounds like a good plan to me – all the newly redeveloped or developed areas are modern classics already, too, because the city planners have learned from the past and are coming up with intriguing concepts that will last. This, of course, will lead to other areas being abandoned and becoming derelict, but it will also be a chance for these areas to reinvent themselves and to be the target of a new revival in the not too distant future.
So all in all you could say that the London of today is a modern classic because our improved living conditions and the international community make our lives so much more worth living. We are offered the great opportunity of living in an era that might once be looked upon as the age of the founding of the first global metropolis. Of course, the chain of events might prove me wrong but then again it was worth the try ... *(442 words)*

3.2 *Here you will have to write a blog entry as Jonathan Gili. Try to bear in mind how Gili wrote his text and make yours a believable new chapter as the task demands. Keep in mind that Gili doesn't seem to be too enthusiastic about changes. Use your knowledge about London and be convincing. Again, use stylistic devices to support your ideas.*

Celebration of the 21st century

After all the unexpected reactions to my "Silver Jubilee" blog I decided to take the time to add another chapter on London. The Olympic Games might be seen as a cornerstone in city development since they have visibly changed the face of the old Lady. However it's not only the face-lift of what the Olympics started, thinking about the Olympic Park, Westlands or our new ArcelorMittal Orbit tower, which might be seen as Britain's Eiffel Tower, but also the Botox that lies underneath. The new transport networks will smooth out old wrinkles in the face of old Mrs. London. Infrastructure projects like the East London Line Extension and the Emirates Line cable car underway, not to mention future projects such as High Speed 2, Overground and the Northern Line Extension, will all apparently leave London better accessible from a whole variety of new affordable housing areas out in the greenbelt. Of course, if we look at all the botoxed celebrities who have had a facelift, we cannot be sure whether a makeover will result in the longed for beauty that was thought lost or rather in Frankenstein's monster, but let's hope for the best.

Second boom of the millennium

So far the focus has been on Milady's recent rejuvenating procedures but there was a set of measures that were taken at the turn of the millennium and you will be surprised at how effective new make-up can be and how a little color can change your face (even if not always for the better) as was the case with the Tower Bridge. Other examples of that era are the London Eye, the Millennium Dome – home to innumerable acts of cultural greatness – the Millennium Bridge connecting the best of the London sights on both sides of the Thames. With Old Spitalfields Market she also shows off what her old Victorian wardrobe still has to offer. It's the observer who has to decide whether he likes the mixed-up style the new buildings and renovations bring with them or if he resents the glitter in the old girl's face.

Working Environment

With the old new Mrs. London taking more and more action to maintain and improve her beauty more and more measures will be necessary, of course, which will provide new jobs in a whole number of fields of employment.
But on the whole with the old Lady still looking modern but not hip and with her fine distinction of patina, she has everything that makes her a modern classic today, as she was yesterday and as she will be tomorrow. *(433 words)*

> Abitur 2012 Schleswig-Holstein – Englisch (Kernfach)
> Aufgabe 4: India – Roots and Challenges

Andrew Buncombe, "India in uproar over decision to include caste in national census", *Independent.co.uk* 2010

Critics say traditional distinctions of class have no place in a would-be global power

For the first time since the days of the British Raj, officials in India are to ask people their caste as part of the national census, the biggest of its kind in the world. It is a move that has triggered intense controversy about a painful, vexing subject that the
5 country cannot leave behind.

Having initially chosen not to include caste, the Indian government apparently gave in to demands from opposition parties and decided that, for the first time since 1931, census officials would ask respondents to say what traditional Hindu grouping they belong to.

10 The decision has sparked fierce debate. Defenders of the move say it will provide up-to-date information about the size and needs of various groups that will be vital for providing grants and reserved jobs and college places for those at the bottom of the caste ladder.

Others are equally adamant that caste should have no place in a country seeking to
15 throw off the shackles of poverty, malnutrition and illiteracy and looking to assume a position as a leading world power.

Among those who have strongly criticised the decision is Amitabh Bachchan, the near-legendary Bollywood actor considered the elder statesman of Hindi movies.

Writing on his blog, Mr. Bachchan said that when census officials arrived at his
20 house in Mumbai, he told them that his caste was "Indian".

"My father never believed in caste and neither do any of us," he added. "He married a Sikh, I married a Bengali, my brother a Sindhi, my daughter a Punjabi, my son a Mangalorean … in his autobiography he had [said] future generations of his family should marry into different parts of the country."

25 In traditional Hinduism there were four main castes and hundreds of sub-groups. In addition there were the "untouchables", who were considered to have no place in society and who are now more usually called Dalits.

For centuries, what job a person did, where they lived, what food they ate and where they were cremated depended largely on their caste. One of those who sought
30 to reform the system was the independence leader Mahatma Gandhi, who, along with social campaigners such as Bhimrao Ramji Ambedkar, argued that caste had no place.

As India has developed, and as more people have moved to the cities, the rigid caste restrictions have loosened slightly. Yet although discrimination on the basis of caste is banned by the constitution, for hundreds of millions of people caste remains a
35 defining, and often debilitating, label. Even now, English-language weekend papers

carry pages of adverts for arranged marriages, all categorised under various castes. And a number of online sites cater exclusively to one caste.

Caste also remains hugely important in the world of business and finance. A recent study by the Indian economist Sukhdeo Thorat and Princeton University sociologist Katherine Newman found that having a low-caste surname significantly cut the chances of winning a job interview.

Caste can have deadly repercussions. Parts of northern India are blighted by so-called "honour killings", incidents in which a young woman is murdered by members of her family for having an affair, or eloping, with a man from the "wrong" caste or clan. In one recent high-profile case, police in Jharkhand arrested the mother of a young female journalist, Nirupama Pathak, who was found smothered to death.

The middle-class family, who were opposed to Ms Pathak's planned marriage to a lower-caste man, say she committed suicide. However, her boyfriend claims she was murdered. The young woman's father, a bank manager, told local reporters: "We were trying to convince her to marry within our own caste. That does not mean we killed her."

Despite its purported wish to move away from caste, India has repeatedly opposed including caste in UN guidelines against discrimination. It insists that it is an internal matter for India. At the same time, caste has increasingly become an important means of organising politically.

Kumari Mayawati, the so-called Dalit Queen who heads the Bahujan Samaj Party (BSP), has four times ridden to the position of chief minister of India's most populous state, Uttar Pradesh, with the support of its poorest and most downtrodden people.

Those who want to include caste in the census say the data gathered can be used to help those in need. Writing in the Hindustan Times Sagarika Ghose, a senior broadcaster, said: "The fight against caste is best fought when we know the enemy. Caste is an immutable, invisible and overwhelming reality in our daily lives. If we continue to act as if caste does not exist, or deny its existence, we would be failing to do battle with one of the most urgent social inequalities of our time."

Some Dalits fighting for empowerment also believe the information will help, especially if it is made publicly available. Pushpa Salaria, head of the Dalit Rights Protection Forum, said: "If we have a census which is centralised then we can have information about weaker sections and minority groups. It will help us know the majority of our country." (836 words)

From: Andrew Buncombe, "India in uproar over decision to include caste in national census", Independent.co.uk, Friday, 14 May 2010 (http://www.independent.co.uk/news/world/asia/india-in-uproar-over-decision-to-include-caste-in-national-census-1973037.html, letzter Zugriff: 10.12.2011)

Assignments

1. Render the pros and cons about the national census and about the question if "caste" should be included in the national census. *(25 %)*
2. Starting out from the text, analyse why the caste system is such a social problem for modern India and why the subject is so "painful" and "vexing" (l. 5). Include your background knowledge. *(35 %)*
3. "Critics say traditional distinctions of class have no place in a would-be global power" (l. 1–2). Referring to India write a comment for the *Independent* on this statement. *(40 %)*

Lösungsvorschläge

1. *For this assignment you must collect the arguments presented in the text and write a logically structured text without quotations. Start with a short introduction to the topic. Don't summarise the whole article!*

The Indian government regularly conducts a national census in order to gather information about the social structure of the population. This time, however, the question of whether respondents should be asked what caste they belong to has divided Indian society.

Supporters see the collecting of information on the socio-economic structure as a means of identifying and fighting social inequality. With the help of this data, the distribution of benefits to the poor could be enhanced and affirmative action programmes could be tailored to the population's needs. Here the text refers to grants, reserved jobs and college places for people from a lower caste.

Politicians also appreciate information on caste membership because it makes it easier for them to target their voters since many political parties cater to specific social groups.

Finally, advocates also claim that while many of the segregative effects of the traditional caste system are fading away in modern India, what caste a person belongs to still largely defines their identity; thus making it natural to include this category in the national census.

Opponents of the plan counter that a categorisation according to caste no longer reflects the everyday life of modern India. While in the past caste membership determined not only people's social status but also who they were allowed to marry and what jobs they were allowed to do, these restrictions are now becoming less widespread, at least in urban areas. They claim that including caste in the census makes the fight against discrimination more difficult because it cements the prejudices in people's heads.

This not only harms India's socio-economic development but also its standing in the international community, as critics claim. They are convinced that categorising the Indian people according to their caste conflicts with the UN guidelines against discrimination, a fact they regard as unworthy of a nation striving for global economic and political leadership. *(311 words)*

2. *Before you start your analysis you should briefly describe the origins and development of the Indian caste system. You should then go on to explain its impact on Indian society. This exercise is closely related to Exercise 1. Try not to repeat yourself and wherever it is possible find different words to express what you want to say.*

The origins of the Indian caste system date back to around 1200 BCE, when society began to organise itself by occupational categories. In the course of time, adherence to a certain group became hereditary, resulting in the emergence of four main social groups, or varnas: the Brahmans as the varna of priests and spiritual teachers, the Kshatriyas as rulers and warriors, the Vaishyas as farmers and the Shudras as servants. These were ranked vertically, with the Brahmans at the top of the social ladder, then the Kshatriyas below them, after them the Vaishyas and the Shudras at the bottom.

These varnas were divided into numerous subgroups, the jatis, a term which is most often used synonymously with the term "caste". These castes determined their affiliates' way of life, for example what food they were allowed to eat and what jobs they were allowed to have, but also who they were allowed to work for or employ. There were strict rules concerning the contacts between members of different castes, mainly due to religious reasons: for members of the upper castes, having your meal cooked by members of certain lower castes, for example, would mean polluting your own purity. Most striking is probably the ban on inter-caste marriages.

These rules resulted in a highly segregated, hierarchical society. At the very bottom, below the Shudra caste, were those people who did the demeaning jobs which were considered impure. They were regarded as belonging to no caste at all and were usually referred to as "untouchables". Even today, when they are officially called "Dalits" or "scheduled castes" and despite the fact that there are anti-discrimination legislation and affirmative action measures to promote the Dalits' living conditions, they still face a lot of disadvantages. As a "recent study […] found […] having a low-caste surname significantly cut the chances of winning a job interview" (ll. 38–41).

But contacts between different castes remain problematic in other respects as well. While young people, especially those from urban communities, tend to look past caste borders, older people or those from rural areas are more likely to uphold traditional values. Thus, there is still a big market for marriage brokers who find suitable partners from the same caste. Sometimes traditional values can be so powerful that families feel justified in reverting to violence in order to enforce obedience. Reports of so-called "honour killings" are unfortunately anything but rare in some parts of the country (ll. 42–45).

Since they find themselves torn between the traditional values of their childhood on the one hand and an individual lifestyle they see enjoyed by their peers when studying abroad or which they see on international TV on the other hand, young, well-educated people especially are driven into an identity crisis that might be hard to resolve. Thus, a whole generation is burdened with the weight of this conflict between the demands of their families and those of the modern socio-economic world. This takes up valuable energy and drains both economic and scientific resources that a country like India, which is still developing, could definitely use elsewhere.

The social segregation caused by the caste system is in all probability harmful for the Indian economy as well. Since it restrains social mobility by keeping everyone in their assigned place, a job might not be given to the most eligible candidate, but to one from the same caste as the employer. Additionally, it might squash people's initiative if they can see no perspective outside their own caste, thus impeding innovation and social change.

Finally, it is also on an international level that the caste system is a "painful, vexing subject" (l. 4) for Indians. With the UN calling for the inclusion of caste in UN guidelines against discrimination, systematic discrimination against large parts of the population, albeit officially prohibited, will in all probability raise some eyebrows among the international community. It is highly inconsistent with India's image as a rising global power that it does not seem to be able to overcome this social segregation.

(671 words)

3. *In this assignment you should start by explaining or maybe challenging the quotation. You should then go on to discuss the validity of the statement. What you have found out in Exercises 1 and 2 may help you here. Do not just repeat the arguments! Try to elaborate on them and include your own point of view. Since this is a comment, you will have to finish by taking a stand on the subject. If you feel insecure about how to write a comment, have another look at page VI. You can find useful tips here.*

When Andrew Buncombe claims that critics say traditional distinctions of class have no place in a would-be global power, he is referring to social reformers like Mahatma Gandhi and Bhimrao Ramji Ambedkar as well as influential artists like Amitabh Bachchan, who have been trying to rally people against the caste system. Along with other critics they argue that the notion of caste is racist and inappropriate for a country striving for global power.

They are, of course, correct. When India became independent in 1947, many elements of the British and US American political system (like the parliamentary system and the federal organisation) were adopted by the Indian constitution, which came into effect in 1950, proclaiming a secular democratic republic. Unfortunately, the political reality does not live up to the theory. Although the constitution grants equal rights to all citizens of India, discrimination by caste or gender still abounds. Admittedly, there are attempts at empowering the so-called scheduled castes, but opponents of these schemes criticise the fact that they cement the status quo rather than achieve more social mobility by pacifying members of these castes. Therefore, holding on to the caste system despite constant criticism by the UN undermines the trust of the international community in India's reliability as a democratic country. Ultimately, it might raise the question of whether India is modern and developed enough to be a partner in international politics and whether it can be trusted with something as dangerous as an atomic bomb.

Apart from the uneasiness spread among its partners, India's failure to abolish the caste system also poses problems for its citizens themselves. As a nation that seeks international influence and economic leadership, India has already started to fight illiteracy and malnutrition successfully. So it is hard to understand why they should impair their own progress by silently acknowledging outdated rules of social segregation. Upholding class distinctions will always lead to disadvantages for those at the bottom of the social ladder. It might also cause social unrest if people who finally got the education they had been fighting for hit a glass ceiling at the next level when they applied for jobs that used to be out of their reach but were still unattainable because the applicant might have the wrong surname, for example.

But it is not only Dalits who feel the negative impact of the conflict between tradition and progress. It also affects young academics. They have to find the balance between family expectations, traditional values and the Western lifestyle that they are confronted with in the media. On the one hand, the fact that young urban citizens are increasingly inclined to adopt this Western lifestyle makes it easier for them to deal with international business partners, but on the other hand they risk their family's disapproval. However, even if they themselves might live a modern life, as long as the caste system dominates India's image in the world, in international transactions they might be faced with ignorance and prejudice concerning the unwritten rules of the Indian society. Business partners from overseas might be unsure about how far the rules apply to them: Would it be a bad idea to send a black colleague? Could they send a woman? These cultural traps are potentially harmful to India's economic development.

In conclusion, critics of the caste system like Bachchan, Ambedkar and Gandhi are to be congratulated on their far-sightedness. If India does not take determined measures against social discrimination, it might end up isolated. And that, I think, we can all agree would be deplorable considering the country's intellectual and economic potential.

(597 words)

> Abitur 2013 Schleswig-Holstein – Englisch (Kernfach)
> Aufgabe 1: India – Roots and Challenges

Chetan Bhagat, *Revolution 2020 – Love. Corruption. Ambition.* 2011 (excerpt)

'Revolution 2020' is the story of three friends, narrated by the protagonist of the story, Gopal Mishra, the 26-year-old director of GangaTech Institute in Varanasi[1], a town in the North of India. The two boys Gopal, Raghav and the girl Aarti grew up together in Varanasi. Both boys love Aarti. Raghav is the smart, intelligent and multi-talented one, while Gopal is the strictly average guy with average skills and average grades. He wants to make it big in life and marry Aarti by becoming an engineer, but fails all the entrance exams, whereas Raghav succeeds with ease and becomes Aarti's boyfriend. Gopal decides to join ranks with a corrupt politician who helps him build the engineering college GangaTech Institute. Meanwhile, Raghav decides to change the country. He chucks his engineering career, takes up journalism and starts up his own paper named 'Revolution 2020'.

A fluorescent pink A3-sized sheet fell out of the morning paper. I thought it was a flyer for a travel agency or tuition classes. However, it had a masthead like a newspaper. Aha, I smirked, Raghav's attempt to change the world. *Revolution 2020,* it said in big, bold font. Below was a letter from the editor, headlined: *"Because Enough is*
5 *Enough".* I read on.

What do you say about a society whose top leaders are the biggest crooks? What do you do in a system where almost anyone with power is corrupt? India has suffered enough. From childhood we are told India is a poor country. Why? There are countries in this world where an average person makes more than fifty times
10 that an average Indian makes. Fifty times? Are their people really fifty times more capable than us? Does an Indian farmer not work hard? Does an Indian student not study? Do we not want to do well? Why, why are we then doomed to be poor?

I laughed at Raghav's self-indulgent trip. I sipped my morning tea and continued to
15 read.

This has to stop. We have to clean the system. Che Guevara[2], the great revolutionary, once said, "Power is not an apple that falls from a tree into your lap. Power has to be snatched from people who already have it." We have to start a revolution, a revolution that resets our corrupt system. A system that shifts power
20 back into the hands of the people, and treats politicians like workers, not kings.
Of course, this won't happen overnight. This also won't happen until the real suffering begins. As India's young population increases, we will need more good colleges and jobs. Soon, there won't be enough. People will realize who is fooling them. It could take ten years. I call it *Revolution 2020,* the year in which it
25 will happen, the movement that will finally shake the muck off India. When the

2013-1

Internet will connect all colleges across the country. When we will go on strike, shut down everything, until things are fixed. When young people will leave their classes and offices and come on to the streets. When Indians will get justice and the guilty will be punished.

And it will all begin in Varanasi. For that reason, we bring you Revolution 2020.
Yours truly,
Raghav Kashyap
Editor

I smiled as I saw a crudely sketched map of India under the article. It had a dot on Varanasi, with arrows connecting it to various cities. The map had a little 'Revolution 2020 potential plan' attached to it. In various cities, it listed the main colleges that would lead the revolution there.

My accountant came into my office for my signatures on the month-end accounts. My amused expression puzzled him.

"What happened, sir? Reading jokes?" he said.

I nodded.

The front page also carried an exposé on cremation shops in Varanasi selling ordinary wood as sandalwood after spraying it with synthetic perfume.

My accountant saw the pink-coloured paper.

"Is this an ad? A poster?" he said.

"I have no idea," I said.

I turned over the *Revolution 2020* page and couldn't help but laugh. In contrast to the bombast in the front, the back page had matrimonial ads! I read one out aloud.

"Wanted beautiful/educated/fair/homely virgin for twenty-five-year Kayasth[3] Brahmin engineer working in stable government job. Girl must be willing to stay in joint family and respect traditional values".

I handed Raghav's paper to my accountant.

"Searching for a girl, sir?" he said.

I looked how I felt – offended.

"Sorry, sir," he said. "Sir, we have more requests for admissions," he sought to change the subject.

"We are full", I said, "you know that. We have as many students as we are authorized to take."

"Sir, if the AICTE[4] can adjust …"

I sighed. "How many more?"

"Five, ten …", he said. "Twenty at the most."

"Take them in", I said. "I'll manage the AICTE when the time comes."

"Yes, sir", he said and left the office.

I picked up the pink rag, ripped it apart, bundled up the shreds and threw them in the dustbin.

***

Every Friday I made rounds of the classes. I kept a three-day stubble to look old enough to be a director. I entered a classroom where a maths class was in progress.

The professor stood lecturing when he sighted me. The entire class of forty students stood up. It felt good. I could go to any of the eight classrooms and the same would happen. Money, status and power – however evil people may say these are – get you respect in life. A few years back I was begging at career fairs for an admission. Today, hundreds stood up to attention when I arrived.
"Good afternoon, Director sir," the professor said.
I nodded in response. (952 words)

Chetan Bhagat: Revolution 2020– Love. Corruption. Ambition.
New Delhi: Rupa Publications India 2011, pp. 205–207

1 *Varanasi:* supposed to be the oldest city in India, situated on the banks of the Ganges, regarded as a holy city by Hindus, Buddhists and Jains
2 *Che Guevara:* Ernesto "Che" Guevara de la Serna, 1928–1967, Argentine Marxist revolutionary who – together with Fidel Castro – was a crucial and prominent figure of the Cuban Revolution in the years 1957–1959
3 *Kayasth:* The members of that high Hindu caste are regarded as Brahmins in the upper Gangetic region and as Kshatriya in the rest of India.
4 *AICTE:* All India Council for Technical Education: a national-wide council, responsible for proper planning and coordinated development of the technical education and management education system in India.

Cartoon

K. Raja

Assignments

1. When Raghav starts his new career he needs to recruit staff for his *Revolution 2020* team. In preparation for their first meeting he distributes an outline of his concept. Write this outline. *(20 %)*

2. Examine in what way Gopal's reactions to *Revolution 2020* reveal his character. *(25 %)*

3. Analyse the cartoon and relate it to both the excerpt of the novel and the situation in India. Use your background knowledge as a basis. *(30 %)*

4. Write a letter to the editor, Raghav Kashyap, in response to his article "Because Enough is Enough". Express your own critical view on the topic. *(25 %)*

Lösungsvorschläge

1. *For this first task you have to describe what "Revolution 2020" stands for by leaving out unnecessary details. This means that you will have to take a close look at the indented (= eingerückt) parts of the text that were written by Raghav and outline the characteristics of present-day India, what you learn there about Revolution 2020, and its goals as described by the editor. Bear in mind that you want to recruit staff for your movement!*

Revolution 2020
Almost everybody in power is corrupt and abuses his position to make a fortune, while most people in present-day India remain poor in spite of their hard work, since wages in India are comparatively low.
We are trying to tackle these problems in the "Revolution 2020" movement which has just been founded in Varanasi and which will continue to spread until the year 2020, e. g. via the Internet or the "Revolution 2020" newspaper. All of India's secondary schools and colleges will propagate the ideas of the movement, and this will eventually lead to a student strike. This will be the beginning of a revolution in which the young generation will shake off corruption, punish those are guilty of that, and put power back into the hands of the people. Our goal is to achieve better learning and working conditions for all of us.
Join us and help us start a revolution! *(154 words)*

2. *Based on the information about Gopal given in the introductory note, you now have to examine carefully the reactions he shows while reading Gaghav's text, what he says about it, and what he does with it after reading. For this task it is important to offer proof taken from the text and to use quotes where appropriate.*

After failing the entrance exams, Gopal chooses to take the easy way out and launch a career with the help of dubious friends who make him director of the GangaTech Institute in Varanasi. This shows how ambitious he is, but it also reveals that he is corrupt and has no moral standards (cf. introductory note).
He knows Raghav well and is obviously amused by his friend's attempt to draw attention to the country's main problems, smirking at the text (cf. l. 3), laughing about it after reading the first part (cf. l. 14) and again about the whole newspaper when he has finished reading it (cf. l. 47). He smiles when he reads about the "Revolution 2020 potential plan" (ll. 35 f.). This shows how safe he feels in his position – one which he obviously does not deserve but obtained through his close connection to a politician. The depths of his arrogance are revealed when he refers to Raghav's manifest as "bombast" (l. 48) and calls it a joke (cf. l. 40) while talking to his accountant.
When Gopal "pick[s] up the pink rag, rip[s] it apart, bundle[s] up the shreds and [throws] them in the dustbin" (ll. 64 f.) it is not clear whether it is rage and aggression that is flaring up in him or whether he really rejects Raghav's ideas and thinks they are ridiculous. There are some signs that his behaviour is due to rage.

Gopal feels annoyed because, when he reads out the matrimonial ad to his accountant, the man misinterprets that as a sign that Gopal is looking for a bride. Since Raghav is married to the woman Gopal once loved and wanted to marry, his aggressive treatment of the newspaper may be a sign of his jealousy. Whatever the case, it certainly shows that Gopal is an emotional person. *(306 words)*

3. *First, take a close look at the cartoon and describe it in detail. Although you probably do not know who is depicted there, try to find a link to the story as well as to the situation in present-day India. This is where you should make use of the background knowledge on this topic that you have gathered over the past few years. When you talk about the text, give references which show that you are able to make a connection.*

The cartoon in question, published on the Internet by the *Public Interest Foundation* on 3 May 2011, shows two men wearing suits and carrying briefcases; they are walking on a carpet that they are rolling out. The part of the carpet in front of them has the word "reforms" printed on it. A little way behind these two men, there are another two who are rolling the carpet up again. Both of them are wearing traditional Indian clothes. Their part of the carpet shows the word "corruption".

The main idea is obvious: many reforms are made with good intentions, but are undermined by corruption, i.e. by people who try to exploit the new situation for their own ends.

In the text Raghav wants to fight this kind of corruption. He sees no other way to put an end to corruption in society than with a (hopefully peaceful) revolution (cf. ll. 16 ff.). In support of his claims, he refers to other revolutionaries who in his opinion had the same goals: to give power back to the people, bring those to justice who are responsible for the current situation, and then to build a new India, one without corruption (cf. ll. 28 f.). His ideals are high, and Raghav sacrifices his engineering career to the higher good (cf. introductory text).

The reasons for Raghav's unease are clear. The economy is booming in India, many people are beginning to earn more money and able to live a more comfortable life. The middle class is growing and might carry India into a better future. The politicians are trying to pave the way with necessary reforms, and India seems to have a bright future ahead of it. This is represented in the cartoon by the two men at the front of the carpet: they stand for change.

There are, however, dark sides to this fast economic growth: many politicians are corrupt. They accept a favour in return for a favour in situations such as elections and often abuse their office. Unfortunately, not only the people in charge but also ordinary citizens take part in this system of favours. In many cases minor civil servants take extra money for a job they should actually do for free. There often seems to be no other way for the average person to speed things up than to bribe the person in charge. This basically works for all administration and is commonly accepted. Even in the field of education corruption is a widespread phenomenon:

you can buy grades at school, a place at a certain university, and even a university degree if you need or want all this without having to do the work. Lawyers, prosecutors, and judges are bribed to influence the result of trials. The truth and the law often have no bearing on the verdict. This is a situation also reflected in the text at hand: Gopal is made director of the GangaTech Institute in Varanasi at the age of only 26, and without any academic degree, by a corrupt politician whom he supports in return. This shows that obviously no further qualification is needed in order to build up an engineering college than loyalty to the person in charge, here the corrupt politician (cf. introductory text). Gopal and the politician stand for the old India and for the corruption displayed in the cartoon by the two men at the end of the carpet, rolling it up and thereby undoing any progress achieved by reforms. That is why people like Raghev hope for a revolution which will bring justice to India and punish those guilty of crimes and corruption (cf. ll. 28 f.). *(609 words)*

4. *Your task here is to write a letter in response to the article by Raghav Kashyap as shown in the text. Usually a letter starts with your own address and the address of the person who receives the letter. As this kind of task is quite commonly set, it might be a good idea if you find out what written addresses usually look like in the countries mentioned in your* Themenkorridor. *If there is no address given and you are not sure how to write an address of a specific country, just start your letter with the date. Refer in the letter itself to what Raghav wrote in the newspaper and present your thoughts in the form of a critique. There are several ways of doing this, as the text allows a number of different critical approaches. Choose one and go for it!*

Simon Beck
Goethestraße 8
24116 Kiel
Germany

Mr Raghav Kashyap
Executive Editor
6/50G, Shanti Path, Cantonment,
Varanasi 221004
India

4th February 2013

Dear Mr Kashyap,

I am a German student, and we have read your newspaper in class. It was shocking for me to find out about the difficulties you have to face in India. After finishing school I would like to study law at university. I do plan to work hard, but I agree with you, I am really not going to work 50 times as hard as an Indian student. I was told that people from India are very hard-working and that, over the course of an average year, they work a lot more than Germans do.

I really admire you for your dedication and for having the courage to start the project "Revolution 2020". I think this is what India needs. You are right: "Enough is Enough", and the situation in present-day India is terrible. However, I am a little worried since I believe that, at some stage in your campaign, you will encounter massive, perhaps even fierce opposition from all those who have much to lose in the corrupt system. How will you be able to prevent the injustice and corruption that dominates India's establishment just now from coming back after "Revolution 2020"? The people newly in office then might just commit the same crimes as their predecessors and be just as open to bribery as they were. How can you guarantee a fair and just India after the revolution?

I wonder, moreover, how you will get the people in high-ranking positions now, the ones who control the police and military, to give up their positions. Just by demonstrating? You will really need to organise massive and permanent protests – and those protests will have to be peaceful, otherwise you will provide a reason for the powers-that-be to shut down the revolution before it has even started. So, how do you mobilise the masses and how can you control the mob? Of course, a peaceful revolution can be done as the history of your country and the more or less peaceful present day revolutions in the Middle East demonstrated, but it is a dangerous gamble. Are you willing to take that risk? If things go wrong, there will be a civil war involving more than a billion people.

Keep these difficulties in mind when you start your revolution! But on the whole I do agree with you: a revolution is probably the only way to change anything at all. Critics may ask: is there no way to change the system from within? I think not. As Jack Terricloth, a wise punk rocker from New York once said "you can't change the system from within, it ends up changing you". So I guess you are on the right path to a better India and I would like to congratulate you once again for your courage in taking this path. Not everyone would be courageous enough to start a revolution, but I am confident that your way is the right way for India.

I am writing today to let you know that there is support for your movement in Europe and that I would be willing to contribute whatever you think is needed and can be done at this distance.

Keep sight of your ideals, stay on track!

Yours sincerely,
Simon Beck *(563 words)*

> Abitur 2013 Schleswig-Holstein – Englisch (Kernfach)
> Aufgabe 2: London – Life in a Changing Metropolis

Ravi Somaiya, "After British Riots, Conflicting Answers as to 'Why'"

London – Outside a London court last week, as those accused of looting and rioting in the most destructive and widespread violence in recent British history faced justice, a mother turned to her 11-year-old son, accused of theft, and asked simply, "Why?"
That question has been at the heart of a fraught national debate as Britons puzzle over what drove even some previously law-abiding people to steal, sometimes risking arrest for nothing more than bottles of water. The debate has often divided people into predictable camps.
The Conservative prime minister, David Cameron, stood up in Parliament as Britain smoldered around him on Thursday and railed against "mindless violence and thuggery." His critics on the left blame deep mistrust of the police in poor communities, and income inequality they say will worsen as his government pursues sweeping cuts in spending and social welfare.
Some commentators have blamed modern society at large. *The Daily Telegraph* struck a popular chord when it blamed a "culture of greed and impunity" that it said extended to corporate boardrooms and the government itself. Many politicians, meanwhile, have lashed out at technology – including the instant messaging that encouraged looting – for whipping up the crowds.
But as more details of the crimes emerge, the picture has become infinitely more complicated, and confusing. In some of the more shocking cases, the crimes seemed to be rooted in nothing more than split-second decisions made by normally orderly people seduced by the disorder around them.
An aspiring social worker, Natasha Reid, 24, turned herself in after stealing a $500 television. Nicolas Robinson, a young engineering student who had never been in trouble with the law, grabbed bottles of water because, his lawyer said, he was thirsty.
The 11-year-old, the youngest looter arrested, stole a trash can.
At several of the riots last week, those perpetrating the violence had no ready explanation for their behavior. One young man, kicking trash cans into the street, shrugged when asked why. And the atmosphere in Hackney's Pembury Road low-income housing projects was sometimes one of adrenaline-driven glee. Looters whooped as they stripped a convenience store bare, yards from the police.
Even some Londoners who had initially condemned the riotous behavior joined in. Bystanders had watched in shock as rioters lined up against police officers on Tottenham's main street last weekend, setting fires and looting. The mood shifted dramatically, though, after officers moved in, dogs barking and horses charging. One man, suddenly emboldened, grabbed a box of pears from outside a convenience store. A

woman carried off an armful of coconuts. Another man, seemingly conflicted, sprinted, then turned back briefly to snatch a crate of bottled water.

Clifford Stott, a social psychologist at the University of Liverpool who studies riots, says that behavior, at least, is not unusual. Bystanders, he said, often turn against the police when they themselves get swept up in a broad crackdown. "That confrontation makes them start to think that the police are wrong, not the rioters," he said.

But he added that crowd dynamics are incredibly complex and cannot be readily reduced to blame people, or to explain away their behavior. […]

So far, the police say more than 1,200 people have been arrested in connection with "violence, disorder and looting." Of those, 725 have been charged and some are being handed stringent sentences by courts that run 24 hours in some areas. Many have prior convictions, and court records reveal that some were armed, or carrying quantities of drugs when arrested – the "criminals" that many political figures have blamed for the riots.

Others, like Ms Reid and Mr Robinson, are not so readily pigeonholed. Ms Reid is a university graduate. She put her head in her hands in court, and her mother told reporters that she had been sobbing in her bedroom since her arrest over the stolen television. "She didn't want a TV," her mother said. "She doesn't even know why she took it. She doesn't need a telly."

Mr Robinson, the engineering student, was walking home at 2:40 a.m. on Monday when he looted a supermarket in Brixton. Mr Robinson, the court heard from his lawyer, "got caught up in the moment" and was now "incredibly ashamed." He was sentenced to six months.

The story of Chelsea Ives, an 18-year-old athlete who had been chosen to be one of the faces of London's coming Olympic Games, has dominated the front pages of newspapers in Britain. She has been accused of burglary, violent disorder and throwing bricks at a police car, according to media reports. She was turned in by her mother, Adrienne. "I had to do what was right," her mother told reporters. […]

Dr Stott said that people, in a rush to judgment, often latch on to the idea that a mob mentality has taken hold. "There's an excitement and an intensity to those situations that are really quite profound," he said, "and the tendency is to say, 'Well, these people are upstanding citizens, like me, something must have gone wrong with their brains. It must be mob mentality.'"

But he said the theory that people in mobs become mindless had been widely discredited, and he warned that focusing on such a simplistic explanation would prevent an important national discussion about the underlying causes of the riots.

When faced with difficult questions about the role that policing, government policies, and societal ills might have played, Dr Stott said: "You can see it becomes very useful to portray it all as just mindless. Why did that young man steal bottles of water? We may never know."

(929 words)

Ravi Somaiya, "After British Riots, Conflicting Answers as to 'Why'"
From The New York Times, 13 August 2011 © 2011 The NewYork Times. All Rights reserved.
Used by permission and protected by the Copyright Laws of the United States. The printing, copying, redistribution, or retransmission of this Content without express written permission is prohibited.

Assignments

1. After the riots people were looking for explanations. Delineate the different approaches to the problem of the riots as presented in the text. *(20 %)*

2. Analyse the author's way of conveying the events and its impact on the reader. *(25 %)*

3. Using your background knowledge, explain why conflicts like the one described in the text keep occurring in London. *(25 %)*

4. Because of her involvement in the riots Chelsea Ives, the young athlete, was excluded from the Olympic Games. In an introductory statement for a press conference of the British Olympic Committee she reflects on what she has done. Write this statement. *(30 %)*

Lösungsvorschläge

1. *This assignment is meant to test your reading skills. Before you start, you should mark the different attempts to explain the rioting in the text and then structure your text logically. Make sure you do not quote from the text but use your own words. Start with a short introductory sentence in which you refer to the text and to its main message.*

In the text "After British Riots, Conflicting Answers as to 'Why'" from *The New York Times*, the journalist Ravi Somaiya takes a closer look at the riots that shook London in 2011 and presents a variety of attempts at explaining the underlying reasons.

Firstly, he describes the points of view of different politicians. Naturally, their opinions differ according to their party affiliation. While Tory Prime Minister David Cameron denounces the rioting as ruthless and criminal behaviour, the Labour opposition interprets it as a reaction towards increasing social inequality, decreasing social benefits and the tense relationship between the police and the general public. Politicians of all factions seem to be united, though, in blaming modern technology like instant messaging as a means of mass agitation.

Secondly, he points out that journalists have taken a more general approach by laying the responsibility at the feet of modern society. *The Daily Telegraph*, for example, expressly discerns a universal tendency towards ruthlessness and selfishness as the root of the problem.

These explanations are contrasted by the opinion of an expert, social psychologist Dr Clifford Stott. He affirms that casual bystanders could be radicalised by witnessing seemingly drastic police operations, but he also claims that blaming group processes for the mass looting is too shortsighted and that the true underlying reasons for the rioters' behaviour might never be found.

Finally, Somaiya outlines the cases of several people who are accused of taking part in the riots. Although the people concerned are from a wide range of social backgrounds – an 11-year-old school boy, a student, a social worker, a young athlete – they all have one thing in common: they have no criminal record and mostly committed minor offences. *(287 words)*

2. *This assignment requires you to do two things: first, you have to find the stylistic devices that characterise this text. Second, you have to explain the intention the author had in using them. Make sure you have an idea of the effect a stylistic device is meant to create before you mention it in your analysis, otherwise you will simply produce a list of meaningless elements of speech.*
Note that "the author's way of conveying the events" does not only refer to stylistic devices, but also to the way he structures his text and the topics he chooses.
When you write your analysis, make sure to use your own words and prove your point by giving quotations. Do not follow the structure of the text, but put your points in a logical order.

In his article, Ravi Somaiya employs a wide range of stylistic devices in order to emphasise the extraordinary character of the London riots in 2011.

The first thing that strikes the reader is the fact that Somaiya begins and ends his text with the question "Why?" (ll. 4, 77), thus expressing the utter perplexity people feel in the face of the rioting. The feeling that this question cannot be answered easily is supported by the multitude of perspectives Somaiya offers: he outlines the views of politicians (cf. ll. 9 ff., 16 ff.), journalists (cf. l. 14 f.) and scientists (cf. ll. 40 ff.) who all offer different explanations for the behaviour of the rioters. These explanations all sound sensible in themselves, but none of them are sufficient to account for the situation in London in 2011. What is more, Somaiya skilfully undermines the speakers' credibility by his choice of words: for example, he describes David Cameron as he prefers making a speech to taking the necessary steps to end the riots ("David Cameron[…] stood up in Parliament as Britain smoldered around him on Thursday and railed against 'mindless violence and thuggery'", ll. 9 ff.). But the author does not take sides – other politicians show nervous agitation as well: they "have lashed out at technology […] for whipping up the crowds" (ll. 17 f.).

In the course of the text the author contrasts these views with the experiences of people who actually took part in the riots. He chooses people from different social backgrounds and presents them all as ordinary, usually law-abiding citizens (cf. ll. 6, 21 f.), thus giving the readers the opportunity to identify themselves with the protagonists, or at least develop sympathy for their situation. What is more, their offences – stealing bottles of water (cf. l. 25) or a trash can (cf. l. 27) – seem insignificant in the light of the media's alarm. As a consequence, the reader might begin to doubt the attempts at explanation made by the officials, thus amplifying the confusion about the underlying reasons for the riots.

Another effect of the multiple perspectives Somaiya presents is an impression of objectivity. This is strengthened by his use of quotations and references to different sources like *The Daily Telegraph* (l. 14) and especially the expert Dr Clifford Stott, a social psychologist. Dr Stott's reflections on the topic lend credibility to the author's thesis that there are no easy answers ("Why did that young man steal bottles of water? We may never know", ll. 76 f.).

All in all, Ravi Somaiya's text leaves the reader with the feeling that even after taking into account all available perspectives the underlying causes of the London riots are hard to find.

(453 words)

3. *This assignment is supposed to test your background knowledge. Here you should choose suitable facts about London and relate them to the 2011 riots. Possible explanations for the tense situation might be:*
   - *London's ethnic and cultural diversity and the racism that might result from it*
   - *London's overall social structure*
   - *The citizens' economic situation, e.g. the widening gap between rich and poor, and the resulting conflicts between the classes like gentrification, violence and crime*

> *Make sure you explain each point thoroughly before you start with the next one. You should also be careful not to deviate from the topic by writing a general analysis of riots during the global financial crisis.*

London has several characteristics that make it especially prone to social unrest, at least more than other European metropolises.

One example of these characteristics is London's ethnic and cultural diversity. There are more than eight million people living in London, belonging to a multitude of ethnicities. On the one hand, this leads to the development of ethnic districts like Chinatown with its rich traditions that make it attractive to millions of tourists. On the other hand, it can also lead to cultural clashes and violence between different ethnic or religious groups. Cultural misunderstandings between these groups and conflicts that immigrants from all over the world bring from home often lead to racism which finds its outlet in gang violence and hatred.

Another example is people's economic situation. As in every major city, there is a wide spectrum of income levels. While employees in the City can enjoy life's amenities, members of the working class struggle to make ends meet, sometimes working more than one job to make enough money. This fuels conflicts between the classes, especially when affluent people move to formerly cheap boroughs because they are suddenly becoming hip. This gentrification leads to increased rents, thus displacing original residents who cannot afford living there any longer.

Finally, London's size and financial power act as a magnet for two very different kinds of migrants: A constant influx of well-educated academics is complemented by rising numbers of refugees, driven by poverty or persecution. These migratory patterns aggravate the chasm between rich and poor, adding to the menace of social unrest.

(259 words)

> 4. *This creative task gives you the opportunity to prove how far you can put yourself in the position of Chelsea Ives. Although it is possible that she is proud of what she has done, the tenor of the newspaper article suggests that Chelsea, like the other people presented in the text, has acted spontaneously and regrets her behaviour by this time. As a consequence, in her statement she should reflect on her behaviour critically and express her remorse for it. She should also assess her mother's reporting her to the police. Finally, Chelsea ought to draw a conclusion for her future behaviour and maybe also refer to her career as an Olympic athlete.*

Good morning,

my name is Chelsea Ives. I'd like to say a few words about my involvement in the riots last month.

Let me start by saying that I am terribly sorry for what I've done. It was wrong, and if I had a chance to undo it, I would take it.

I am not a criminal. When I left home on August 7, I had no intention of breaking the law. I just wanted to meet my friends. When we reached the main street, we heard glass breaking and shouting. People were carrying stuff out of a Sainsbury's. We thought it was funny and joined them. When the police arrived and started arresting people, I felt threatened because the officers were wearing armour. It was then that I started shouting and throwing stones at the police car, which I'm really sorry for. I'm relieved that nobody was hurt.

I'm still at a loss for an explanation for my behaviour. It must have been the general atmosphere of excitement and recklessness that drove me to it.

I know that there is no excuse for my actions, but still I'd like to apologise to the people who have been hurt in the riots or whose property was destroyed. I'd also like to apologise to the police officers who were only doing their job. And finally I'd like to apologise to the National Olympic Committee for violating the Olympic Spirit. Although it makes me sad, they were right to exclude me from the games.

I would also like to thank my mother. She did the right thing when she reported me to the police. Although I was shocked at the time, I understand her motives now and I'm grateful to her because she showed me the right way.

All in all, I can only say that I hope you can all forgive me over time. I have learned my lesson. I will never do something like this again, and I hope I can prove that I'm worthy of becoming a part of the Olympic team again.

Thank you for your attention. *(349 words)*

> **Abitur 2013 Schleswig-Holstein – Englisch (Kernfach)**
> **Aufgabe 3: London – Life in a Changing Metropolis**

Andrea Levy, "Loose Change"

The narrator, a Londoner, and Laylor have met by accident in the lavatory of the National Portrait Gallery where Laylor has lent the narrator some change. They end up in the cafeteria of the museum where the narrator intends to return the money.

[…] I wanted to be released from my obligation.
"Look, let me buy us both a cup of tea," I said. "Then I can give you back your money."
She brought out her handful of change again as we sat down at a table – eagerly passing it across to me to take some change for the tea.
"No, I'll get this," I said.
Her money jangled like a win on a slot machine as she tipped it back into her pocket. When I got back with the tea, I pushed over the twenty-pences I owed her. She began playing with them on the tabletop – pushing one around the other two in a figure of eight. […]
"Where are you from?" I asked.
"Uzbekistan," she said.
Was that the Balkans? I wasn't sure. "Where is that?"
She licked her finger, then with great concentration drew an outline on to the tabletop. "This is Uzbekistan," she said. She licked her finger again to carefully plop a wet dot on to the map saying, "And I come from here – Tashkent."
"And where is all this?" I said, indicating the area around the little map with its slowly evaporating borders and town. She screwed up her face as if to say nowhere. "Are you on holiday?" I asked.
She nodded.
"How long are you here for?"
Leaning her elbows on the table she took a sip of her tea. "Ehh, it is bitter!" she shouted.
"Put some sugar in it," I said, pushing the sugar sachets toward her.
She was reluctant, "Is for free?" she asked.
"Yes, take one."
The sugar spilled as she clumsily opened the packet. I laughed it off but she, with the focus of a prayer, put her cup up to the edge of the table and swept the sugar into it with the side of her hand. The rest of the detritus that was on the tabletop fell into the tea as well. Some crumbs, a tiny scrap of paper and a curly black hair floated on the surface of her drink. I felt sick as she put the cup back to her mouth.
"Pour that one away, I'll get you another one."
Just as I said that a young boy arrived at our table and stood, legs astride, before her. […] They began talking in whatever language it was they spoke. Laylor's tone pleading – the boy's aggrieved. Laylor took the money from her pocket and held it

up to him. She slapped his hand away when he tried to wrest all the coins from her palm. Then, as abruptly as he had appeared, he left.

Laylor called something after him. Everyone turned to stare at her, except the boy, who just carried on.

"Who was that?"

With the teacup resting on her lip, she said, "My brother. He want to know where we sleep tonight."

"Oh, yes, where's that?" I was rummaging through the contents of my bag for a tissue, so it was casually asked.

"It's square we have slept before."

"Which hotel is it?" I thought of the Russell Hotel, that was on a square with uniformed attendants, bed turning down facilities, old-world style. She was picking the curly black hair off her tongue when she said, "No hotel, just the square."

It was then I began to notice things I had not seen before: dirt under each of her chipped fingernails, the collar of her blouse crumpled and unironed, a tiny cut on her cheek, a fringe that looked to have been cut with blunt nail-clippers. I found a tissue and used it to wipe my sweating palms.

"How do you mean just in the square?"

"We sleep out in the square," she said. It was so simple she spread her hands to suggest the lie of her bed. She nodded. "Tonight?"

The memory of the bitter cold still tingled at my fingertips as I said, "Why?" It took her no more than two breaths to tell me the story. She and her brother had had to leave their country, Uzbekistan, when their parents, who were journalists, were arrested. It was arranged very quickly – friends of their parents acquired passports for them and put them on to a plane. They had been in England for three days but they knew no one here. This country was just a safe place. Now all the money they had could be lifted in the palm of a hand to a stranger in a toilet. So they were sleeping rough – in the shelter of a square, covered in blankets, on top of some cardboard. [...] She'd lost a tooth. I noticed the ugly gap when she smiled at me saying, "I love London."

She had sought me out – sifted me from the crowd. This young woman was desperate for help. She'd even cunningly made me obliged to her. [...]

But why me? I had my son to think of. Why pick on a single mother with a young son? We haven't got the time. Those two women at the next table, with their matching hand bags and shoes, they did nothing but lunch. Why hadn't she approached them instead? [...]

I didn't know anything about people in her situation. Didn't they have to go somewhere? Croydon, was it? Couldn't she have gone to the police? Or some charity? My life was hard enough without this stranger tramping through it. She smelt of mildewed washing. Imagine her dragging that awful stink into my kitchen. Cupping her filthy hands round my bone china. Smearing my white linen. Her big face with its pantomime eyebrows leering over my son. Slumping on to my sofa and kicking off her muddy boots as she yanked me down into her particular hell. How would I ever get rid of her? (1,008 words)

From: Andrea Levy, "Loose Change", http://www.teachingenglish.org.uk/sites/teacheng/files/loosechange_print.pdf (letzter Zugriff 28. 9. 2012)

Assignments

1. Outline the course of the conversation between the two women. *(20 %)*
2. Characterize the narrator. *(25 %)*
3. Using your background knowledge contrast problems and opportunities refugees like Laylor face when they choose London as "a safe place". *(25 %)*
4. "How would I ever get rid of her?" Write the ending of the story. *(30 %)*

Lösungsvorschläge

1. *In this task you have to summarise the conversation between the two characters in your own words. It is important to focus only on the conversation, not on the thoughts. Find a logical structure and avoid interpretation. Write an introductory sentence that clarifies what you are writing about.*

The conversation in the given text is between an English woman, the narrator, and a woman from Uzbekistan named Laylor who has lent the narrator some change. They now end up in the cafeteria where the narrator wants to pay back her debt and invites Laylor to a cup of tea. The small talk at the beginning reveals that Laylor comes from Uzbekistan, which the narrator believes to be somewhere in the Balkans. The narrator's question of where exactly it is remains unanswered, Laylor describing the form of its borders and the location of its capital instead by using spit on the table. The narrator goes on to ask Laylor about the purpose of her visit to London, assuming that she is a tourist, which Laylor answers with nodding agreement. The English woman pushes on, asking the girl how long she has already been in London, but instead of an answer Laylor complains about the bitterness of the tea, which the narrator responds to by offering her some sugar. Laylor asks if it is for free, which the narrator agrees to. When Laylor makes a mess trying to put the sugar in her tea and manages to put whatever else is on the table into her cup as well, the narrator is disgusted and offers her another cup of tea. In this situation their conversation is interrupted by a boy who talks to Laylor in a language that the narrator is not able to understand. When she is asked who the boy was, Laylor says it was her brother, who was asking where they would sleep that night. Taking up their conversation again the narrator asks where that would be. The answer is ambiguous: "the square". The narrator thinks that they are staying at a hotel on a square, but as it turns out Laylor and her brother sleep rough. They are not tourists after all but refugees who came to London with fake passports after their parents, who are journalists, had been arrested in Uzbekistan. They have been sleeping rough in London for three days because they do not have enough money and do not know anybody. The conversation in this excerpt ends with Laylor saying that she loves London.   *(371 words)*

2. *Now the task is to characterise the narrator. First of all scan the text for useful information in this context, and concentrate not only on the direct descriptions but also on what the conversation and the narrator's thoughts reveal (= indirect characterisation). Give proof from the text to support your ideas.*

The narrator is a single mother of a young son (cf. ll. 67 f.) who lives in London and is visiting the National Portrait Gallery (introductory note). At first glance she seems to be good at heart, because when she borrows some money from a person she does not know she is willing to make it up to her by buying her a cup of tea in the gallery cafeteria to give her back the change that she lacked earlier on (cf. introductory note). It seems that she means well but in fact she is only trying to be released from her "obligation" (l. 1), which shows that she is desperately trying to do what is right. It also seems as if she does not carefully check whom she is dealing with because in the train of events she ends up in disgust at Laylor's outer appearance (cf. ll. 49 ff.) and behaviour (cf. ll. 29 ff.). This shows how superficial she is, not only because she does not really register the person she asks for the money but also because of the way she thinks about the Uzbek woman: in the end she wants to get rid of Laylor (cf. ll. 77 f.), because she has "filthy hands" (l. 75) and would drag an "awful stink into [her] kitchen" (l. 74), would smear her linen (cf. l. 75) and drag her down (cf. l. 77) if she took her home. She even goes so far as to think that Laylor only lent her the change in the first place to make her "obliged to her" (l. 66).

The narrator does not seem to be well educated either, since she does not know that Uzbekistan in not in the Balkans (cf. l. 13) and that there is an Uzbek language (cf. l. 34). During the small talk the London mother shows another of her bad character traits, which is ignorance. The way she speculates about Laylor's origins and her background (cf. ll. 13, 34) already reveals ignorance, but when she asks Laylor about where she would stay it becomes even more evident, since at first it does not even occur to her that Laylor might really be homeless and sleeping out on the square (cf. ll. 45 ff.). The way the conversation between the two goes on lets the reader speculate about the certain wealth that the narrator seems to have acquired when she speaks of her kitchen, bone china, white linen and her sofa and how she wants to protect her belongings from this strange homeless Uzbek lady and her brother by trying to prevent them from getting close to it (cf. ll. 74 ff.). It also becomes obvious that the narrator envies people who are better off than her, such as the ladies at the neighbouring table with "their matching hand bags and shoes" (ll. 68 f.) who – an obvious prejudice – in her opinion do not have anything else to do but go out for lunch (cf. l. 69). Still, as said at the beginning, the fact that she at least thinks about maybe taking the homeless refugees to her home shows that there is a spark of good in her, because she shows a certain feeling of responsibility for those in need, even though she does not really know how to cope with the situation and is trying to find a way to sneak out of it somehow.

(570 words)

3. *Here you have to use your background knowledge about Britain in general and London in particular. Write about the opportunities but also the difficulties that a refugee might encounter. If possible, give examples.*

London – capital of the British Commonwealth. It is one of the financial capitals of the world and, with all its sights and history, a tourist magnet. However, London is also one of the major cities in which hopeless people from all over the world seek refuge. For many of them London offers the hope of a better life. Of course, at first sight London seems a good choice, because people there speak English, which many of the refugees speak as well, at least to some extent. That makes it easier to find a way into work and maybe even society. Besides that, compared to many other countries in the world, London in particular and Britain as a whole have a high standard of living, including the infrastructure, with all its hospitals, schools and universities etc. Furthermore, most importantly for many people like Laylor, legal security is guaranteed in democratic countries like Britain. You can officially seek asylum in Britain but that also implies the possibility of being turned down and sent home. This is where the problems start for many refugees – they are in London illegally. Many of them have no idea where to go or how to start and when the police pick them up, the only thing they can do is to apply to the human rights convention. Unfortunately, as the last report of the European Commission showed refugees are not treated according to human rights in Europe. They are locked up in small, crowded rooms for longer than necessary and have to cope with racial assaults by officials before they are sent home to the countries they came from.

Even if they are not caught, their situation is made worse by their illegal status, because they always have to hide from the authorities. Usually they live in some of the infamous, almost slum-like suburbs of London, such as Southall for example. Like Laylor they often have no roof over their heads. In the suburbs they also have to cope with assaults and racial violence, usually from British people at war with the system, who feel that they have no future and who claim that the refugees are taking away their jobs.

Moreover, the number of refugees does not make their situation easier – they mostly have to start their new existence with an illegal job, which of course will be badly paid. If they do not take up such offers, there is a queue of other refugees behind them who are willing to put up it.

So all in all you could say that there are definitely opportunities for those who seek a new start or safety in London, but that there are also many obstacles to be overcome. Nevertheless, the hopelessness of their situation makes people take the risk and try. *(464 words)*

4. *Now you have to finish the story. Does the narrator get rid of the woman or will she help her? Bear in mind what you wrote in tasks two and three and write a text that is both convincing and fitting considering the given situation. Basically both endings are possible but they have to be achieved logically. Try to adopt the style of the text. You can easily achieve this by mixing a description of what happens with an inner monologue of the narrator as seen in the text.*

How would I ever get rid of her? I wouldn't. She was disgusting, but was it her fault? On the other hand, was it my problem? Well, right now it kind of was since she was sitting right in front of me ... What could I possibly do? Send her to a homeless shelter, maybe? But she would probably get into trouble there even if it was only for not being British. That was another problem – she was here illegally. Should I tip off the police and have her sent home? No, there she would probably be arrested and have to live under much worse conditions than she was having to deal with now.

"I love London," Laylor said again. "We will find some way of surviving here – there are so many opportunities."

Yeah, right, I thought, they are all waiting for someone like you. But what was I going to do? I would have to call Steve. He would know what to do – he was still a prick for leaving me and Brian for that bitch Nicole, but he worked in the municipal district office. Let the lazy bugger figure this one out.

I supposed I could put them up in the shed for a couple nights and throw out Steve's stuff. That would serve him right. What did I care …

She was sipping at her tea. "So nice and warm …," she said. "Well, yes," I replied, "I especially like my tea when it's still hot." "… in here," she finished.

True, I thought, it was only March and still quite cold outside – I would have to do something about that, too. This was going to be terrible.

Her brother came back and started an argument with her. That was my chance. Now or never, I thought.

"Sorry, I have to pick up my son," I said, grabbed my bag and rushed past them towards the exit, not looking back. I really felt terrible, but what could I do?

(332 words)

> Abitur 2013 Schleswig-Holstein – Englisch (Kernfach)
> Aufgabe 4: India – Roots and Challenges

Lydia Polgreen, "Digital ID Program benefits the poor", *China Daily,*
18 September 2011

Kaldari, India
Across this sprawling, chaotic nation, workers are creating what will be the world's largest biometric identity database, a mind-bogglingly complex collection of 1.2 billion individuals. But even more radical than its size is the scale of its ambition: to reduce the inequality corroding India's economic rise by digitally linking every one of India's people to the country's growth juggernaut.

The program will enable citizens to access welfare benefits, open a bank account or get a cellphone in remote villages, something that is still impossible for many people in India.

For decades, India's sprawling and inefficient bureaucracy has spent billions of dollars to try to drag the poor out of poverty. But much of the money is wasted. Now, using the same powerful technology that transformed the country's private economy, the Indian government has created a tiny start-up to help transform – or circumvent – the crippling bureaucracy that is a legacy of its socialist past.

"What we are creating is as important as a road," said Nandan M. Nilekani, the billionaire software mogul whom the government tapped to create the database. "It is a road that in some sense connects every individual to the state."

The program, in which citizens are assigned a 12-digit ID number after their irises and fingerprints are digitally scanned, is an ingenious solution to a particularly bedeviling problem. Most of India's poorest citizens […], are trapped in a village-based identity system that makes migration, which is essential to any growing economy, much harder.

The ID project also has the potential to reduce corruption. With electronic transmission and verification of many government services, the identity system would make it much harder for corrupt bureaucrats to steal citizens' benefits.

The new system, known as Aadhaar, or foundation, would be used to verify the identity of any Indian anywhere in the country within eight seconds, using inexpensive hand-held devices linked to the mobile phone network.

It would also help build real citizenship in a society where identity is almost always mediated through a group – caste, kin and religion. Aadhaar would for the first time identify each Indian as an individual.

India may be the world's second-fastest-growing economy, but more than 400 million Indians live in poverty. Nearly half of children younger than 5 are underweight. India's expensive public welfare systems are so inefficient that warehouses overflow with rotting grain despite malnutrition rates that rival those of Africa. Much of it is siphoned off to the private market before it reaches the hungry. […]

Technology, the identity project's supporters believe, would provide people with a way to interact with the state without depending on local officials who are now the main gatekeepers of government services. […]

The Indian government has created a highly unusual hybrid institution: a small team of elite bureaucrats who are working with veterans of Silicon Valley start-ups and Bangalore's most-respected technology companies. No more than a few hundred people will work on the project, and private contractors will enroll citizens. It costs the program about $ 3 to issue each number, and more than 30 million have been issued so far. The process is free and voluntary.

Leftists fret that the database will lead to an erosion of the state's role in helping the poor. But powerful and corrupt bureaucrats, politicians and businessmen have yet to object publicly, though they almost certainly will once the challenge to the way they operate becomes evident.

The man in charge of the project, Mr Nilekani, is a co-founder of India's most famous start-up. In 1981 he pooled 10,000 rupees in capital, or $ 1,100 to $ 1,200, with six colleagues to start Infosys, the outsourcing giant. Infosys is now a $ 30 billion company with more than 130,000 employees worldwide.

Mr Nilekani stepped down as chairman of Infosys to oversee the effort. "I am an entrepreneur within the system," he explained.

The notion of a businessman in government was once unthinkable. Mr Nilekani, 56, came of age in an era when almost all private industry in India was smothered under License Raj, the old system that governed India's closed economy. This meant entrepreneurship was almost impossible.

[…] When the government decided to create the unique-identity system, Mr Nilekani leapt at the chance to run it. Though he would hold cabinet rank, he would be in charge of a small and seemingly arcane government authority.

"People who are not familiar with technology don't understand how big this is," one official said.

Privacy advocates fear that the government will use the program to track citizens. India lacks robust laws to protect privacy. So the database has been designed to contain as little information as possible – only a name, date of birth, sex and address. When anyone tries to confirm a person's identity using the number, the database will supply only a yes-or-no answer.

Many influential critics argue that it is costly – $ 326 million is budgeted for the next financial year, and the project will take a decade to complete – and unnecessary because there are easier ways to check corruption. […] But the project has enjoyed an unusual degree of support from the highest officials in India.

Under an overpass in the shadow of New Delhi, the homeless lined up to be counted. Mohammed Jalil, a rickshaw puller, has no bank account, making it hard to save money. Poor people like him are entitled to subsidies for food, housing and health care, but he has no access to them.

Mr Jalil hopes Aadhaar will allow him to open a bank account. He could get a driver's license and a cellphone.

"That will give me an identity," he said. "It will show that I am a human being, that I am alive, that I live on this planet. It will prove I am an Indian." (964 words)

Lydia Polgreen, "Digital I.D. program benefits the poor" From The New York Times,
2 September 2011 © 2011 The NewYork Times. All Rights reserved.
Used by permission and protected by the Copyright Laws of the United States. The printing, copying, redistribution, or retransmission of this Content without express written permission is prohibited.

Assignments

1. As a consultant write a paper to brief the new secretary of the Indian-German Society on the key issues of the new Aadhaar programme. *(30 %)*

2. Compare the concept of identity behind the Aadhaar programme with notions of identity in traditional India. Include your background knowledge *(30 %)*

3. As a civil liberties campaigner with a profound knowledge of Indian society and fervent critic of the Aadhaar project you are invited to take part in a panel discussion. Write your initial statement for a TV-panel discussion in which, among others, government officials as well as Mr Nilekani take part. Take into account your background knowledge. *(40 %)*

Lösungsvorschläge

1. *In this assignment you are supposed to outline the main points of the ID programme described in the given text. However, the assignment is more challenging than a simple summary, because you are asked to assume the role of a consultant briefing an outsider. Therefore it is not only important to get all the facts right, it is equally important to use the correct register and structure. The original text contains information on the programme that is not vital for the secretary. Stick to the information that is necessary to understand what the project is about. Since your text is addressed to a foreigner you should occasionally explain Indian peculiarities that might otherwise confuse your reader.*

Aadhaar – a digital ID programme to combat corruption and enhance people's initiative

The Aadhaar ("foundation") project is an ambitious ID programme devised to register every Indian citizen and provide everyone with a means of unambiguous identification. For this purpose, every citizen will first be biometrically identified and then receive an individual 12-digit identification number. Clear identification and registration of every participant are vital in order to prevent mistakes and misuse, which unfortunately are common in India's bureaucracy.

Besides cleaning up the records, the project aims at containing corruption and streamlining administrative work. The ID number will make it possible for citizens to exercise their civic rights and claim social benefits, for example, without being held back by administrative barriers.

Taking action in this field has become necessary because of the extremely fast economic growth rate India has experienced in the last ten years. Local officials and traditional systems of identification based on people's position in the community have become insufficient, because citizens' increased mobility demands a means of identification independent of group membership. For example, signing contracts outside of their community is only possible if people are able to verify their identity easily, without having to refer to local administrators. Another important advantage is the fact that the project makes use of the mobile communications network, thus making it flexible and cheap to use.

In the long run, the programme is expected to reduce poverty by creating a society in which everybody is guaranteed equal rights, regardless of their social status.

(251 words)

2. *When you approach this task, you should either first give an outline of traditional concepts of identity you have come across in your studies about India and in a second step describe the concept underlying the Aadhaar programme, or you could start with the Aadhaar programme and then go on to delineate traditional notions of identity. Whichever way you choose, in your conclusion, you should compare the different notions by examining their impact on people's lives.*

"Identity" is a complex construction in India. Traditionally, Indian citizens define themselves by their membership in numerous social groups, the most important being caste, religion and ethnicity (cf. l. 30). Consequently, a person can at the same time belong to a majority (e. g. as a member of the Hindu community) and to a minority (e. g. as a Brahmin). Thus, the word "identity" carries a multitude of connotations which can differ individually because they always depend on the social context somebody is moving in at any given moment.

The individual identification of people as it is practiced in Western societies is contingent upon a functioning administration. In India, administrative efficiency can differ widely due to the country's dimensions and the infrastructural challenges that ensue. Especially in rural areas people are largely dependent on local officials, who, finding themselves in a position of power, might be tempted by corruption or nepotism. As a consequence, slow or unreliable administration could hamper business transactions across communities and complicate migration (cf. ll. 20 ff.).

The Aadhaar programme has been devised to tackle exactly these problems. In contrast to the traditional concepts, it is a very utilitarian approach to the notion of identity. It is based on the premise that all citizens have equal rights and thus should be treated equally, regardless of their social status ("Aadhaar would for the first time identify each Indian as an individual", ll. 30 f.). Consequently, the project focuses on identifying people by their biometric data and then issuing each applicant their distinctive ID number. In contrast to the traditional notion, this project does not provide people with a concept of who they are, but it aims at empowering them in their daily life. The ID number will enable its bearer to take the initiative in dealing with authorities or in business transactions.

(305 words)

3. This task gives you the opportunity to prove your knowledge of Indian society as well as your text production skills. In contrast to the preceding assignments, you should not stay neutral here. Instead, you should take a decided stand against the Aadhaar programme.
The following list contains suggestions for your argumentation against the ID programme:
   – high costs
   – modern technology puts the uneducated at a disadvantage because they cannot assess the risks
   – there is no sufficient privacy legislation yet/risk of data abuse

Make sure you meet the formal requirements of this kind of text by assuming and maintaining the perspective of a fictional speaker, by addressing your fictional audience and by responding to the situation. Since your fictional speaker intends to win the audience over, your style should be critical, emotional and emphatic rather than neutral. Do not forget to employ well-chosen rhetorical devices that support your arguments effectively, e. g.
   – addressing your audience directly
   – addressing and invalidating possible counterarguments

- *emotive and/or figurative language*
- *exaggerations*
- *rhetorical questions*

Dear ladies and gentlemen,
Dear Mr Nilekani,

it is an old saying that things that seem too good to be true usually are too good to be true. And I'm afraid this simple rule also applies to the Aadhaar project.

Mr Nilekani here promises us that his programme will save our country from corruption and poverty. And all for less than $ 3 per capita. Isn't this simply too good to be true?

It must be clear to you that the seemingly low costs must add up to millions at the end of the day – $ 326 million for this year alone, and who can say where the clock will stop? There have to be more efficient ways to combat corruption. This problem seems to be inherent to our country. It is almost traditional! Simply issuing ID numbers to everyone won't weed it out! We need better legislation, and it must be enforced determinedly!

However, the Aadhaar project is the opposite determination. At least, the government declares that participation is voluntary. But how much is this voluntariness worth when it comes to social welfare? If you need the new ID number in order to access social services, then of course you will apply for one, for who can afford to place their principles above their economics? You must be really credulous to believe that there is a real choice here.

But it is always stunning how gullible otherwise intelligent people can be when modern technology is involved. People who would not lend their car to a neighbour in an emergency are ready and willing to give up their personal data to total strangers! This is inexcusable naïveté! Most people are only too ready to see the advantages of new technology, but they never see the risks involved.

The Aadhaar database is not transparent for the average consumer, let alone for the less educated. How are they to know what happens with their data? The advocates of Aadhaar claim that the numbers created are arbitrary and cannot be used to create profiles. But can we trust them?

How safe is our data? What precautions are taken in order to preserve them from falling into the wrong hands?

This is relatively new territory for us. Therefore, it is no wonder that India has no efficient privacy laws yet. But that is why we have to be really careful! In a legal vacuum like this, data abuse is bound to occur. I am sure there are companies who are dying to get their hands on the personal data of millions of consumers. Only think of the possibilities … being able to relate age, income and place of residence – that would make market research much easier. And I simply don't want to imagine what corrupt government officials could get up to … Big Brother is only a step away!

Therefore, I appeal to all of you to make up your minds and raise your voices – don't let the government turn you into a number!

Thank you for your attention.

(505 words)

> **Abitur 2014 Schleswig-Holstein – Englisch (Kernfach)**
> **Aufgabe 1: Ireland – A Country between Tradition and Modernity**

Brian John Spencer, *Belfast Riots Are the Symptom of a Community Left Behind*

The ugly scenes of rioting that have returned to Belfast's streets 14 years after the signing of the peace agreement are a sorry sight. But they tell a story of poor political leadership and of a demographic section of society left behind.

The riots follow a democratic decision taken by the Belfast City Council to reduce the number of days which the Union flag should fly at the city hall. For a capital city and a province of the United Kingdom that counts well over half of its citizens as loyal to the union with Britain, somewhat naturally, the flag removal decision irked a lot of people.

However, there is a demographic section of Northern Ireland for which the decision has been more than irksome. For some it has been seen as a direct assault on their Britishness; an assault […] that's triggered a return to arms, violence, riots, death threats and petrol bombs. Something many of us thought that we'd seen the back of. But as the BBC NI correspondent Mark Simpson said, there's now a real sense that Belfast is going backwards.

But if you dig a little deeper into Northern Ireland society, you will see that there are some people and communities who had never gone forward. And so in a sense the riots have been an event waiting to happen. Yes we have a peace agreement. Yes we have shared institutions. But we remain a divided and often backwards looking society; a divided and backwards looking society not only in terms of politics but also in terms of economics.

Unionists and nationalists who have the economic fortunes on their side have taken the post-1998 continuation of division in their stride. However, those who live in economically deprived areas, especially protestant[1] unionist working class areas, remain a people that time has forgotten. These are a people who without opportunity are devoid of ambition, drive and any sense of personal betterment.

As the reverend Robert Beckett rightly pointed out on BBC Radio 4, this community wide[2] economic deprivation is a direct remnant of the Troubles which stained Belfast for nearly 40 years.

Reverend Beckett called it an underlying deterioration in the social fabric of working class unionism. Something which he said began during the Troubles when a great many fathers were imprisoned for sectarian crimes, which caused the breakup of many families. Protestant working class children grew up without proper and normal parental discipline and routine.

It destroyed the moral fabric and made dysfunction the norm in Protestant areas. This cycle of dysfunction continued over the years and decades and so the peace process has paid little dividend to a generation of young Protestants who're now almost totally disconnected from the society around them.

But as well as familial and moral breakdown, Protestants have chronically underachieved at education. This contrasts with the working class Catholic community whose members largely value education and seek to better themselves. As a result, when the young Protestant men and women leave school they have no qualifications, poor literacy and numeracy skills and only have the capacity for low-paid menial work.

And these difficulties have only been compounded by the ongoing economic difficulties which have caused widespread unemployment. That in turn has caused boredom. And as the saying goes: the devil makes work for idle hands.

And that's the issue. Yes we've had genuine protesters who feel genuinely aggrieved by the decision to remove the Union Jack from the front of the Belfast city hall for all but 15 days of the year. However, we have another type of protester: the young working class loyalist who's been left behind.

And so the rioters we've seen on our screen have been bored and disengaged re-creational rioters. These are misguided, opportunistic young men orchestrated[3] by loyalist paramilitary groups who seek to be seen as relevant again. The irony is that the culture that they seek to defend is being pulling[4] through the mud by their very doing.

Just as the summer riots of 2011 unveiled a discontent and social rot, the flag-riots have done the same. So we must address the cause, fix the illness and so stop anything like this happening in the future. We need to step down to these people and help them to help themselves. Otherwise Northern Ireland will remain a society forever divided and at a conflict stalemate. (727 words)

Spencer, Brian John: "Belfast Riots Are the Symptom of a Community Left Behind." In: Huffington Post United Kingdom (15.12.2012). http://www.huffingtonpost.co.uk/brian-john-spencer/belfast-riots-are-the-symptom-of-a-community-left-behind_b_2304275.html

1   *protestant:* grammar taken from original version; should be "Protestant" (capitalised)
2   *community wide:* community-wide
3   *orchestrated:* instrumentalised
4   *is being pulling:* grammar taken from original source; should be: "is being pulled"

Assignments

1. Sketch the causes for the "illness" (l. 55) referred to, directly or indirectly, in the blog. *(25 %)*

2. Examine the effects the text might have on the reader and analyse how they are achieved. *(35 %)*

3. The week before the "democratic decision" (l. 4) and the final vote a group of Belfast Unionist students start the peaceful online blog "Save Our Union Jack". You as the leader of the group post the initial blog entry in which you assess the impact of the flag-flying reduction on the citizens and evaluate the importance of this symbol for Northern Ireland then and now.
Also taking into account your background knowledge, write this blog entry. *(40 %)*

Lösungsvorschläge

1. *This task is sort of a summary. You have to scan the text for its argumentative structure and rephrase it. Concentrate on the main causes of the new troubles and make sure that you point out the different layers and the complexity of this negative development. However, remember not to interpret the text or add new facts that cannot be found in the original text.*

The causes of what is referred to as the "illness" that infects mainly Northern Ireland's young uneducated Protestant Unionist working class originate from the eruption of the Troubles in the early seventies.
Back in the seventies many families got torn apart because the fathers got locked away in Northern Ireland's prisons for committing sectarian crimes. In those broken families many children were neglected, which led to a loss of moral standards. As large numbers of disrupted families lived in the same neighbourhood in Protestant areas, their way of life was broadly accepted in their secluded parts of society.
According to the text many Protestants lack qualifications and do not have the same level of education as Catholics. This is why they were hit harder by the financial crisis and many of them are unemployed. The author suggests that because they do not have a real purpose in life and do not know what to do with their time, they are drawn to loyalist paramilitary groups.
The government before and after the peace agreement of 1998 failed to reach out to these people to offer them a way out, and drove them back into the open arms of the same paramilitary groups that have been troubling peace in Northern Ireland for generations. The resurrection of these groups might be seen as an illness and consequently you might say that many Protestant Unionist working-class families still carry the virus that they were infected with back in the seventies. *(246 words)*

2. *To solve this task you have to go through the text again and decide which general impression the text leaves on the reader. Keep in mind that the readers come from different backgrounds and that the impression Protestants get might differ from the one Catholics get. Next, you explain how the author tries to influence the effect of the text by his use of content, language and structure (e.g. stylistic devices). You can collect your findings in a cluster and then choose which elements you would like to mention in your solution and how they can be structured. Try to write a logical, coherent text. Give proof from the text to support your arguments.*

The author, Brian John Spencer, tries to come across as a reliable and serious expert on the problems in Northern Ireland. He quotes quality TV sources like BBC NI correspondent Mark Simpson (cf. ll. 13 f.) or sources of a high moral standard like Reverend Robert Beckett, one of the pastors of north Belfast's Protestant problem areas (cf. ll. 26 ff.). Spencer uses their credibility to explain the situation in the areas where present day troubles are evident: "Belfast is going backwards" (l. 14) and the reason for this is the broken families (cf. ll. 29 ff.). As he refers to reliable sources, many readers might accept his theory as fact.

Spencer tries to emphasise that there is a certain urgency to face the problems by using alliterations like "sorry sight" (l. 2) and "rioting [...] returned" (l. 1) to describe the general situation, the "ugly scenes" (l. 1) as he calls them. Later he uses similarly drastic words to describe the family situation of those he has made out as the source of the troubles: the young, Protestant, Unionist working class (cf. ll. 48 f.). He refers to the "destroyed [...] moral fabric" (l. 34) that has led to "dysfunction" (l. 35) and makes them emerge as "bored and disengaged recreational rioters" (ll. 50 f.), for example. Due the negative way in which the rioters are described, the readers will distance themselves from the protesters.

However, the author does not point the finger at these families. To him they have been "left behind" (l. 49), are "without opportunity" (l. 24) or "qualifications" (l. 41) and only have the "capacity for low-paid menial work" (l. 42), which of course is frustrating. He describes them as victims whom we are supposed to reach out to and help overcome their self-inflicted misery (cf. ll. 48 ff.). Instead of simply condemning what the rioters did, the audience is supposed to pity them.

However, although Spencer avoids blaming the members of the Protestant working class directly, he claims that we have to "step down" to them (l. 56). By using these unfortunate words he puts himself and everybody else in a higher position, which is an insult to those he is trying to reach out to. If they read the article, they will probably reject the offer due to wounded pride.

The author also uses parallelism (cf. ll. 17 f.) and contrasts (cf. ll. 9 f., 21 ff.) to point out the urgency to change things. He appeals to the readers to start doing something to solve the cause of the new troubles and to overcome Northern Ireland's segregation (cf. ll. 55 ff.). By using the inclusive "we" here he aligns with his audience, which is supposed to see the causes of the troubles the same way he does.

(468 words)

3. *Now you have to be creative and show that you can imagine how an educated Northern Ireland Unionist must feel about the upcoming flag-flying regulations. To do so you have to bear in mind the history and your background knowledge of Northern Ireland. Your task is to put this into a first entry of a new peaceful online blog. That means in general that you are supposed to write in a factual manner but that you are also allowed to add personal thoughts or ideas. Of course it helps to use stylistic devices to make your point.*

Keep the flag flying!

The decision that will be made at Stormont next week is bigger than many of our elected politicians may think. It is going to be a decision about our future in Northern Ireland – our home! The Union Jack has been the symbol of the Union with England since 1801. This has grown historically and has to be seen as a fact that is not negotiable. The reason for that is simple: First we take the flag down – our flag – for a few days. Next thing we raise the Irish tricolour next to our flag and in the end our flag will stay down permanently. You ask why? The reason for that – again – is simple. With the rise in Nationalist power in N. I. the balance that ensures our peace right now will be disrupted. And that will lead to new troubles.

The 1998 Agreement made us – both – Nationalist and Unionist a lot of promises. We held our part of the deal: the RUC was turned into the PSNI, and nationalist districts are prospering. And what about us? Do we live in prosperity? No! Young Unionists are already leaving their homes to get out of the misery here and make their fortune abroad. That, of course, further weakens Northern Irelands balance of power to our disadvantage and in the end we will be strangers in our own country that will have to stand their ground once again. It is not a coincidence that the UVF and the UDA are returning to duty and increasing activities in our neighbourhoods right now.

We do not want to scare off the Nationalist part of our population – we appeal to them urgently to accept what is historically right and to reach out to us – the part of the population that is left behind. Help us to preserve our heritage. The flag flying is a symbol of great importance to us Unionists. If we lose that, many will return to darker places, darker rhetoric and most likely N. I. will also return to darker times. This is the last chance to reason and to keep the peace that we have. So, or honourable Unionist Members of Parliament at Stormont, listen to the voice of the people and use your majority of votes in Parliament to vote for the Union, vote for the Union Jack, vote for our heritage and vote for our home! Vote for PEACE!

(404 words)

> **Abitur 2014 Schleswig-Holstein – Englisch (Kernfach)**
> **Aufgabe 2: Canada – A Land of Many Nations**

Jamie Bastedo, *Eco-Warrior – Empire Oil*[1] *Trailer*

As I sloshed a full jerry can of stolen gas on the trailer floor, it occurred to me that this would be one expensive fire. Not for the big oil bastards. They were filthy rich. But for Dad. It was his gas I stole. Not exactly cheap up here. Nothing is, especially when every snowmobile, comic book, and cucumber is either flown in, barged in, or trucked in over a temporary ice road. How people are supposed to survive in the High Arctic is beyond me. Especially now with our climate falling apart.

But I wasn't in the mood to chew on such heavy questions. I had serious work to do.

The trick was to make sure I'd covered as much of the floor and walls as possible to get the whole trailer going up in flames. I wanted to knock this sucker clean off the map. My basic idea was to stop a southern Goliath[2] from crushing our village.

For good measure I dumped gas on a stack of pipeline engineering plans, a row of fancy computers, and a huge box of Empire Oil PR brochures that promised economic paradise to all northerners.

A flashing red light above a computer screen caught my eye. A Webcam winked at me. I doused it with my last dribbles of gas and dove out the window I'd smashed.

It didn't take long to figure out my escape. Run for Anirniq Hill – Angel Hill – the most sacred landmark along a hundred miles of sea coast. Where the veil between us and the spirit world was said to be paper thin. Where, according to our Elders, light-filled drum dancers, or *tuurngaq*, popped out of the rocks every Christmas and New Year's and partied. Where Empire Oil wanted to build a humongous compressor station. To pump natural gas out of our land, right past our back doors, all the way to California. So they could power their electric can openers, gobble barbecued pig's tails, and drive their Hummers to the beach while we froze in the dark.

My plan was to sit back and watch the fire show from the top of Anirniq Hill. Just me and a stone inukshuk[3], an audience of two.

The first rule of the eco-warrior: *Nobody gets hurt*. I hadn't seen a light in the trailer since a bunch of Empire executives dressed like lumberjacks flew back to New York after a big pipeline powwow[4]. The event had been organized by our moneygrubbing mayor, Gordon Jacobs. The front page of *News North*[5] showed him slapping their backs as they stepped onto their private jet.

No Empire butts would burn.

The second rule of the eco-warrior: *Don't get caught*. I'd always worked alone in this business of monkey-wrenching[6] – pulling up stakes marking the compressor station site, dumping sand in the gas tanks of Empire bulldozers, chucking their toolboxes into the sea. Our house was empty. My parents, Gabe, and my little brother Pauloosie had taken our boat to Inniturliq for their annual shopping spree – no thrill for me. I'm allergic to shopping. And now that darkness had returned to the night sky, no matter how crazy things got once the flames took off, Ashley the Arsonist would be invisible up on Anirniq Hill. Besides, nobody climbed up there much anymore, let alone in the middle of a wet, foggy night.

I'd wait until things died down, sneak back home, and go straight to bed. I would tell no one of my perfect crime.

Except maybe Rosie and Becca. How could I not tell them?

I wasn't scared. Never once thought I'd get caught.

I was mostly just angry.

I lit a match. Then, for good measure, the whole book of matches.

I tossed the little fireball through the smashed window.

There was a great whoosh of flames. Another window popped out, just like in some old war movie.

I ran like hell to the top of the hill. I shook with nervous laughter all the way, thinking: *How easy was that!* (670 words)

Reprinted with permission from Sila's Revenge, written by Jamie Bastedo, published by Red Deer Press, Markham, Ontario.

1 *Empire Oil:* fictional company
2 *Goliath:* in the Bible, a giant (= extremely tall man) who was killed by the boy David throwing a stone at him
3 *inukshuk:* "Inuktitut": a stone figure constructed by Inuit across North America and Greenland; used for navigation, hunting marker
4 *powwow:* also "pow-wow"
5 *News North:* North Canadian newspaper
6 *monkey-wrenching:* colloquial expression to express sabotaging business plans

Assignments

1. The following day *News North* publishes a report about the crime. Write that report. *(20 %)*

2. Analyse Ashley's personality. *(20 %)*

3. Based on the text and taking into account your background knowledge speculate on Ashley's motives for her "perfect crime". *(30 %)*

4. Later in the novel Ashley attends a conference on climate change. She is to give a speech in front of over 30 scientists. Write the script for her speech starting with the following quote taken from the novel:

   "Ladies and Gentlemen, there is no more time to pussyfoot around with carbon targets fifty years from now. Most of you will be dead by that time. We are the ones who'll still be there." *(30 %)*

Lösungsvorschläge

1. *Your task is to report for a local newspaper on the crime that has happened. Bear in mind how such articles read. They are impersonal and stick to the facts, yet they are interesting enough for the reader to finish reading them. You should also remember to find a fitting headline. Here you will simply have to show that you have read and understood the text and can reduce the story to the facts. Of course you are allowed to embed the facts given in the original text with minimal side information that makes your article sound more realistic.*

Fire blast destroys Empire Oil trailer near Inniturliq
Friday night a fire blast destroyed an Empire Oil storage trailer near Inniturliq in the Northern Territories. High-tech equipment for the future pump station on Anirniq Hill was destroyed along with office supplies. An Empire Oil spokesman explained that this incident was a setback in the company's construction plans for the natural gas resources pipeline from the High Arctic to California. The fire occurred only days after the developmental meeting of local mayor Gordon Jacobs with Empire Oil officials.
According to police spokesman Peter Miller, this incident marks the current peak in a series of earlier acts of sabotage against Empire Oil's development plan. Forensics found out that the perpetrator entered the trailer late Friday evening through a smashed window, thoroughly doused the interior in gasoline and lit it with a box of matches after leaving through the same window as before. A destroyed web cam that is being analysed at the moment might offer a first lead to identify at least one of the unknown saboteurs. *(175 words)*

2. *In this task you are also asked to show that you have read the text properly and understood the details. This time you are asked to characterise Ashley using the information given in the text. Make sure that you also include the indirect hints that the text offers. Give references concerning where in the text the information that you use is to be found.*

Ashley is obviously a native inhabitant of a village near Anirniq Hill (cf. ll. 11, 17 ff.). She seems to be in her late teens, since she still lives with her family of five. While the rest of the family has gone on a shopping trip to the next city, she is old enough to stay at home alone because she does not like shopping (cf. ll. 36 ff.). She is worried about what the gasoline that she uses to set fire to the trailer costs her father, whom she stole it from (cf. l. 3). She knows and cares about the Inuit Traditions as told by the Elders (cf. ll. 17 ff.) and seems capable enough to critically question the political (cf. ll. 29 ff.) and economic (cf. ll. 1 ff., 5 f., 11) developments of our time. The impotence of having no control over these developments obviously leads to a radicalisation that results in her commitment to being an "eco-warrior" (l. 27), as she calls it, to stand up for her political, ecological, economic and her traditional beliefs. Being an eco-warrior, she acts considerately, in that she makes sure that nobody gets hurt (cf. l. 27) and carefully, in that she does not leave any traces so that she does not get caught (cf. l. 33). She does not think about the consequences for herself if she ever gets caught (cf. l. 45). Besides that, she seems to be a normal teenager, who is sometimes funny, saying for instance, "I'm allergic to shopping" (l. 38), who likes colloquial language to express precisely what she thinks, for example "to knock this sucker clean off the map" (ll. 10 f.) and loves to share important things with her best friends (cf. l. 44). *(294 words)*

3. *To do this task you have to look at the text again and check what hints are to be found as to Ashley's motives. Then you will have to make connections between the knowledge that you have about Inuit, the economic relations between Canada and the US or the climate changes and the pollution of the environment, especially in the Arctic. Give proof from the text to support your ideas.*

Ashley's motives seem noble. She loves her home and wants to preserve it. She would like to prevent the "climate [from] falling apart" (l. 6). To do so she fights against *Empire Oil*, a big oil company from the United States which has plans to build a pipeline to exploit the natural gas in this area, which would destroy not only the nature there but also villages (cf. l. 11) and Inuit sacred landmarks that are in their path (cf. ll. 17 ff.). In connection to these ecological reasons to fight *Empire Oil*, there are also economic reasons, which become obvious in the text when Ashley speaks about the natural gas that will be pumped out of their land to maintain the Californians' luxury lifestyle (cf. ll. 22 ff.) while people up North "fr[eeze] in the dark" (l. 24). It becomes obvious that there is a lot of money pushed back and forth between government officials (including the "moneygrubbing mayor" of her village, ll. 29 f.) and global companies that hardly ever reaches the people living in the areas to be exploited. To her, all this seems unfair, which she clearly expresses in the text when she says, "I was mostly just angry" (l. 46).

Her fight also seems to be propelled by the idea of just doing something, even though the fight against what she calls "a southern Goliath" (l. 11) seems quite hopeless. Several scandals, such as the oil sands scandal in Canada, have proven that "the big oil bastards" (l. 2) usually get what they want and that the first nations hardly stand a chance of fighting them and their hedge lawyers. So logically she fights underground as an eco-warrior, trying to be ethically correct, hurting the big player but making sure that people and the environment remain unharmed (cf. l. 27). *(305 words)*

4. *In order to solve this task you now have to take the ideas from the original text that you have already described and analysed in tasks 1–3 and go one step further, transforming them into whatever Ashley could possibly have to say on this conference after her character's development throughout the book. That means that you can either stick closely to the ideas you have already written down earlier or concentrate on a new, specific issue that is somehow related to the text, e. g. land reclamation. In any case you have to bear in mind that Ashley is or was an*

eco-warrior who fights for the protection of the environment and for justice for the man on the street. You should also bear in mind whom you are talking to. You are delivering a speech, which means that you have to address someone. You should use stylistic devices to make your arguments more credible.

Ladies and Gentlemen,

There is no more time to pussyfoot around with carbon targets fifty years from now. Most of you will be dead by that time. We are the ones who will still be there and we won't stand by and watch our heritage being destroyed further. We have to stop here and now – the world is my witness. A long time ago it was an ecological paradise with an infinite diversity of life forms given to my ancestors by the raven. The water was clean and the supply of natural food was endless. What do we have now? Ancient villages that sink in the floods caused by global warming and the exploitation of the ground they were built upon, erosion that washes away fertile soil and takes away the never-ending food supply, melting permafrost that causes pipelines in the remotest inaccessible areas to become instable and break and cause mayor pollution of even more soil and our clean waters ... We in the North already live in a paradise lost, but why don't you people from the South want to see this? The signs are already there for everybody to see. Agriculture is fighting heat wave after heat wave every summer, losing millions of dollars in the process. The extreme weather conditions with tornados, hurricanes and floods kill many people every year and cost the insurance companies billions of dollars in damage but nothing happens. Funny, isn't it? Usually losing money is our wake-up call ... friendship ends when it comes to money. But in this situation ... the world keeps turning and as long as there is big money to be made for the global players, the collateral damage of a few thousand people or a few billion dollars doesn't matter. But ladies and gentlemen, there is no future in present-day economics ... we will have to start thinking about our future – invest in it and stop the deterioration of our living conditions to reach a crucial point from which there is no return ... So what can we do? First of all, we will have to leave the inaccessible natural resources that the ground still holds where they are for the generations to come, as they will have more advanced techniques for retrieving them without destroying vast areas. Secondly, we will have to restore the land that has already been destroyed. Thirdly, we, the people, will have to work hand in hand with our governments to stop those global companies from crossing borders to conveniently do as they like – leaving our land and future to foot the bill. Make them invest in science – let them pay for the research that we need to regain the future of our once green planet. Let this conference be the start. Advise your governments to start the three-step programme now before it is too late. Thank you for allowing me as a representative of this country's future to deliver the opening speech at the *Resources and Sustainability Conference* this year, which my generation hopes to mark the end of yesterday and the beginning of a better future. Three steps – now!!!

(520 words)

Abitur 2014 Schleswig-Holstein – Englisch (Kernfach)
Aufgabe 3: Ireland – A Country between Tradition and Modernity

Poor Pat Must Emigrate

Fare you well poor Erin's Isle, I now must leave you for a while;
   The rents and taxes are so high I can no longer stay.
From Dublin's quay I sailed away and landed here but yesterday;
   Me[1] shoes, and breeches and shirts now are all that's in my kit
I have dropped in to tell you now the sights I have seen before I go,
   Of the ups and downs in Ireland since the year of ninety-eight;
But if that Nation had its own, her noble sons might stay at home,
   But since fortune has it otherwise, poor Pat must emigrate.

The divil[2] a word I would say at all, although our wages are but small,
   If they left us in our cabins, where our fathers drew their breath,
When they call upon rent-day, and the divil a cent you have to pay.
   They will drive you from your house and home, to beg and starve to death.
What kind of treatment, boys, is that, to give an honest Irish Pat?
   To drive his family to the road to beg or starve for meat;
But I stood up with heart and hand, and sold my little spot of land;
   That is the reason why I left and had to emigrate.

Such sights as that I've often seen, but I saw worse in Skibbareen[3],
   In forty-eight (that time is no more when famine it was great),
I saw fathers, boys, and girls with rosy cheeks and silken curls
   All a-missing and starving for a mouthful of food to eat.
When they died in Skibbareen, no shroud or coffins were to be seen;
   But patiently reconciling themselves to their horrid fate,
They were thrown in graves by wholesale which cause many an Irish heart to wail
   And caused many a boy and girl to be most glad to emigrate.

Where is the nation or the land that reared such men as Paddy's land?
   Where is the man more noble than he they call poor Irish Pat?
We have fought for England's Queen and beat her foes wherever seen;
   We have taken the town of Delhi – if you please come tell me that,
We have pursued the Indian chief, and Nenah Sahib[4], that cursed thief,
   Who skivered babes and mothers, and left them in their gore.
But why should we be so oppressed in the land of St Patrick blessed.
   The land from which we have the best, poor Paddy must emigrate.

There is not a son from Paddy's land but[5] respects the memory of Dan[6],
    Who fought and struggled hard to part the poor and plundered country
35 He advocated Ireland's rights, with all his strength and might,
    And was but poorly recompensed for all his toil and pains.
He told us to be in no haste, and in him for to place our trust,
    And he would not desert us, or leave us to our fate,
But death to him no favor showed, from the beggar to the throne;
40   Since they took our liberator poor Pat must emigrate.

With spirits bright and purses light, my boys we can no longer stay,
    For the shamrock is immediately bound for America,
For there is bread and work, which I cannot get in Donegal,
    I told the truth, by great St Ruth[7], believe me what I say,
45 Good-night my boys, with hand and heart, all you who take Ireland's part,
    I can no longer stay at home, for fear of being too late,
If ever again I see this land, I hope it will be with a Fenian band[8];
    So God be with old Ireland, poor Pat must emigrate. (605 words)

anonymus, "Irish refugee, or, Poor Pat must emigrate" published by A. W. Auner in "American ballads of the nineteenth century", Philadelphia 1847.

1. *me:* dialect for "my"
2. *divil:* spelling taken from the original source
3. *Skibbareen:* most southerly town in Ireland
4. *Nenah Sahib:* led the Kanpur rebellion during the Indian Rebellion of 1857
5. *but:* here: who does not
6. *Dan:* Daniel O'Connell (6 August 1775–15 May 1847); was an Irish political leader in the first half of the 19th century. He campaigned for Catholic Emancipation and repeal of the Act of Union which combined Great Britain and Ireland.
7. *St Ruth:* Charles Chalmont Marquis of St Ruth (circa 1650–12 July 1691) was a French general. Early in his military career, he fought against Protestants in France. Later, he fought in Ireland on the Jacobite side in the Williamite wars, where he was killed at the Battle of Aughrim.
8. *Fenian band:* The term Fenian is still used today, especially in Northern Ireland and Scotland, where its original meaning has widened to include all supporters of Irish nationalism. It has also been used as a demeaning term for Irish Catholics and Catholics in general in the British Isles. Irish nationalists, while honouring the 19th century Fenians, more often describe themselves as "nationalist" or "republican".

Assignments

1. Outline the reasons for emigration referred to in the ballad. *(20 %)*
2. Analyse the image of the Irish created by the author. *(25 %)*
3. Examine to what extent 19th century circumstances and driving forces for emigration still match today's emigration motives. *(30 %)*
4. You as an Irish student have graduated from Trinity College, Dublin. As you do not see any job perspectives at home emigration has become an option. Write a letter to an American relative in which you explain your dilemma and seek orientation as to whether to stay in Ireland or to leave. *(25 %)*

Lösungsvorschläge

1. *In this assignment you are supposed to demonstrate your reading skills by summing up the main points of the ballad. Use an objective style. Do not quote at this point and do not add information that is not in the original text. Start with a short introductory sentence in which you say what you will concentrate on in the summary.*

The speaker in the ballad describes the circumstances in 19th century Ireland which induce people to emigrate. The driving force for emigration is the dire economic situation: while the cost of living is increasing, people are paid insufficient wages, thus making them unable to meet all their expenses. On a national scale, this leads to poverty and hunger when people can no longer afford to buy food, and even homelessness when they are forced to leave their homes because they can no longer pay the rent. At the end of the day they might have no other alternative but to sell their property in order to be able to afford to emigrate.
Another factor is Ireland's social situation: due to the high death toll of the Great Famine it has become necessary to dispose of bodies in mass graves instead of holding individual funerals. The survivors are often reduced to begging, without any hope of political change, since there are no leaders to fight for Irish rights and improve the situation.
In the light of these problems, attempting a new start overseas becomes the only way out for many Irish men and women. *(193 words)*

2. *In order to write your analysis you must explain the numerous images and allusions on a more abstract level. Do not limit your analysis to the content level but examine the language and style of the ballad as well.*

The author of the ballad paints a thoroughly positive picture of the Irish people: he describes their character as "noble" (ll. 7, 26), "honest" (l. 13; "I told the truth" l. 44), patient ("patiently reconciling", l. 22) and religious ("God be with old Ireland", l. 48).
He also stresses the Irish people's patriotism by lovingly addressing Ireland as "Erin's Isle" (l. 1) and "land of St Patrick blessed" (l. 31), while emphasising the emigrants' ties with their country by likening them to "shamrock[s]" (l. 42). He deplores the loss of family homes, "where our fathers drew their breath" (l. 10), as well as the loss of leading figures like Daniel O'Connell, who he calls "our liberator" (l. 40) and whose memory is still cherished decades later ("respects the memory of Dan", l. 33).
The author also praises the courage and reliability of the Irish ("fought for England's Queen and beat her foes wherever seen", l. 27) as well as their solidarity in the fight for their own rights when he describes Daniel O'Connell ("he would not desert us, or leave us to our fate", l. 38).
In contrast to that, Ireland and the Irish are also presented as victims of oppression and exploitation by the British when the author refers to Ireland as a "plundered

country" (l. 34) and O'Connell as Ireland's "liberator" (l. 40). The impression of lacking prospects is supported by the frequent use of "poor Pat" (e. g. ll. 8, 40) as the speaker of the poem and a representative of all Irish emigrants.
The rhetorical questions (cf. ll. 13, 25, 26), which make the reader feel personally addressed by the speaker, support the communicative style of the text. The speaker also directly appeals to the listeners to "believe [him] what [he] say[s]" (l. 44) while calling them "my boys" and "all you who take Ireland's part" (l. 45). Thus reader will feel the Irish are a sympathetic people you can identify with.

(326 words)

3. *In this assignment you are required to compare your findings from assignment one with your background knowledge about emigration today. You should discuss similarities as well as differences between people's motivations for leaving their home countries. Probably the easiest way to solve this task is by rephrasing the reasons mentioned in assignment one and immediately comparing them to the situation today.*

In the 19th century there were three main factors which drove people to emigrate. Firstly, the economic crisis and consecutive crop failures led to poverty and starvation, leaving many Irish no other choice but to leave. In the 21st century, Ireland also faced an economic downturn due to the banking crisis following the Celtic Tiger years. Since the state had to make expenditure cuts (e. g. reducing welfare payments and health spending) during the recession, a significant part of the population lives in danger of poverty. The situation is not as drastic as in the 19th century, but emigration is still high.
Secondly, low wages and high unemployment in the 19th century led young people to seek a better future overseas. In the 21st century, it is again the young who have few opportunities on the job market. Traditional jobs like in the construction sector no longer offer a long-term perspective since the property bubble first boosted prices and then crashed in the banking crisis, ruining businesses and making many people redundant. Foreign workers hired during the economic boom and when there was a shortage of labour are now vying for jobs with school leavers. Other parts of the economy are also affected, i. e. the banking sector or the service sector: it is a fact that companies outsource their call centres to developing countries in order to cut down on wages, thus reducing jobs for people in Ireland. These changes in the job market are also responsible for a distinct difference between the two phases of emigration: while it was mostly workers who left Ireland in the 19th century, today's emigrants often have university degrees, thus causing what is known as a "brain drain".
Thirdly, political motives were an important push factor behind emigration in the 19th century because people were dissatisfied with their lives under British rule. Those motives no longer play any role for modern-day emigrants. In contrast to that, the pull factors have gained more weight compared with the 19th century. While the emigrants of 150 years ago often simply relied on their luck when they

left home, their counterparts in our globalised world can plan ahead more easily since they may find a job in the same sector or even the same company abroad. Additional pull factors are a positive attitude towards increased mobility and the fact that Irish applicants face no language problems when working in Anglophone countries. *(404 words)*

4. *This assignment tests your writing skills. Apart from the formal rules of letter writing you should focus on creating a personal atmosphere in your letter. Try to put yourself into the position of a possible emigrant, imagine what the recipient and your relationship with them are like. You should make your dilemma clear to your reader and ask them for advice.*

71 Baggot Street
Dublin

Mary Larkin
118 North Jefferson Street
Petersburg
Virginia, USA

29th March 2014

Dear Mary,

How are you? We're all fine. It's a shame you couldn't be here for Grandma and Granddad's anniversary – we had so much fun! And they would really have loved to have seen you again. But it's no use crying over spilt milk, so we'll just hope you can make it next time … Which, actually, is coming up pretty soon since Sharon is pregnant and the baby is due in September, so maybe you and Alex would like to visit us over Christmas and meet my brand-new nephew or niece? We could have a "cousin reunion" like in the good old days. I'm sure everyone would be delighted!

On the other hand, maybe you and I could meet even sooner. As I told you in my last letter, I'm going to graduate in Computer Sciences this summer. Unfortunately, I still don't see any job opportunities coming my way … Jobs in this sector are pretty scarce here these days, since a lot of companies are outsourcing their IT to India or the Philippines.

That's why I've been wondering what the perspectives are like in Virginia. I mean, I'm not thrilled about the idea of leaving my family behind (especially now I'm going to be an aunt), but I've seen enough friends with excellent degrees move from one unpaid internship to the next, always hoping for a permanent job. I worked too hard for my grades to be a checkout girl at SuperValu!

So do you think it would be realistic to look for work around Petersburg? And would I need a Green Card in order to apply for a job? I've heard you can only get them in a kind of lottery.

Maybe you even know someone working in IT or statistics? So you could find out whether I would stand a chance if I applied for a job near you? I've already tried careerbuilder.com, but actually I'd prefer some personal information from someone working in the sector, especially since I'm not familiar with job definitions and wage agreements in the US.

Actually … if it's not too pushy … Could you imagine having me over for a few weeks in the summer so I could have a look around myself? I've still got some funds left from my savings plan, so I could pay my own expenses, and it's not as if I've got much to do after my graduation except wait for rejections … And if nothing works out, I could still mow your lawn or make myself useful while we spend some time together. I'd love that!

Please write back soon – I'd really appreciate your advice.

Lots of love,
Aoife   *(461 words)*

> Abitur 2014 Schleswig-Holstein – Englisch (Kernfach)
> Aufgabe 4: Canada – A Land of Many Nations

James Mackay and Niigaanwiwedam James Sinclair:
Canada's First Nations: a scandal where the victims are blamed

The response of the Canadian government to the emergency in Attawapiskat shows why indigenous communities are in trouble

In October, the Attawapiskat[1] First Nation declared an emergency. And no one came to help.

The community, situated in far northern Ontario and made up of 1,800 mostly Cree citizens, has announced that its situation is dire, due to a "severe housing shortage". The community has been visited by an Opposition MP and filmed. The images relayed back are horrifying. There are generations of families living in flimsy tents or shacks built from mismatched plywood and covered with tarpaulins. Mould seeps through insulation and runs down the walls. Pails of excrement are being thrown in ditches. Children have chronic skin diseases brought on by poor living conditions, others have third-degree burns caused by cheap stoves. A hundred people live in a prefab trailer, crammed into rooms with just four bathrooms for all. The temperature drops a few more degrees below zero every day. It gets as low as – 40° C in the winter – without the wind chill. Mothers say baby shampoo freezes sitting on the shelf.

Most citizens of Attawapiskat have endured these desperate conditions since a sewage overflow drove them from their homes in 2009. Some have lived this way for longer. Now, with most temporary accommodations deteriorating, the situation has become critical. But despite repeated calls to the department of Indian and northern affairs, their issues have been ignored.

There are more problems. Schooling takes place in temporary constructions, erected after a diesel fuel leak took the main building in 2000, and even after an energetic campaign by students, no plans to build a new one have been made. Unemployment, alcoholism and crime are rife. Disaster officials are now working at the scene. To add to the irony, a few miles away (and on Attawapiskat land), the DeBeers[2] diamond mine extracts hundreds of millions of dollars in resources, delivering valuable tax dollars to governments – but, while it employs a small part of the community, the riches, for a variety of reasons, remain in the hands of others. It's a scene one frequently sees in the developing world. But here it is, in Canada.

For all the extremity of the Attawapiskat situation, perhaps the biggest disgrace for Canadians is that poor living conditions, mediocre educational systems and deprived health are the norm for many First Nation communities. As the MP Charlie Angus notes, there are numerous "Bantustan[3]-style homelands in the far north" of Canada.

The federal government's response to the crisis has been a combination of arrogance and bullying. The prime minister, Stephen Harper, stood up in parliament to argue that widespread corruption on the part of band leaders was to blame, stating: "This government has spent some $ 90 m since coming to office just on Attawapiskat. That's over $ 50,000 for every man, woman and child in the community. Obviously we're not very happy that the results do not seem to have been achieved for that."

As the author of the Apihtawikosisan blog points out, this figure not only conflates the amounts allocated for education, maintenance, healthcare and social services but ignores the cost difficulties brought about by Attawapiskat's remote location and the fact it is over a number of years. Full government-sponsored audits since 2005 are available on the official Attawapiskat website.

Then Harper placed Attawapiskat in third-party management. Last Monday, when the controller arrived, he was promptly asked to leave by the community – and did. Now, the aboriginal affairs minister, John Duncan, has given Attawapiskat two choices: either hand over control of their affairs directly to the federal government (at a cost of $ 180,000 to the community), or evacuate the needy families. As chief Theresa Spence states in a press release: "It is incredible that the Harper government's decision is that instead of offering aid and assistance to Canada's First Peoples, their solution is to blame the victim, and that the community is guilty, and deserving of their fate."

All this speaks to the reasons why Canada's indigenous peoples are in such a difficult situation today. After centuries of federal practices and policies that robbed First Nations of their children, their languages and their right to self-determination, the disastrous consequences will not be undone easily. At the same time, Canadians continue to benefit tremendously from resources and land extracted from First Nations while failing to fulfil their obligations through the treaties that gave them access to these riches[4].

As recommended by Canada's royal commission on aboriginal peoples, massive investment and a true commitment to supporting First Nation self-government and self-sustainability are required to reverse the damage wrought by this history. A national meeting between First Nations leaders and the federal government – where issues like health, housing, and education will be discussed – has been announced for early 2012.

Meanwhile, Attawapiskat, and so many communities like it, call for help and hope for change. (816 words)

Mackay, James and Niigaanwiwedam James Sinclair: "Canada's First Nations: a scandal where the victims are blamed." In: The Guardian (11.12.2011).
http://www.theguardian.com/commentisfree/2011/dec/11/canada-third-world-first-nation-attawapiskat

1 *Attawapiskat:* An isolated First Nation located in northern Ontario
2 *DeBeers:* Name of a privately-run family of companies operating diamond mines worldwide
3 *Bantustan:* Territory set aside; formerly for black inhabitants in South Africa, to concentrate members of an ethnic group; today used to describe a region that lacks any real legitimacy
4 *riches:* Used as plural in the original source

Assignments

1. Outline the living conditions of the Attawapiskat First Nation as presented in the article. *(20 %)*

2. Analyse how the authors try to win support for the interests of the indigenous people. *(30 %)*

3. Referring to your background knowledge, compare the two value systems that clash in this conflict. *(20 %)*

4. On behalf of the elders of the Attawapiskat First Nation, Chief Theresa Spence urges the Canadian government to improve their situation. Write this petition.
(30 %)

Lösungsvorschläge

1. *For this assignment, you are required to sum up the main information from the article in a neutral and abstract way. Do not quote from the text or give your own opinion at this point.*

The article "Canada's First Nations: a scandal where the victims are blamed" from The Guardian Online describes the living conditions of the Attawapiskat First Nation in northern Ontario.

The community's 1,800 members mostly live in detrimental conditions: adequate housing is scarce and the majority are makeshift quarters lacking proper insulation and basic safety standards. Hygiene is also poor, since living quarters are overcrowded and the number of facilities is insufficient. All of these factors lead to widespread health problems in the community.

The poor infrastructure also affects the educational system: lessons have taken place in makeshift structures since the school building was destroyed, with no prospect of improvement.

As a consequence, social problems abound in the Attawapiskat community. There are few job opportunities, and in combination with the poor living conditions the resulting widespread unemployment fosters criminal behaviour and substance abuse.

There does not seem to be any prospect of improvement yet, although the First Nations' hopes rest on a national summit with the federal government in 2012.

(168 words)

2. *In your analysis you should concentrate on the stylistic devices the author employs in order to make a case for the First Nations. You should also examine the effect of these devices on the reader. Don't forget to support your arguments by giving quotes from the text.*

In their article, Mackay and Sinclair aim to persuade their readers of the First Nations' rightful cause by universally taking their side. Throughout the text they refer to the Attawapiskat citizens as "victims" (headline) who "have endured" (l. 14) the critical living conditions for years. They describe these conditions vividly and in detail in order to create compassion for the Attawapiskat community ("There are generations of families living in flimsy tents or shacks built from mismatched plywood and covered with tarpaulins." ll. 6 f.). Additionally, they use a large number of adjectives depicting the Cree's desolate situation, e. g. "dire" (l. 4), "horrifying" (l. 6), "flimsy" (l. 6), "desperate" (l. 14), "critical" (l. 17), "poor" (l. 29), "deprived" (ll. 29 f.), "incredible" (l. 50), "disastrous" (l. 57). The effect is heightened by the paratactic structure of the first part of the text (ll. 5 ff.), which intensifies the impression of an unbearable situation by condensing the information into as few lines as possible.

An intentional choice of rousing or persuasive expressions is noticeable throughout the whole article, such as the use of the nouns "scandal" and "emergency" in the headline followed by "extremity" and "disgrace" (l. 28), which are also intended to sway readers' opinions in favour of the indigenous people.

Another important rhetorical device in this text is the use of opposites. The authors contrast the poor living standards of many First Nations communities (e. g. "Unemployment, alcoholism and crime", ll. 21 f.), which one politician even likens to black ghettos in apartheid South Africa ("Bantustan-style homelands", l. 31) with the wealth created by the exploitation of resources from land belonging to the indigenous people without their benefiting from it. They also point out the "irony" (l. 23) of the fact that this exploitation should happen in the developed country of Canada, while, according to general opinion, such things are characteristic of developing countries. The contrast is heightened by the opposition of the historic discrimination against the First Nations as described in ll. 55 ff. to the position of the Canadian government regarding the situation in Attawapiskat. The authors criticise it as "a combination of arrogance and bullying" (ll. 33 f.), with the prime minister accusing Attawapiskat officials of corruption instead of living up to the obligations that result from the way the First Nations were treated in the past (cf. ll. 33 ff., 51 ff.). This stylistic device serves to persuade readers of the validity of the First Nations' claims.

Finally, there are also contrasts on a semantic level: on several occasions, the authors add afterthoughts, comments or twists in their train of thought using dashes instead of connecting them by linking words. This is supposed to make readers follow the authors' argument and convince them of the latter's opinion.

To sum up, the authors of the article consistently support the cause of the Attawapiskat community and aim to influence their readers' attitudes in its favour.

(489 words)

3. *As a first step you ought to give an outline of the First Nations' values as compared to "Western" values. After that, you should demonstrate the basic incompatibility of the two in many areas of life. Remember to include your background knowledge adequately.*

In the conflict between the Attawapiskat First Nation and the Canadian government, two diametrically opposed value systems have become apparent.

For one, there is the question of lifestyle. On the one hand there are the First Nations, who traditionally strive to live in harmony with nature, which has religious importance for them. In their natural religion, animals, plants and sometimes even parts of the landscape are regarded as animate and thus entitled to respect. This entails the necessity of a sustainable lifestyle which uses resources like food (traditionally acquired by hunting or fishing) responsibly, without taking more from the ecosystem than can be replaced naturally.

On the other hand, there are Canadian entrepreneurs and government officials who seem to regard nature as a resource that can be exploited to their own advantage. This view might be rooted in the Christian belief that humans were created to rule the earth, giving them natural primacy over animals and plants, which are regarded as inferior and inanimate.

This conviction is probably also the cause of the tendency of "white" Canadians to impose their lifestyle and values on the indigenous people. Relationships between the descendants of settlers and aboriginals used to be characterised by the former's determination to eradicate First Nation culture by, firstly, prohibiting their traditional lifestyle and forcing them to adopt a westernised, settled lifestyle. Secondly, it was official policy to forcibly remove First Nation children from their homes and raise them in special "Indian residential schools", estranging them from their ancestral language and their cultural background, for instance, by giving them new Christian names. The aim was to turn them into "mainstream" Canadians and eradicate aboriginal culture within one generation.

Considering this background, the conflict between the federal government and the Attawapiskat citizens will be hard to resolve. It still seems to be difficult for non-aboriginals to put themselves into the position of the First Nations and to understand their needs, while the First Nations are still suspicious of the government, whose inaction concerning their living situation confirms their feeling of social disadvantage.

(342 words)

4. When you write the petition, consider your audience, addressing their concerns while you try to convince them of your arguments. Your tone should be polite and objective, but at the same time you ought to find a way to appeal to the government to improve your people's situation.

Dear Prime Minister,

The Attawapiskat First Nation needs your help. Our situation is desperate: we live in homes unfit for the Ontario winter; we suffer from ill health because there is no sanitation or waste management; we can't educate our children properly because we have no schools. Many of us are out of work. We live on land that is nominally our own but we cannot live our own way of life.

We appeal to you, sir, to help us change our situation. We need your help to help ourselves.

Our ultimate aim is self-government. We are aware that our current situation does not seem as if this could be an option in the near future, but remember that history has loaded us with a lot of weight which does not show us in the best light.

In order to reach our aim, we ask you for more participation. It is not acceptable for us to live under government control. Instead, we ask you to install a supervisory committee consisting of representatives of both the government and the Attawapiskat community. This way, we could manage our own affairs and give our people a heightened feeling of empowerment. We know the royal commission on aboriginal peoples is on our side when we demand a greater commitment by the government to making amends to the First Nations for the injustice done to them in the past. But we do not need any more experts telling us how to handle our problems. Let us handle them ourselves, giving us the opportunity and means to tackle corruption and aimlessness. That way, the Attawapiskat community will be more likely to accept any measures taken.

In exchange for increased self-sustainability we offer the government the opportunity to benefit from our resources, providing that we can accede to a fair agreement in terms of sustainability and yields. This would require the government to respect our culture and traditions. Our land is sacred to us, so any use of it needs to adhere to our rules. Your apology of 2008 was a demonstration of respect that did not fall on deaf ears, but now you have to live up to it. The First Nations are willing to open a new chapter in the relations with the government, but we need a sign from your government that our culture will be appreciated as a valuable part of Canada's heritage.

For the short term, immediate relief is needed. We urgently request that you support our investment programme to improve the sanitation and general infrastructure in the Attawapiskat community. Help us give our children homes which deserve that name and perspectives besides unemployment and substance abuse.

The future of the Attawapiskat community depends on you!

Sincerely,

Chief Theresa Spence *(458 words)*

Abitur 2015 Schleswig-Holstein – Englisch (Kernfach)
Mediation

Wenn sich Personaler nicht mehr für Persönliches interessieren

Frau im gebärfähigen Alter? Mann kurz vor der Rente? Egal! Bei anonymisierten Bewerbungen zählt alleine die Qualifikation. Sie haben große Vorteile für Jobsuchende, sie lassen weniger Raum für Vorurteile. Doch die individuellen Akzente fehlen – das birgt auch Risiken.

Die Bewerbungsmappen kommen einfach zurück, und es sind viele. Keiner schrieb Yana Peil warum. Allenfalls ein mageres „Dankeschön" und „alles Gute für die Zukunft" richten die Personalabteilungen aus. So ging das monatelang. Bewerber aussortieren, weil sie eine Frau sind, weil sie Yilmaz oder Oblomow heißen statt Obermüller, ist verboten – und so sind die Firmen wortkarg geworden.

Yana Peil kann sich also nur zusammenreimen, was ihr all die Absagen einbrockt: Es liegt nicht an ihrem guten Abschlusszeugnis von der Hochschule in Kempten, wo sie Tourismus studiert hat, nicht an ihrem Deutsch, das sie mit leichtem Akzent, aber fließend spricht. Wohl eher daran, dass sie Ukrainerin ist, dass die Chefs im Bewerbungsgespräch immer nach ihrer Aufenthaltserlaubnis fragten. Zu allem Überfluss lautete ihr Nachname damals, vor ihrer Heirat, Fedoryuk. „Bei Bewerbungen war das eine Katastrophe", sagt Peil. [...]

Peils schwarze Serie endete bei einer Bewerbung, wo all das keine Rolle spielte: Der Münchner Geschenkedienstleister Mydays erprobt seit gut einem Jahr anonymisierte Bewerbungen. Wer eine Stelle in der internationalen Internetfirma will, der darf keine übliche Bewerbung mit Namen, Alter und Porträtfoto schicken, sondern muss sich online an einem vierseitigen Formular abarbeiten. „Vermeiden Sie Angaben, die Rückschlüsse auf Ihren Namen, Ihr Alter, Ihr Geschlecht, Ihren Familienstand oder Ihre Herkunft zulassen", heißt es da. Der Bewerber darf sich nur mit Zeugnissen, Abschlüssen, Berufserfahrung oder sonstigem Engagement präsentieren.

Mydays nimmt an einem Pilotprojekt teil, das auch der DGB[1] unterstützt. Zusammen mit der Telekom, der Post und drei weiteren Konzernen erproben sie eine Bewerbungskultur für die Migrationsgesellschaft – oder, je nach Sichtweise, für die alternde Gesellschaft, oder eine, die Frauen mehr Chancen gibt. [...] Ist das Experiment erfolgreich, könnte dies der Anfang einer völlig neuen Bewerbungskultur im Lande sein. In anderen Staaten wie den USA oder Kanada sind solche Bewerbungen längst verbreitet.

Peil empfand die Anonymität als „Segen". Das Angstwort „Ukrainerin", das bei vielen Firmen offenbar Ablehnung erregte, fiel weg. Peil wurde zum Vorstellungsgespräch eingeladen – und selbst da fragte niemand nach ihrem Visum. Heute kauft Peil für Mydays Erlebnisangebote ein. [...]

Die neue Sachlichkeit hat jedoch ihren Preis – auch für Bewerber. Sie können kaum noch persönliche Akzente setzen. Fotos fallen ebenso weg wie das Anschreiben, keine Bewerbungsmappe lässt mehr Rückschlüsse darauf zu, wie fleißig der

Kandidat Sekundärtugenden wie Fleckfreiheit oder Liebe fürs Detail pflegt. Selbst Schriftart und Farbe sind beim Onlineformular vorgegeben. Die Bewerbung mutiert zu einem kühlen Akt der Datenprüfung – allerdings nur in der ersten Stufe. Denn beim Bewerbungsgespräch wird vieles sichtbar – und dieses fällt auch bei der anonymisierten Bewerbung nicht weg.

Melanie Koschorek organisiert die Bewerbungen bei Mydays und sie verteidigt den Abschied vom Persönlichen. Vor diesem Projekt dachte die 35-Jährige, sie gehe objektiv an die Kandidaten heran. „Jetzt merke ich, welche Macht dieses Bewerbungsfoto hat", sagt sie. Koschorek meinte, aus dem Foto herauslesen zu können, ob er oder sie zur Kultur der Internetfirma passt. Doch nun hat sie erkannt, wie sehr ein Foto täuschen kann, noch dazu in Zeiten atemberaubender Manipulationsmöglichkeiten per Photoshop. „Manchmal lag ich richtig, aber es gab Fälle, wo sich mein Eindruck überhaupt nicht bestätigt hat." Die Anonymität schließt die persönlichen Assoziationen aus. „Das menschliche Element verleitet zu Fehlern", sagt Koschorek. „Es hilft mir, mich selbst zu umgehen."

Natürlich hat das neue Verfahren mehr Aufwand gebracht, doch er ist überschaubar. Koschorek schätzt ihn auf 15 Prozent. So muss sie die Kontaktdaten der Bewerber stets getrennt von dem Bewerbungsbogen abspeichern. Manche Abteilungsleiter laden zudem mehr Leute zu Bewerbungsgesprächen ein. Auch die Bewerber selbst sind nicht durchweg begeistert. Manche schicken stur ihre Bewerbungsmappen im alten Stil, als kürzlich die Marketing-Spitze gesucht wurde, beschwerten sich ein paar Männer. „Man hat rasch gemerkt, die stellen sich gerne dar", sagt Koschorek. [...]

(641 words)

Roland Preuß: „Anonyme Bewerbungen – Wenn sich Personaler nicht mehr für Persönliches interessieren." In: Süddeutsche Online (22.2.2014). http://www.sueddeutsche.de/karriere/anonyme-bewerbungen-wenn-sich-personaler-nicht-mehr-fuer-persoenliches-interessieren-1.1289223

1 *DGB*: Deutscher Gewerkschaftsbund

Assignment

Im Rahmen des internationalen Schulprojekts "School's over, what's next?" beschäftigen Sie sich u. a. mit Bewerbungen und Bewerbungsverfahren.

Für die Website verfassen Sie einen Artikel mit der Überschrift "Anonymized job applications – a chance for everyone?"
Stellen Sie auf der Grundlage des vorliegenden Textes in Ihrem Artikel dar, was anonymisierte Bewerbungen sind und welche Erfahrungen Stellensuchende und Firmen mit diesem Verfahren in Deutschland machen.

Lösungsvorschläge

Your task is to write an article. The headline is already provided. The aim of this assignment is an objective text outlining the nature of anonymised job applications for a diversity of readers. In addition, it should discuss the pros and cons of anonymised job applications, as stated in the assignment.

Anonymised job applications – a chance for everyone?
Applying for a job can be difficult – especially when you somehow deviate from the norm. Anonymised applications seem to be the only solution.
In Germany, where applicants are required to give personal data as well as add a photo to their application, HR representatives often judge by an irrational first impression. Consequently, possibly suitable applicants are not considered for a position.
Anonymised applications solely focus on applicants' qualifications for the job, i.e. school reports, diplomas and prior work experience. Giving any personal information regarding gender, ethnicity or age is undesirable. Candidates are not allowed to add a photo to their application or even give their name in the documents they submit because it could influence HR representatives.
While anonymised applications are very common in Canada and the US, the concept is quite new to Germany. In a pilot scheme several companies are testing its viability in the German job market. The advantages for candidates seem obvious: with standardised applications, they all stand the same chances of being asked to attend an interview. Nevertheless, there are still a great number of applicants, mainly men, who prefer the traditional way of presenting themselves. They feel it gives them the opportunity to stand out from the crowd with little personal details, or even layout choices in their applications.
The companies involved in the scheme have had overall, positive experiences with the new concept. Although the amount of work in Human Resources departments has increased because they have more job interviews to conduct and anonymised job applications require a little more bureaucracy, this is outweighed by the fact that there is a better chance of finding the best person for the job.
All in all, anonymised job applications really seem to be an important step in the direction of equal opportunity employment. *(299 words)*

> Abitur 2015 Schleswig-Holstein – Englisch (Kernfach)
> Aufgabe 1: Canada – A Land of Many Nations

Richard Wagamese[1], "Native despair: face to face with ennui on a reserve",
***The Globe and Mail*, newspaper commentary, Aug 24, 2013**

The hardest battle in our fight to save our native children is against ennui. If you haven't encountered that word before, it means something about a ton heavier and a lot deadlier than simple boredom. It means a lifelong sort of tiredness. It means lassitude, an unrelenting feeling of nothingness. It means you give up trying, dreaming or seeing yourself doing something better.

I encountered it head on recently. I was at a northern reserve to deliver a workshop called Empowering Community Through Story. It was designed to allow native youth to gather and tell stories about themselves and their community in a variety of different media. The program offered the chance to use art, photography, video and oral and written story to create a comprehensive image of their home. It would have allowed them to see and share how they viewed their reserve in the past, present and future.

Because I believe so much in the healing power of story, I created the program so that native youth would discover that stories can be told in any number of ways. I designed it so they could choose how they wanted to tell them. I aimed it right at technology and art. If I had the relevant experience, I would have used dance, theatre and music to achieve the same goals. It was a grand initiative with incredible potential for change and empowerment.

Not a single youth registered. It was a free program with no registration fee. It wasn't really their fault, because no one on the reserve got the word out. There were no posters or anything, so that when we arrived, no one was expecting us. There wasn't a single person from administration, community development or health and wellness to show us where to go. We were a special program with no participants. So months of creating and planning went down the drain and we had to create something out of nothing.

When word did get out that we were there, reserve families simply sent their young children to us so that we could act as a sort of casual daycare. The program wasn't designed for tots or those under 15, so it collapsed and became something far different. It became a face-to-face encounter with ennui.

The youngsters wanted stimulation. That was the good news. So we created an art program on the fly and got them painting, making collage and decorating hula hoops. But their level of interest and ability to concentrate and focus flagged very quickly and every art session devolved into noise and mayhem after about 30 minutes.

When I tried to get the community to show up at free lunches so I could take photographs for a community album, no one showed. When we attempted to get the health workers to arrange interviews with elders for a video that would go in their museum, no one showed – except when they knew they would be paid. Everything we tried to accomplish for that community fell flat. In the end, we created a small but vibrant community photo collage, and a short video with three elders talking and telling stories. But it was only through our energy. The community itself never showed.

When we left, there was no one there to receive the projects. There was no one interested enough to come see what we had created for them even though we'd been there for 10 days. Our bright, shiny projects that showed such hope and promise were left with no one to view them. It was sad – heartbreaking, even, because that's what's at the core of dysfunctional and ineffective reserve communities. Ennui. A thousand-pound word that means you simply just don't care any more.

It's the system that brings a people to that. It's the Indian Act[2]. It's an imposed welfare mentality. It's generation after generation of crushing isolation and poverty. It's the deeply ingrained belief that there is nothing else possible and that no one sees us or cares about us anyway. It's the entire history of Canada and her relationship with native people focused despairingly on our most vulnerable.

It's killing us, starting with our youngest. It's foisted upon our youngsters and our youth and robs them of vision. Those kids in that art class didn't lose their focus because they weren't interested. They lost it because in the larger picture of their lives it had no place. It would end as all things end. It would flare as all promises flare and then gradually slip away never to be repeated.

Ennui. The acceptance that this is all there is and all there ever will be. Fighting that is where our greatest battle has yet to be fought. (785 words)

Wagamese, Richard: "Native despair: face to face with ennui on a reserve." In: The Globe and Mail (24.8.2013).

1 *Richard Wagamese:* author and journalist from the Ojibway Wabasseemoong First Nation. His most recent book is the novel *Indian Horse*.
2 *Indian Act:* The act defines who is an "Indian" and contains certain legal rights and legal disabilities for registered Indians.

Assignments

1. Outline the effects that, according to the text, living on a reserve has on the natives. *(30 %)*

2. Analyse the means the author employs to emphasise his message. *(35 %)*

3. You are a host student in Canada and have read the article "Native despair: face to face with ennui on a reserve".

   Write a letter to the editor of *The Globe and Mail* expressing your view on the complexity of the topic. Take into account your background knowledge. *(35 %)*

Lösungsvorschläge

1. *Of course you have to summarise important aspects of the text as the task "outline" suggests. But here the tasks is rather demanding as the aspects you have to find are more part of the underlying theme of the text than in the centre of it. The author uses his experience at the camp to describe what is wrong with the attitude of the Natives in the camp in general. So do not just describe the events (e. g. nobody knows about the project, they do not take part in it), but analyse what they stand for (e. g. both individuals and the administration are unwilling to take responsibility for their lives and community, they only show interest in things if they are paid for them or gain a personal advantage, such as daycare for their children). You should also mention the reasons for this apathy according to the author (the Indian Act, welfare mentality, isolation and poverty) as he makes clear that he considers Canadian history and the government's role in it to be responsible for the Natives' misery.*

In his newspaper commentary "Native despair: face to face with ennui on a reserve" Richard Wagamese describes how living on a reserve affects First Nations people. When he arrives on the reserve, in order to work with teenagers on an art project dealing with their people's history, his predominant impression is that of an all-encompassing atmosphere of boredom and lethargy. People on the reserve seem devoid of all motivation to take responsibility for their lives, a fact that the author attributes to the long history of poverty and isolation natives on the reserves have been experiencing, and not least by the lack of interest shown by the Canadian government. While residents are glad to take advantage of Wagamese's art project as entertainment for their children, they are not interested in participating themselves, or supporting the project in any way, even though it aims at preserving First Nation culture. The only way of encouraging them to take part is by paying them; an attitude the author blames on the effects of the Indian Act which robs natives of their initiative by making them dependent on state welfare. In the end, this lack of initiative leads to a general sense of hopelessness in the face of a future without prospects. *(208 words)*

2. *To solve this task you have to understand the message of the text first. Why does Richard Wagamese write about his experience at the camp? It is (not only) to describe how disappointed he was when no one showed up for his project. He wants the reader to understand why no one showed up and that there has to be something done about this problem – and that, since it is not the Natives' fault that they have lost all hope and aspiration, they cannot solve the problem on their own. You do not have to include all the aspects mentioned in the following solution to write a good text. Concentrate on the aspects that catch your eye when you read the text and on explaining why the author uses them.*

The central theme of Wagemese's article is the feeling of "ennui" which seems to dominate the entire community on the reserve as much as it dominates the text, where it is used repeatedly (cf. headline, ll. 1, 29, 45, 57). After introducing this theme in the headline, the author further acquaints readers with the phenomenon in his first paragraph, underlining its all-encompassing character by using numerous synonyms and related expressions like "boredom" (l. 3), "tiredness" (l. 3), "lassitude" (ll. 3 f.) and "nothingness" (l. 4).

In the course of the text, the monotony Wagamese experiences on the reserve is reflected in his style as well, for example when he uses anaphora in his definition of "ennui" in ll. 2–4 ("it means [...] It means"). There are also a number of parallel structures which add to the feeling of lethargy and uniformity when Wagamese enumerates the factors he believes are causing the feeling of "ennui", starting every sentence with "It's" (ll. 47–53) or "It would" (l. 55) or describes the little effect his project had on people on the reserve ("When I tried", l. 34; "When we attempted", l. 35; "When we left", l. 41).

The author also tries to share his own feelings of disappointment with the readers when he contrasts depictions of his plans with the lack of reaction from the inhabitants of the reserve, again employing parallel structures, e. g. in ll. 13–15 "I created the program", "I designed it", "I aimed it" and ll. 34–41 "When I tried to get [...] no one showed. When we attempted to get [...] no one showed. [...] When we left, there was no one [...] There was no one".

However, the author doesn't content himself with deploring the situation, he also wants to improve it and rouse his readers to take action themselves. To this end, he stresses the gravity of the situation, introduced in the headline as full of "despair", by his use of adjectives depicting duration like "lifelong" (l. 3) and "unrelenting" (l. 4), or weight ("a ton heavier", l. 2; "thousand-pound", ll. 45 f.; "crushing", l. 48). In addition, he personifies the feeling of "ennui", thus turning it into an enemy that needs to be defeated (e. g. "face to face with ennui", headline; "something a ton heavier and a lot deadlier", ll. 2 f.; "I encountered it head on", l. 6; "a face-to-face encounter with ennui", l. 29), an impression that is also supported by the expressions from words related to war he employs in the first and last paragraph, thus creating a frame for the entire text by referring back to his opening statement ("The hardest battle", l. 1; "Fighting that is where our greatest battle has yet to be fought," ll. 57 f.).

Wagamese also reinforces his appeal when he tries to create a sense of togetherness and solidarity among his readers and people on the reserve by the repeated use of the first person plural, e. g. l. 1 "our fight [...] our native children", l. 51 "our most vulnerable", l. 52 f. "It's killing us, starting with our youngest. It's foisted upon our youngsters and our youth", l. 58 "our greatest battle". What is more, with this technique Richard Wagamese also offers himself as a kind of link between the indigenous culture of the people on the reserve and the cultural background of his readers. On the one hand, he is a member of a First Nation while on the other he is a journalist working in mainstream Canadian culture. This enables him to gain the interest of a wider range of readers in the problems of the Canadian First Nations.

(613 words)

3. *In a letter to the editor you should always mention which article you are referring to. You can either do this in the first sentence of your letter or in a headline as in the following example. If you do not know the name of the editor nor the gender, you can start your letter by writing "(Dear) Sir or Madam".*

Reference: "Native despair: face to face with ennui on a reserve"

Sir or Madam,
on reading the article by Richard Wagamese I was very moved by his impressions of life on a reserve. Being a host student here in Canada I am very interested in Canadian culture, especially the First Nations' heritage, and I am touched by the misfortunes and injustices they have suffered to this very day. Not only were they deprived of their own land when the settlers started claiming it for their own needs, they were then penned up in reservations where they suffered from poverty and isolation.

What is more, even their basic human rights have been violated ever since: they were not allowed to practise their religious rituals and restricted in freedom of movement, thus barred from living their traditional way of life. If it was not enough to kill their culture, from the mid-19th century on, First Nation's children were taken from their families and placed in so-called residential schools, where they were supposed to lose all ties with their people's traditional way of life and assimilate completely into Canadian society. It is almost unbelievable that this violation of human rights did not end until 1996, with the Statement of Reconciliation following a little later – a token gesture, maybe, but a first step in the right direction – which finally acknowledged the fate of the First Nations and the abuse they suffered at the hands of the Canadian government.

Nevertheless, there is still much to be done. The problems Wagamese describes are far from solved. These days, it is not settlers that profit from the First Nations land, but big companies mining resources without compensating the real owners. In return, the First Nations suffer from pollution and disease from the poor safety standards on the sites. The money that is made from mining goes elsewhere – the First Nations do not see any of it.

That is why they are trapped in what Wagamese calls "welfare mentality". Instead of earning their own money (be it from their own work or by selling their resources), they are dependent on the state's goodwill, a situation which kills all initiative and ends in the circumstances he describes: lethargy and lack of motivation as well as a deep distrust of all things official. Maybe that is also where Wagamese might have gone wrong. If he had been less convinced of his own ideas and more open for the ideas of the people on the reserve, he might have been more successful. However, he arrived on the reserve determined to do good by its inhabitants, fully convinced that he knew what would be best for them. Is it really so surprising they did not welcome him with open arms?

The solution to the problems on the reserves surely lies elsewhere. Instead of forever keeping people dependent on state welfare, they should have the chance to develop their own ideas and turn their dreams into reality. This is what the Canadian government should concentrate on: investing in the infrastructure and education on the reserve, so people are on par with the rest of the Canadian people. This is the only way to give them the chance to take their lives into their own hands and solve their problems themselves.

Yours sincerely,

N. N.
Ottawa, Canada/Kiel, Germany *(554 words)*

> **Abitur 2015 Schleswig-Holstein – Englisch (Kernfach)**
> **Aufgabe 2: Ireland – A Country between Tradition and Modernity**

Text 1: Joni Mitchell, "The Magdalene Laundries", 1994

Introductory Note: In 1994, Joni Mitchell recorded the song "The Magdalene Laundries" on her album Turbulent Indigo. *From the 18th century till the late 1990s "Magdalene Laundries" were a network of laundries where women worked and lived. These supposed rehabilitation centres were located throughout Europe and North America.*

1 I was an unmarried girl
  I'd just turned twenty-seven
  When they sent me to the sisters
  For the way men looked at me.
5 Branded as a Jezebel[1],
  I knew I was not bound for Heaven
  I'd be cast in shame
  Into the Magdalene laundries.

  Most girls come here pregnant
10 Some by their own fathers.
  Bridget got that belly
  By her parish priest.
  We're trying to get things white as snow,
  All of us woe-begotten[2]-daughters,
15 In the streaming stains
  Of the Magdalene laundries.

  Prostitutes and destitutes
  And temptresses like me –
  Fallen women –
20 Sentenced into dreamless drudgery …
  Why do they call this heartless place
  Our Lady of Charity?
  Oh charity!

  These bloodless brides of Jesus,
25 If they had just once glimpsed their groom,
  Then they'd know, and they'd drop the stones
  Concealed behind their rosaries.
  They wilt the grass they walk upon.
  They leech the light out of a room.
30 They'd like to drive us down the drain
  At the Magdalene laundries.

Peg O'Connell died today.
She was a cheeky girl,
A flirt
They just stuffed her in a hole!
Surely to God you'd think at least
    some bells should ring!
One day I'm going to die here, too,
And they'll plant me in the dirt
Like some lame bulb
That never blooms come any spring,
Come any spring,
No, not any spring …   (223 words)

Text: Joni Mitchell. Copyright: Crazy Crow Music/Siquomb Publishing Corp.Sony/ATV Music Publishing (Germany) GmbH, Berlin

1 *Jezebel:* a biblical princess; an immoral woman, who tries to attract men sexually
2 *woe-begotten-daughters:* desperate daughters

Text 2: Patrick Soraghan Dwyer, "I'm Not a Fallen Woman", 2009

TB[3] devoured my happy home
In the year of 43
Took Mam and Dad and the baby
O Why O Why did it not take me?

CHORUS
I am not a fallen woman
I never fell from grace
I only fell from hunger
It's a national Disgrace

The state did not protect me
took away my human rights
gave me to the church for free
To do with me as they liked.

CHORUS

They gave me a number and stole my name
I knew my life would never be the same
I never knew a loving touch
Fit for beatings, fit for work

CHORUS

I am just a small piece in your great plan
Their hate and anger I will never understand

Far removed from God's Holy Bible
Rome said nothing and the state stood idle

CHORUS

25 The sin was collusion and collusion is rotten
We were betrayed, brutalized and forgotten
and now silence grows like a cancer
It is not good enough now we want answers   (167 words)

Patrick Soraghan Dwyer, "I'm Not a Fallen Woman", 2009.

3 *tuberculosis, or TB*: is a widespread, and in many cases fatal, infectious disease that typically attacks the lungs.

Assignments

1. The *Irish Recorded Music Association* (IRMA) is promoting an album with a collection of Magdalene songs by various artists. On their homepage they introduce the topic of the laundries in an informative text.

   Sketch the relevant information from both songs for this text.   *(30 %)*

2. Examine how the lyrics of the two songs support the songwriters' intentions and the possible effects they have on the recipient.   *(40 %)*

3. In your English class you have dealt with the Magdalene laundries in connection with the topic Ireland. For your class magazine you are to write an article on the circumstances that contributed to allow the Magdalene laundries to exist for such a long time.

   Write this article. Include your background knowledge.   *(30 %)*

Lösungsvorschläge

1. *Basically what you have to do here is scan both songs for any information on Magdalene laundries that you can find. Based on this information write a short neutral text on what they are. To do so you will have to generalise what the texts say about Magdalene laundries and make it look like facts. Make sure to mention the information given in the introductory note. Do not use any knowledge that you might have on this topic since this task is supposed to test your general understanding of the texts.*

Magdalene laundries were a network of rehabilitation centers for women throughout Europe and North America from the 18th century to the late 1990s that was managed by the Catholic Church and tolerated by various national governments. The general idea was to create something that would give women that were considered immoral the chance to rehabilitate and to offer poor women charity in return for their labour in these laundries. In reality many of the often pregnant girls and women who were sent to the laundries were victims of abuse by relatives or priests. The network turned into a very profitable nun run business which was rooted out major crimes such as false imprisonment, servitude, abuse and social exclusion. *(118 words)*

2. *In this task you have to read the text again and search for any information you can find on the songwriters' intentions and the effects that they might have on you, the recipient. You not only have to examine the content but also the language used since it – just like in a poem – might carry vital information. It is imperative that you explain where in the texts you have found the information that you use and by doing so support your interpretation of the songwriters' intentions. Make sure that you sum up your results at the end.*

The songwriters try to confront the listener with the truth about the Magdalene laundries, i. e. that they were not only a place for rehabilitation and charity as they were meant to be, but also a place of misery for most of the women that spent their lives there.
First of all, the question that needs to be asked is who are the women speaking and who do they speak for? In text one a young, unmarried, obviously good looking woman who calls herself a "temptress[]" (T1 l. 18) was brought to a Magdalene laundry because she drew too much attention from men (cf. T1 ll. 1 ff.). She reports as a first person narrator that she stayed there with other unmarried women most of which were pregnant (cf. T1 l. 9), which was outside the moral standards of the Catholic Church. Often they were victims of abuse (cf. T1 ll. 10 ff.), but there were also prostitutes, poor women (cf. T1 l. 17, also T2 ll. 6 ff.), orphans (cf. T2 ll. 1 ff.) and other "fallen women" (T1 l. 19, T2 l. 6), who did not meet social standards.

This obviously was enough reason to lock them away under the supervision of the Catholic Church (cf. T2 l. 12) and keep them out of sight. These women did not do anything wrong, but they did not have a voice, a chance to speak up, so they were kept imprisoned for life (cf. T2 ll. 9 ff., 20).

The texts show the questionable methods that were used by the people in charge as the treatment the women received was inhumane. The girl in the second text states that they "gave [her] a number and stole [her] name" (T2 l. 15). She says that the personnel in these Magdalene laundries in its "hate and anger" (T2 l. 21) were obviously "far removed from God's Holy Bible" (T2 l. 22). The woman in text one sees the leadership similarly and refers to the nuns that ran these institutions with a biblical alliteration as "bloodless brides of Jesus" (T1 l. 24) who hide behind their rosaries and make the lives of the inmates miserable (cf. T1 ll. 25 ff.). Both texts show that the inmates were oppressed and had lost all hope. They had to serve until they died (cf. T1 ll. 32 ff.) and not even then could their souls find peace since dead bodies were "stuffed […] in a hole" (T1 l. 35) without any ceremony (cf. T1 ll. 36 f.). So a listener might agree with the sarcasm that swings in the rhetorical question asked in the first song "Why do they call this heartless place Our Lady of Charity?" (T1 ll. 21 f.). The church's methods "to get things white as snow" (T1 l. 13) – an image with a double meaning as the women had to work as laundry women while the sins of their lovers or abusers were "whitewashed" – seemed to involve all sorts of violence which was not prosecuted (cf. T1 l. 30, T2 ll. 18, 26).

But not only is the church to blame here – the state also failed to protect its citizens. The inmates were deprived of their human rights and "given" to the church (cf. T2 ll. 10 ff., 25 ff.) to work for the rest of their lives, hence the alliteration, "dreamless drudgery" (T1 l. 20).

All in all, these songs were written to dig up a dark chapter of Catholic and Irish history and to demand some answers (cf. T2 l. 28) about the "collusion" (T2 l. 25) that kept the cruelty and the violence against the inmates of the Magdalene laundries under a veil of secrecy for so long. They want to criticise the behaviour of all the people and institutions involved and leave the listener compassionate toward the victims. *(639 words)*

3. *Now you are to write an article which means that you will have to meet the formal criteria of a (newspaper) article, i. e. title, place and date, your name, opening paragraph, main text and conclusion. Make sure you use the appropriate language. In this article you can use your background knowledge on Ireland and its society. Starting where the texts end, point out the circumstances that led to the long existence of the laundries and draw your conclusions from there.*

This is WHY!
By Peter Petersen

When we talked about the Magdalene laundries in class during the last few weeks we all asked ourselves "WHY?" or "How was it possible to keep this corrupt system going for such a long time?" For me the short answers were not acceptable and so I dug a little deeper and found various reasons WHY.

First of all, there was the one reason that we all speculated about, Irish society. Ireland society has been based on two pillars for a very long time: Church and Tradition. The Catholic Church used to pervade almost every sector of private and professional life. From kindergarten, to school, to marriage and finally death it was omnipresent. Priests and nuns would educate you to become good Christians and you would seek their council on all kinds of matters, particularly moral questions like sin etc. Due to that, the traditionally high number of believers was kept within an extremely conservative set of moral standards that met those of the Catholic Church. This became very evident when talking about sexuality and birth control. The condom, for example, was only available on prescription until 1990.

Another factor that has to be taken into account is that Ireland was, for a very long time, a rural society with very old traditions which of course influenced the structure of relations significantly. To free oneself and break out of these traditional networks was practically impossible. A brazen attempt might have led a young woman directly to a Magdalene laundry. Women were especially at risk because if they did not bow to their husbands in this patriarchal society that Ireland was until at least the 1980s, they were seen as trouble-makers.

Even then this showed that this backward society bore quite a bit of the blame for the situation in the Magdalene laundries. Nobody investigated information that eventually leaked from these institutions. The state failed in its fiduciary capacity, and, as investigations showed in fact in the late 1990s, it used the Magdalene laundries to get rid of inconvenient female cases. Society was also involved as people held in high esteem the low budget high quality laundries, particularly before – and this is another major reason for the Magdalene laundries long survival – the washing machine became a common piece of equipment in the household.

It was only in the 1990s that people began to ask the right questions in order to reveal the full range of wrongs that had been kept under wraps for decades. All in all, the Magdalene laundries ran on a cocktail mixed with old traditions, entrenched habits, a slowly grown network of social relations, a reactionary Catholic Church and a passive state that turned a blind eye to the situation. *(465 words)*

> **Abitur 2015 Schleswig-Holstein – Englisch (Kernfach)**
> **Aufgabe 3: Ireland – A Country between Tradition and Modernity**

Text 1: Chris Jenkins, "Belfast's immoral 'conflict tourism'", *The Guardian*, May 7, 2012

Buses drive into Belfast to allow tourists to gape at the massive walls and sites of bombings. This is simply exploitation.

Visit Northern Ireland. Come to Belfast and see our magnificent city – rejuvenated, regenerated and re-energised. Take a walk through the streets in the shadows of the division walls. Why not stop to get your photo taken beside a mural of men in balaclavas? If you really want, why not write a message of hope and peace on one of our walls, a truly symbolic sign of human solidarity?

It is surprising that, given the lack of humility in Northern Ireland's exploitation of conflict, an advertising campaign using the language above has not been launched yet. Tourism in Northern Ireland has rocketed within the last decade. The continued perception of increased stability and relative peace has attracted people from all over the world to see the many things that Northern Ireland should and does advertise to the world – the Giant's Causeway, the Antrim glens, the Fermanagh lakes.

However, there is something deeply immoral about the rapidly expanding "conflict tourism" sector. Buses drive into the heart of inner city Belfast to allow tourists to gape at the massive walls dividing Belfast's communities – murals depicting violence. Tourists take photos of the division lines that are not consigned to history, but are a part of living Belfast: children play football against the walls that tourists flock to. The places and the people themselves have become a spectacle, an attraction.

If this were history perhaps it would be more acceptable – but it's not. These lines are still a very real part of everyday life for communities in Northern Ireland. Our politicians may say otherwise – that we are now at peace, and that nothing will destabilise our progress – but divisions aren't removed.

As a country, we have come to realise the financial gains that can be made by marketing our conflict while also exaggerating the "stability" of Northern Ireland; painting a picture of those who dissent as being in a vast minority with no support whatsoever. The reality is manipulated, history exploited.

Just last week Peter Robinson, Northern Ireland's first minister, described the redevelopment of the Maze prison site (infamous for housing political prisoners during the Troubles) as being a "mecca for tourists". The Maze/Long Kesh site needs a role within our remembrance process, but not a commercial role. The proposed "conflict resolution centre" for the site (at a cost of £20 m) is not just another example of politicians U-turning all over the place[1], but also of the entire trend of ethics being sidelined for supposed financial gain.

I am not against tourism – quite the opposite in fact. But it seems to me that aspects of the current rebranding of Belfast are not only highly immoral, but also detract from the reality and the severity of our history. We need remembrance and we need reflection – such things will aid our reconciliation as a society. But we don't need the exploitation of our conflict. (502 words)

Jenkins, Chris: "Belfast's immoral 'conflict tourism,'" In: The Guardian (7.5.2012).

1 *u-turning all over the place:* changing their minds to the opposite direction

Text 2: David de Sola: "Belfast: After the fighting ends, the tourists come" *CNN online,* April 14, 2011

[…] Another option for tourists interested in learning about the troubles is the political tours offered by former prisoners groups from both sides of the conflict. Coiste[2] offers a detailed walking tour of the Falls Road neighborhood told from a Republican perspective, while their Loyalist counterparts from the Ex-Prisoners Interpretative Centre (EPIC) offer a similar tour of the Shankill Road.

"We get our history not from having read a book or something like that, we've actually been involved directly. As a result of that involvement, most of us have spent long terms of imprisonment," said Seamus Kelly, Coiste political tour coordinator.

"It's about people who are actually able to give a living history, and I keep repeating that because I think it's important people get a feel for how people became involved in a conflict, why they became involved in it, and where they see themselves in the present day."

Ultimately the tours are about closure and contributing to the peace for the guides who give them.

"It helps us to cement the peace process, to get an understanding of our former enemies. It also gives them the same opportunities. We're involved in a peace process, so therefore you have to be looking at every aspect of how (to) build peace, how (to) ensure that we won't return to what people describe as the bad old days," Kelly said.

So how does it sit with locals that so many sites that were flashpoints in the conflict have now become tourist attractions? Taxi driver Patterson said tourism is better than the alternative.

"I think it's better people come here, get a bit of an insight into it, the murals that are on the wall, it's the biggest outdoor art gallery in the world, and that's how people now express themselves. I think it's better them doing that with a paintbrush in their hand rather than a gun." (315 words)

David de Sola: Belfast: After the Fighting Ends, the Tourists Come. From CNN.com, 4/4/2011 © 2011 Turner Broadcast Systems, Inc. All rights reserved. Used by permission and protected by the Copyright Laws of the United States. The printing, copying, redistribution, or retransmission of this Content without express written permission is prohibited.

2 *Coiste:* company offering political guided tours

Assignments

1. Sketch the concept of conflict tourism and the arguments for and against it as presented in the texts. *(25 %)*

2. Examine how each author conveys his view on the different peace process measures. *(35 %)*

3. You are a pupil representative of *Lagan College,* the first integrated Irish school initiated by parents in Belfast in 1981.

   With its 35th anniversary ahead, you are asked to talk about the measures and events that have contributed to "increased stability and relative peace" (Text 1, l. 9) and to underline the importance of reconciliation.

   Taking into account your background knowledge, write the script for this opening speech. *(40 %)*

Lösungsvorschläge

1. *This task is designed to test if you understood the text and are able to rephrase the main ideas. Start with the concept and describe in brief what "conflict tourism" is according to the given texts. Then sum up the pro and contra arguments on "conflict tourism" as given in the texts. Avoid any interpretation.*

"Conflict tourism" in Belfast is what the organised tours are called that take tourist to the historically and politically renowned places of the Irish troubles. Some of these tours are organised and executed by former combatants from both sides.

In his text "Belfast's immoral conflict tourism" Chris Jenkins describes conflict tourism as unethical. He believes that this form of tourism is some sort of voyeurism that abuses history and shows disrespect for what happened. He also points out that the financial profits do not reach the victims of the troubles and sees it as some kind of manipulation of reality. His worst case scenario is that tourism might disturb the remembrance process which is necessary to reconcile the conflict.

However, he does not only point out contra arguments but also sees some in favor of conflict tourism. As already mentioned there is the financial gain which Mr. Jenkins sees as a positive side effect and he also sees certain signs of solidarity in that development which are to be welcomed. In contrast to Chris Jenkins, David de Sola sees "conflict tourism" as very positive. In his text "Belfast: After the fighting ends, the tourists come" he points out several arguments in favor of conflict tourism. He thinks that these tours help people to understand the conflict. The tours are offered by Republicans as well as Nationalists and provide different perspectives from people who were actually involved in the troubles. De Sola believes that these tours help people to gain a deeper understanding on both sides, not only the tourists but the guides as well. He concludes that this form of tourism can be seen as an active contribution to the peace process. *(282 words)*

2. *Here, "peace process measures" refers to conflict tourism and its implications for the peace process. Read the texts and find out how both authors make their points. Make sure to structure your text in a way that it is logical and functional. Give proof from the texts.*

Chris Jenkins questions the idea of conflict tourism in Belfast. He introduces his text with a fictional, rhetorically very effective and sarcastic advertisement for a conflict tourism tour (cf. T1 ll. 1 ff.). By doing so he reveals his point of view on the topic. He also contrasts the classic destinations in Northern Ireland which he approves against the relatively new form of conflict tourism which he opposes (cf. T1 ll. 8 ff.). In his text he likes to judge the tourists that go on conflict tours and the organisations that offer them, e. g. as people that "flock to" (T1 ll. 16 f.) certain sights and do something "deeply immoral" (T1 l. 12) when they stare at the murals (cf. T1 ll. 13 f.), or on behalf of the organisations that exploit the conflict (cf. T1 ll. 6 f.). By doing so the tourists take home, as the author puts it in a parallelism, "a picture" in which the "reality is manipulated, history exploited"

(T1 l. 25). He sees things differently. Mr. Jenkins obviously wants to be seen as an objective journalist and uses common methods to express his point of view. Starting with practical examples he describes what the tourists see and then explains the current situation as it is, e. g. people see kids playing football against diversion walls in Belfast and believe that the diversion belongs to the past, even though it does not. According to Chris Jenkins, segregation is still very real (cf. T1 ll. 15 ff.) even though Northern Ireland politicians say otherwise. In this context the writer speaks as "we" (T1 l. 22 also later, l. 35) making it seem as if he spoke for all the Northern Irish.

His quote from Ireland's first minister gives his argumentation more credibility (cf. T1 ll. 26 ff.). The author's repeated use of the word "but" in order to contrast his beliefs is striking (cf. T1 ll. 21, 29, 31, 33 and 36) and does not miss the point he is trying to make against conflict tourism. Mr. Jenkins ends his article with a personal well defined position and a plea on the matter that makes him seem reasonable. His last words are a repetition of his general opinion on conflict tourism (cf. T1 ll. 33 ff.).

David de Sola's approach to the topic is completely different. He sees troubles tourism as one option among others to learn about the troublesome history of Northern Ireland (cf. T2 l. 1) and praises the tours as something positive that has evolved from the conflict. He gives the example of Republican Coiste Tours, which he has obviously taken, but also mentions the Loyalist Ex-Prisoners Interpretive Center, who offer similar tours on their turf, which gives his text a certain credibility (cf. T2 ll. 2 ff.). The whole text is more positive, as is to be expected, since he writes in favor of conflict tourism. The positive atmosphere is supported by his use of optimistic words, e. g. another "option" (T2 l. 1) that is offered, "opportunities" (T2 l. 16) that are given, or that the tours are "contributing" (T2 l. 13) to the peace. De Sola gives statements (cf. T2 ll. 13 f.) and supports them with quotes to gain credibility (cf. T2 ll. 15 ff.). All the quotes that he uses (cf. T2 ll. 6 ff., 15 ff. and 23 ff.) in his text are statements by people who are involved in the matter, which of course shows that he did research and adds to the tenability of the point he wants to make. Therefore, the quotes he chooses are positive ones that are in favor of the tours.

De Sola introduces his final statement by addressing the reader directly with a question which seems contrary (cf. T2 ll. 20 f.) but, again, is invalidated by a quote of one taxi driver who represents all people that live in the vicinity of trouble sites (cf. T2 ll. 21 ff.). *(659 words)*

3. *You are supposed to write an anniversary speech for a cross community school which was planned for both Catholics and Protestants (and other beliefs as well). You not only need to mention the anniversary, but also the peace process and the necessity to forgive in order to make things better. Use your background knowledge to fill your speech with content that is appropriate to the topic. Do not forget to address your listeners at least twice, in the beginning and at the end, and use stylistic devices to emphasise important points.*

Ladies and Gentleman,

I have the honor to stand before you today to deliver the student's speech. Our student's point of view of course is different from those we have already heard. For us students it is normal to stand together, Catholics next to Protestants. We have learned that we are all the same – despite our beliefs – and let's be honest, we all pray to the same God. Politically, we might not share the same points of view, there are still Republicans and Loyalists, but we have learned to talk about the goals for a bright and peaceful future in Northern Ireland. The troubles – let's hope – lie behind us. We have heard official excuses from both sides, started a process to deal with our past and encouraged several cross community peace projects. That is good, but we still have no reason to celebrate since we still have a long way to go. A way that our generation will have to pave. Here at Lagan we appreciatively picked up the tools from those parents who had a vision of a peaceful, anti-sectarian society 35 years ago and founded this institution. Back then in 1981, life here was far from what we now know. Their vision was to build a road where there was none – only rocks. But history was in their favor and they helped to pave what was about to become the stony road that led here. They did what others were about to do after them. They talked, joined hands and understood the importance of reconciliation – the Anglo-Irish Agreement, Good Friday Agreement, St Andrew's Agreement and the Hillsborough Agreement – to mention but the most important cornerstones. It was their generation's vision and determination to change things our way that have brought some normality – Catholics and Protestants working together toward the same goal: a peaceful society. On their behalf, Trimble and Hume received the Nobel Peace Prize for just that. The parents of the founding generation laid the groundwork that later was adopted by DUP and Sinn Fein's power-sharing and which we all directly profit from.

Of course, we also have to thank our teachers, especially Mr. Mc Mullen, the only teacher from that founder's generation who is still on the staff today, a teacher who, along with others, shares the founder parents' vision and determination. Together with our parents they fought and are still fighting against all odds for a Northern Ireland that now can look back with pride and look ahead with great hope.

Let's proudly mount the bulldozers and lay the foundation for a wide and scenic path toward a bright and colorful future. Let's make our parents and our teachers proud. Let's hope that in 15 years from now – our schools 50th anniversary – we can send our kids here and lay out their plans. Let's hope, that one day the aversion we can still feel today will be a footnote in history. Let's hope that on this day a future generation of students will be given the opportunity to make our road a boulevard. Thank you and God bless us all. *(515 words)*

> **Abitur 2015 Schleswig-Holstein – Englisch (Kernfach)**
> **Aufgabe 4: Canada – A Land of Many Nations**

Drew Hayden Taylor: "Strawberries"

Introductory Note: Drew Hayden Taylor is a contemporary Canadian author writing predominantly about the First Nations' culture. This is the extract from one of the short stories in the collection Fearless Warriors.

1 "So, what will we have next?" I asked.
 We'd been asking each other that question for the last two hours and it still brought deep thought and even deeper study of the drink menu. As was our yearly ritual, Joby Snowball and I were blowing our first paycheque of the season on abso-
5 lutely nothing worthwhile. It was a time-honoured tradition we loyally kept. I had just started a new job at the band office, occupying specifically the well-respected title of Day Camp and Regatta Coordinator for all the little ankle-biters of the village[1]. It was work on the reserve, therefore no income tax to worry about, and it was close to home so I could save even more money for my next year of college.
10 Joby's paycheque was different from mine. [I]n many ways we had drifted apart. I did the collegiate thing while he had remained on the reserve being a working man, doing odd jobs, mostly seasonal things. […]
 But that was a long time ago.
 "Well, what do you think?" It was Joby's turn to ask the famous question. I
15 couldn't decide. We were having a drinking contest. A sophisticated one of sorts. I was showing off, ordering a variety of interesting yet bizarre drinks I had learned about during my brief excursion into the equally interesting and bizarre Caucasian world. Joby on the other hand was matching me exotic drink for exotic drink, having watched many a soap opera and movie. We had just finished a Vodka Martini, shaken,
20 not stirred. I believe Joby had picked that up in a movie for the same reason he referred to his pickup truck as his 'Austin Martin'[2].
 We had been there two hours but we weren't drunk by any measure. Joby was a beer person through and through, and I still had an affinity for rye and Coke, the mix I was weaned on. So with all these new liquors and liqueurs, we were taking it slow
25 and carefully, as all scientists do with their experiments. So far we had also tried White Russians, Black Russians, Brandy Alexanders, Sea Breezes, Singapore Slings and Manhattans[3]; we prided ourselves in 'how international' we were being.
 Now the ball was in my court. "How about a Strawberry Daiquiri? I hear they're pretty good."
30 Joby stiffened like I'd slapped him. "The hell they are. My strawberry days are over. Pick another one."
 "What do you got against Strawberry Daiquiris?"
 He looked at me for a moment. I could tell he was remembering. Not the kind of memory that follows a story line or pattern, the sort you see in movies, but the kind

that brings back a random series of emotions and experiences. Sort of like having a pail of water suddenly dumped on you when you heard the right word or saw the right image. Judging by the look on Joby's face, the water was cold.

"You were lucky," he said, "all through high school you got to work at the band office. Just ten minutes from home, air conditioning, and a chair to boot. You forget what I did all those summers."

Then I remembered. The fields.

"For three goddamned years I picked strawberries. I'd come home with my hands stained blood red, my back ready to break from bending over all day. A sixteen-year-old shouldn't have back problems, it ain't right. When I turned seventeen, I swore I'd never pick another strawberry in my life, or eat one, or look at one, or think of one."

That's the way it used to be when we were young. Local strawberry farmers would send in these huge flat-bed trucks to our reserve to pick up the Indian kids to pick strawberries. We used to be like those migrant workers except we weren't migrant. We lived on the edge of the fields. [...]

"One time my sister had her room wallpapered with pictures of that toy character, I think her name was Strawberry Shortcake. I coulda killed her. There were strawberries all over her room," he was getting excited. "All over it. I think that was her way of making sure I never went into her room. I had nightmares for a week. Andrew, to this day, I've never eaten a strawberry or even touched one and I hope I never do. To me they're the Devil's own food. Now for God's sake, pick another drink."

Trying to be sympathetic (it's remarkably easy to be sympathetic in a bar), I ordered a Grasshopper. We were quiet for the next little while, the spirit of our adventure having been spoiled by the berry from Hell. We tried to recapture the fun of our outing, but the moment had been lost to a bad memory. We had a few more drinks, then went our separate ways. As he walked away, I realized how much I missed the closeness we had shared as kids. No amount of this new age "male bonding" can ever come close to two fourteen-year-olds trying to convince our day camp counsellors to go skinny dipping[4] with us. And I couldn't even swim. [...] (885 words)

Drew Hayden Taylor: „Strawberries". In: Fearless Warriors: Stories, Burnaby, BC: Talonbooks, 1998, pp. 49–54.

1 *village:* (here) reserve
2 *Austin Martin:* actually called Aston Martin: a British manufacturer of luxury sports cars
3 *White Russians, Black Russians, Brandy Alexanders, Sea Breezes, Singapore Slings, Manhattans:* names of alcoholic drinks
4 *to go skinny dipping:* to go for a swim

Assignments

1. Describe Andrew and Joby's encounter. *(25 %)*
2. Analyse the relationship of the two protagonists and how it is presented in the text. *(35 %)*
3. Shortly after, Andrew, then a student at the *University of Ottawa*, is awarded the *Burt Award for First Nations*[5].

   To honour his outstanding achievement, Andrew is asked by the event planners of the *Assembly of First Nations (AFN)* to deliver a speech on the occasion of their annual meeting entitled: "Being a First Nation, a vicious circle?"

   Write the script for this speech taking into account your background knowledge. *(40 %)*

   5 *Burt Award for First Nations:* annual award given to English-language literary works for young adults written by First Nations

Lösungsvorschläge

1. *This task is supposed to test your reading comprehension skills. Your text should present the information concisely and well-structured. Make sure to use your own words and avoid interpretations as well as personal evaluations!*

Andrew and Joby are two First Nations characters from Drew Hayden Taylor's short story "Strawberries". They were close friends at high school but after that their lives developed in different directions. While Andrew has gone on to college and only returns to the reserve for the holiday season to earn some money, Joby has never left the reserve and tries to make ends meet with temp jobs.
Nevertheless, they traditionally celebrate their annual reunion by spending their first paycheques together; in the situation presented in the text, they are having cocktails in a bar. To add a twist to the situation, they have decided to take turns in choosing drinks; as a consequence, each tries to outdo the other in picking unfamiliar drinks. This is when their different lives become apparent: while Andrew attempts to show off his cosmopolitanism, he attributes Joby's knowledge of exotic drinks to his excessive TV consumption. The evening ends on a bad note when Andrew suggests a strawberry daiquiri, which reminds Joby of his three-year summer job as a strawberry picker. His memories are of hard work which caused health problems, making him detest strawberries ever since. The gap between the friends widens when Joby reminds Andrew that they do not share this experience because Andrew always had indoor jobs with the band office. When they say good-bye, Andrew realises that their childhood friendship has cooled.

(231 words)

2. *In this task, you are required to examine the way the author presents the relationship between Andrew and Joby. Hence, after analysing the content of the extract, you must also analyse its structure and stylistic devices. Remember not to just list the devices, but always explain their intended effect.*

In the given text, the relationship between Andrew and Joby, who used to be close friends at school, takes a serious turn for the worse when they realise how different their lifestyles have become.
The encounter is described from Andrew's point of view. At the beginning, the friends still seem to be close despite their differences, when Andrew mentions their "yearly ritual" (ll. 3 f.) of spending their first paycheque together and describes it as a "time-honoured tradition" (l. 5). This feeling of togetherness is also supported by his frequent use of the first person plural pronouns "we" (cf. ll. 1, 2, 5) and "our" (cf. ll. 3, 4).
In the course of the evening, however, things become tense between the friends. Their meeting turns into a competition (e.g. "drinking contest", l. 15; "showing off", l. 16; "Now the ball was in my court," l. 28) with each trying to outdo the other in their choice of drinks. Andrew states that his and Joby's lives have developed in different directions ("in many ways we had drifted apart", l. 10), a fact

that is also reflected in their incomes ("Joby's paycheque was different from mine," l. 10): while Andrew goes to college, Joby has never left the reserve for higher education, but stayed on the reserve making a living from temp jobs (cf. ll. 10 ff.). Consequently, Andrew remarks that while he derives his education from first-hand experience ("during my brief excursion into the equally interesting and bizarre Caucasian world", ll. 17 f.), Joby's information comes from James Bond movies ("a Vodka Martini, shaken, not stirred. I believe Joby had picked that up in a movie for the same reason he referred to his pickup truck as his 'Austin Martin'", ll. 19 ff.). Andrew's decision to quote Joby's mistake about the correct name of Bond's car, an Aston Martin, as well as his reference to Joby as a "beer person" (l. 23), imply that Andrew feels intellectually superior to his friend.

The friendly character of the meeting comes to an end when Andrew unthinkingly suggests drinking "a Strawberry Daiquiri" (l. 28) and triggering bad memories in his friend. Joby then verbalises the distance between them when he contrasts their different work experiences during high school ("'You were lucky,' he said, 'all through high school you got to work at the band office. […] You forget what I did all those summers. […] For three goddamned years I picked strawberries,'" ll. 38 ff.) in order to underline why he is not satisfied with Andrew's choice.

After this fauxpas, the atmosphere is ruined. Although they try to reconcile, Andrew realises that they might not regain the friendship they had when they were children and had the same interests, e. g. seeing girls naked ("No amount of this new age 'male bonding' can ever come close to two fourteen-year-olds trying to convince our day camp counsellors to go skinny dipping with us", ll. 62 ff.). Still, he deplores the loss of "the closeness we had shared as kids" (l. 62). *(509 words)*

3. *In your speech, try to present the problems of Native Americans, but avoid saying anything that would insult your friends and family. Therefore, you may refer to aspects mentioned in the story, but avoid adding information that would make Joby look bad. Also refer to problems of Native Americans in Canada you have heard about in class or you have come across while preparing for the exam. In your speech you should address the audience and show gratefulness for receiving the award. Use suitable rhetorical devices like repetition, anaphora, similes, metaphors etc.*

Ladies and gentlemen,

I'd like to thank the Assembly of First Nations for inviting me. I am very pleased to be here tonight at your annual meeting and I am deeply honoured to receive the *Burt Award for First Nations*.

As a First Nation person myself, I know that not everyone is as privileged as I am. Although I grew up on a reserve, my parents always gave me the feeling that there was nothing I couldn't achieve. So when I finished high school and went on to university, I felt singled out, but also entitled to be part of the academic community.

At first, I felt lost. I was the only First Nations person in my semester. But my fellow students were great. They accepted me as one of their own, and I soon became comfortable. But the more time I spent away from home, the less I thought about my old friends. I came to this painful realisation a few weeks ago, when I met my oldest friend Joby. We spent our entire childhood together, and man, the secrets we shared! But our meeting, which was planned as a reminiscence of our glory days, reminded me of all the things I had tried to forget …

The poverty that forced elementary school kids to start lessons on empty stomachs, not allowing them to tap their full potential and dooming them to a future of unqualified jobs – a vicious circle.

The unemployment that forced school leavers to either leave the reserve or make do with aforementioned unqualified jobs – a vicious circle.

The families disrupted by the so-called Indian Residential School system, with children that never returned home, others so estranged from their roots that they were unable to find their place in society again, and parents so traumatised as to be unable to provide a stable environment for their own children – a vicious circle.

The feeling that no matter how hard you worked you would never amount to anything much because nobody was really interested in you, not your neighbours, not the people outside the reserve, and especially not the government.

Our people have been used to being treated like second-class citizens since the colonial days when we were deprived of our land and our culture. We've become so used to it that many of us lack the energy to break out of this circle, what is more, we even perpetuated it. After the Prime Minister offered a formal apology for the Residential School system, why did we not raise our voices, seize the opportunity and get the help we need to achieve a settlement? Why did we not strive to restore our infrastructure and take our lives into our own hands on the reserves with all the subsidies the government has been paying? Why do people still just sit around and wait for the day to end instead of taking the initiative and improve the living conditions of their community?

Seize the opportunity; the time has never been as good as now. Take your lives into your own hands, and don't take no for an answer. If you feel discriminated against, speak out. If you feel you're not getting the chances you deserve, protest. If you have the chance to fulfil your dream, don't let it go. Go after it, like I did, and break out of the circle. Do it not only for yourself, but also do it for those who will come after you. Show them that anything is possible.

Thank you for your attention. *(589 words)*